Race and the Yugoslav region

THEORY FOR A GLOBAL AGE

Series Editor: Gurminder K. Bhambra, Professor of Postcolonial and Decolonial Studies in the School of Global Studies, University of Sussex

Globalization is widely viewed as a current condition of the world, but there is little engagement with how this changes the way we understand it. The *Theory for a Global Age* series addresses the impact of globalization on the social sciences and humanities. Each title will focus on a particular theoretical issue or topic of empirical controversy and debate, addressing theory in a more global and interconnected manner. With contributions from scholars across the globe, the series will explore different perspectives to examine globalization from a global viewpoint. True to its global character, the *Theory for a Global Age* series will be available for online access worldwide via Creative Commons licensing, aiming to stimulate wide debate within academia and beyond.

Previously published by Bloomsbury:

Connected Sociologies
Gurminder K. Bhambra

Eurafrica: The Untold History of European Integration and Colonialism
Peo Hansen and Stefan Jonsson

On Sovereignty and Other Political Delusions
Joan Cocks

Postcolonial Piracy: Media Distribution and Cultural Production in the Global South
Edited by Lars Eckstein and Anja Schwarz

The Black Pacific: Anti-Colonial Struggles and Oceanic Connections
Robbie Shilliam

Democracy and Revolutionary Politics
Neera Chandhoke

Published by Manchester University Press:

Debt as Power
Tim Di Muzio and Richard H. Robbins

Subjects of modernity: Time-space, disciplines, margins
Saurabh Dube

Frontiers of the Caribbean
Phillip Nanton

John Dewey: The Global Public and Its Problems
John Narayan

Race and the Yugoslav region

Postsocialist, post-conflict, postcolonial?

Catherine Baker

Manchester University Press

Copyright © Catherine Baker 2018

The right of Catherine Baker to be identified as the author of this work has been asserted by her in accordance with the Copyright, Designs and Patents Act 1988.

Published by Manchester University Press
Altrincham Street, Manchester M1 7JA
www.manchesteruniversitypress.co.uk

British Library Cataloguing-in-Publication Data
A catalogue record for this book is available from the British Library

Library of Congress Cataloging-in-Publication Data applied for

ISBN 978 1 5261 2660 3 hardback
ISBN 978 1 5261 2662 7 paperback
ISBN 978 1 5261 2661 0 open access

An electronic version of this book is also available under a Creative Commons (CC-BY-NC-ND) licence

First published 2018

The publisher has no responsibility for the persistence or accuracy of URLs for any external or third-party internet websites referred to in this book, and does not guarantee that any content on such websites is, or will remain, accurate or appropriate.

Typeset
by Toppan Best-set Premedia Limited
Printed in Great Britain
by CPI Group (UK) Ltd, Croydon, CR0 4YY

Contents

Series editor's introduction	vi
Preface	viii
List of abbreviations	xi
Introduction: what does race have to do with the Yugoslav region?	1
1 Popular music and the 'cultural archive'	31
2 Histories of ethnicity, nation and migration	57
3 Transnational formations of race before and during Yugoslav state socialism	94
4 Postsocialism, borders, security and race after Yugoslavia	122
Conclusion	166
Bibliography	189
Index	229

Series editor's introduction

In this exceptional book, *Race and the Yugoslav region: postsocialist, post-conflict, postcolonial?*, Catherine Baker brings together her extensive scholarly expertise on former Yugoslavia with theoretical work in postcolonial and postsocialist studies to offer us a novel and distinctive insight into how the region is configured by, and through, race. Moving beyond a simple engagement with key concepts from within postcolonial theory to describe the current situation of the Balkans, Baker is more interested in examining how global colonial histories have themselves been integral to the formation of geopolitics and culture there. She argues, for example, for the Yugoslav region to be understood as entangled with more extensive histories of coloniality and, thus, as shaped by 'transnational racialized imaginations' as many other parts of the world.

Baker skilfully fulfils the task she has set out for herself by first investigating what the demographic transformations of, and in, popular culture reveal about the historical legacies of coloniality and racialisation in the region. She locates the discussion of the cultural archive also in the question of how, as a consequence of the Non-Aligned Movement, people were able to move into and through spaces historically constituted as white. She then goes on to examine the multiple and intersecting connections of ideas and peoples within the historical contact zone of the Balkans. She weaves together discussions of historical migrations and myths of nationhood to present a complex and compelling account of the longer history of the region. In this way, Baker is adeptly able to highlight the ways in which historically constituted racial formations organise the ground of Yugoslav politics in the present.

One of the key aims of the Theory for a Global Age series is precisely to ask what difference theory makes, and is made to theory, when we start from places other than the Euro-centred West. Here, Baker uses postcolonial theory to better understand a region seen to be unmarked by processes of colonialism and uncovers both a richer history of the region and the basis for sharpening theoretical concepts and categories in the process. It is an outstanding contribution to the series, providing new insights, theoretical clarification and a rich narrative.

Gurminder K. Bhambra
University of Sussex

Preface

This book has a single author but rests on many shoulders, often those whose position in the political economy of academic knowledge is more marginal than mine. I owe the perspective I have been able to express in this book to two women in particular: the feminist writer and cultural critic Flavia Dzodan, whose writing first confronted me with very different meanings of 'Europe' from those that dominated the study of the Yugoslav region and my own experience, and the philosopher Zara Bain, whose explanations of her research on the critical race theory of Charles Mills first suggested to me that the spatialised hierarchies of modernity with which the literature on 'balkanism' was so familiar were also part of global formations of race. These interactions, through online platforms in the early to mid-2010s, came about at a novel moment in the history of digital media and feminism, yet the perspectives they enabled me to form were not in themselves new: Anikó Imre and Miglena Todorova elsewhere in east European studies, and Dušan Bjelić and Konstantin Kilibarda in post-Yugoslav studies themselves, had all written on race, whiteness, postcoloniality and postsocialism before I had even begun questioning the absence of race in the debates to which I was contributing. I hope that their work will be cited at least as often as this book.

My first rough notes of topics a book like this might cover were written while listening to Julija Sardelić (who directed me towards Imre's work on whiteness and antiziganism) discuss her research on post-Yugoslav Romani minorities at a workshop organised by the Europeanisation of Citizenship in the Successor States of the Former Yugoslavia project at Edinburgh in June 2013. In 2014, the 'Why Is My Curriculum White?' campaign by students at University College London challenged me and other academics to rethink how we could redesign our teaching to integrate race into topics where, due to the structural whiteness of the academy itself, it had traditionally been erased. Talking to postgraduates including Olivia Hellewell and Laura Todd in Russian and Slavonic

Studies at Nottingham after I first presented an early version of this book's argument, in March 2015, showed me that arguing for race to be explicitly part of the agenda of post-Yugoslav studies invited others to re-reflect on racialised representations they had encountered in their own research. The contributions of all participants at a workshop on '"Race" and Racialisation in the Study of South-East Europe' I held at Central European University in February 2016, at the invitation of the Department of Gender Studies, reflected a combination of situated knowledge and critical engagement that it would be rare to find at any other university, and were decisive in persuading me that the argument should be book-length. Amid a suddenly expanding body of research on postcoloniality and race in Yugoslavia, conversations with Srđan Vučetić, Jelena Subotić and Sunnie Rucker-Chang across several conferences – and a guest lecture at the University of Cincinnati – in 2016 enabled me to sharpen the book's claims from questions into potential answers. This book appears in the 'Theory for a Global Age' series thanks to the enthusiasm of Gurminder Bhambra at a time when it has probably never been more politically urgent to understand how global coloniality and the marginalisation of postsocialist Europe have interlocked.

While writing this book, I have been indebted to the encouragement and critical feedback of Elissa Helms, Marsha Henry, Konstantin Kilibarda, Jelena Obradović-Wochnik, Sunnie Rucker-Chang, Julija Sardelić, Paul Stubbs and Srđan Vučetić, and to conversations with Anna Agathangelou, Petra Bakoš Jarrett, Dušan Bjelić, Wendy Bracewell, Dario Brentin, Alex Cooper, Susan Cooper, Elizabeth Dauphinée, David Eldridge, Lucian George, Michael Gratzke, Amela Hadžajlić, Tea Hadžiristić, Olivia Hellewell, Aida Hozić, Vladimir Kulić, Tomislav Longinović, Jo Metcalf, Jasmin Mujanović, Astrea Pejović, Joy Porter, Jemima Repo, Melanie Richter-Montpetit, Jelena Subotić, Sara Swerdlyk, Marianna Szczygielska, Laura Todd, Miglena Todorova, Naum Trajanovski, Rosemary Wall and Peter Wright. Responsibility for the book's interpretations, of course, remains my own. Parts of the argument have been presented at the University of Nottingham, Central European University, University College London (School of Slavonic and East

European Studies), the University of Hull, the University of Graz (at a conference supported by the Leverhulme Trust), the London School of Economics and Political Science (at the annual conference of *Millennium: Journal of International Studies*), the Association for Slavic, East European and Eurasian Studies annual convention, and Cincinnati. I am grateful to staff at the British Library (especially Milan Grda) and Hull's Brynmor Jones Library for assistance with bibliographic research, and to what is now the School of Histories, Languages and Cultures at Hull for providing an intellectual environment where situating the Yugoslav region within global formations of race seemed all the more essential. I am also grateful to Caroline Wintersgill, Alun Richards, David Appleyard and Diane Wardle for the smoothness and speed of this book's journey through production. This book owes its earliest origins to the anti-racist engagement of my mother, Helen Baker, from whom I first understood that the legacies of colonialism and slavery shape the global present.

List of abbreviations

ARBiH	Army of the Republic of Bosnia-Herzegovina
EU	European Union
HDZ BiH	Croat Democratic Union, Bosnia-Herzegovina branch
HVO	Croat Defence Council
IFOR	Implementation Force
IPTF	International Police Task Force
IR	International Relations
ISIS	Islamic State in Iraq and Syria
NAM	Non-Aligned Movement
NATO	North Atlantic Treaty Organization
NDH	Independent State of Croatia
RS	Republika Srpska
SDA	Party of Democratic Action
SDS	Serb Democratic Party
SFOR	Stabilization Force
SKJ	League of Communists of Yugoslavia (until 1953 known as the Communist Party of Yugoslavia (KPJ))
TCN	Third Country National
TLZP	*Tvoje lice zvuci poznato* (television programme)
UNESCO	United Nations Educational, Scientific and Cultural Organization
UNPROFOR	United Nations Protection Force
USA	United States of America
USSR	Union of Soviet Socialist Republics
VJ	Army of Yugoslavia
VRS	Army of the Bosnian Serb Republic
WPS	Women, Peace and Security

Introduction: what does race have to do with the Yugoslav region?

The Yugoslav region – or so one would infer from most works about the territories and identities that used to be part of Yugoslavia – apparently has nothing to do with race, and race apparently has nothing to do with the Yugoslav region. The region has *ethnicity*, and has *religion*; indeed, according to many texts on the Yugoslav wars, has them in surfeit. Like south-east Europe and Europe's ex-state socialist societies in general, the Yugoslav region has legacies of nation formation, forced migration and genocide that invite seeing its past and present through the lens of ethnopolitical and religious conflict. Moreover, as part of 'eastern' rather than 'western' Europe, and without its own history as an imperial power, it did not experience the mass migration from outside 'Europe' of millions of people whose identities would be racialised as non-white. Studies of how ideas of 'race' have circulated and been adapted across the globe, for their part, themselves still almost always pass over the east of Europe and its state socialist past. The paradox is all the greater because, ever since the 1990s, south-east European cultural critique has been deeply informed by a translation of postcolonial theory into a way of explaining the historic and present-day structural peripheralisation of the region and its people. And yet, in domains from everyday cultural artefacts to often-forgotten nodes of transnational history, the Yugoslav region has been as entangled in global 'raciality' as any other part of the planet.

These entanglements, moreover, have created conditions for shifting, ambiguous identifications with symbolic histories and geographies of race. They include not only identifications with 'Europe' as a space of modernity, civilisation and (critical race studies would insist) whiteness, but also analogies drawn between 'Balkanness' and 'blackness' in imagined solidarity, as well as the race-blind anti-colonialism of Yugoslav Non-Alignment (which, under Tito, cast the leader of this European country as a model of national liberation for the Global South). The Yugoslav region is increasingly likely to be thought of as 'post-conflict' and 'postsocialist', the product of ethnopolitical conflict *and* the collapse of state socialism, at once – yet it is less commonly placed in the global context of the legacies of colonialism and slavery that should emerge from the refusal to divide the planet into separate 'postsocialist' and 'postcolonial' worlds that Sharad Chari and Katherine Verdery (2009) describe as 'thinking between the posts'. The foremost of those legacies, as Charles Mills (1997) and others write, is the global pervasiveness of 'race'. At a time when the juncture of 'postsocialist' and 'postcolonial' lenses for making sense of ex-Yugoslavia, 'the Balkans' and 'eastern Europe' has been inspiring reinterpretations of the region's transnational and global history that multiplied even as this book was being written, it is no longer possible – and never should have been – to contend that the Yugoslav region stands somehow 'outside' race. The question is *where* it stands, and why that has gone unspoken for so long.

My own research has reproduced this disregard for race, a sense that race was not something south-east European studies 'needed to know'. In 2006 or 2007, reading archived newspapers and magazines in the National and University Library in Zagreb during my PhD on popular music and identity in Croatia, I was stopped short by an interview with a music presenter, Hamed Bangoura, from one tabloid's entertainment supplement in 1993. Referencing the English-language title of Bangoura's show, *DJ Is So Hot*, the headline, also in English, called attention to his skin colour and Guinean heritage with a directness that, growing up in a white, British, anti-racist family, I believed had been 'left behind': 'DJ is so black.' My postgraduate training had equipped me to note even the most 'trivial' invocations of 'Europe' and 'the Balkans', 'Westernness' and 'Easternness', modernity and backwardness, as everyday rearticulations of nationhood; yet south-east European studies' theoretical literature seemed to have posed no questions to which 'DJ is so black' might be the answer. Indeed, a white liberal reflex of 'You can't *say* that!', confusion over how I would bridge my home discipline's literature with work that explained it, plus fear that I was inappropriately projecting British identity discourses on to somewhere which, by not sharing Britain's colonial history, also lacked Britain's insecurities about race, meant I did not even write down a citation.

Scholarship by feminist and queer writers of colour, and campaigns to decentre Eurocentrism and whiteness at UK universities, would challenge me to rethink my past work on post-Yugoslav identities, as would listening on Twitter to a philosopher of critical race theory I had first followed for her disability activism, and trying to understand what I had meant when, teaching at my old department in 2011–12, I asked Master's students 'How would south-east European cultural studies look if it had been based on Paul Gilroy instead of Edward Said?' Planning to mention Bangoura's interview during a paper at a conference on 'Racialized Realities in World Politics' in 2016, I revisited my handwritten notes from Zagreb. It might be in that daily newspaper or this magazine; I've remembered, accurately or not, it was 1993. If it was, I failed to record it. I did find – and this time had noted – an interview with a forgotten dance-music vocalist called Simplicija, part of a mid-1990s Croatian movement that adapted 'Eurodance' pop as evidence that Croatia was culturally Western and European while Yugoslavia and Serbia were not. Simplicija, alias Dijana Vunić, said her on-stage gimmick, devised by a well-known 'Cro-dance' backing dancer, Tomislav Tržan, 'isn't just new in Croatia, but even in European and worldwide circles' (Morić 1995). The gimmick – collapsing multiple European and American caricatures of blackness into one soft toy – involved a grinning monkey puppet known as Dr Rap.

Ephemeral even for 1990s Croatian pop, explicit in mobilising colonial advertising tropes as perverse association with Afro-European Eurodance and African-American hip-hop modernities, 'Simplicija' placed a caricatured racialised imagination in plain sight, just as, two decades later, a Serbian/Croatian/Slovenian celebrity talent-show franchise, licensed from Spain, regularly dressed contestants in blackface to impersonate African-American, Caribbean or Afro-European stars. There could hardly be blunter instruments proving the Yugoslav region is not 'outside' race, but is deeply embedded in transnational racialised imaginations and therefore a global history of coloniality; indeed, such obvious expressions of racism do not even constitute the whole range of ambiguous and shifting roles that race has played in the Yugoslav region, before, during and after Yugoslavia itself. If the Yugoslav region is somewhere where television blackface goes unmarked and football fans have hurled racist abuse at black players, it is also somewhere where state socialism identified with the decolonising Global South more than eastern Europe through Non-Aligned ideology, and where Aimé Césaire, the theorist of Négritude, could identify a Dalmatian shore, Martinska, in anti-colonial solidarity with his own Martinique. And yet, compared with ethnicity and religion – which in many other settings are intricately linked to race – 'race', or the politics of racialisation and whiteness which constitute it, is rarely a subject of study for the Yugoslav region.

The contrast with ethnicity is stark. After years of research explaining the late Yugoslav crisis through social inequalities and the intricacies of 'workers' self-management', the rise of ethnopolitics in the Yugoslav public sphere in 1985–91 made studying Yugoslavia synonymous with studying ethnicity and nationalism even before the wars began.[1] The wars, and post-war ethnonationalist elites' persistence in power, tightened the bond further – as, when millions had been targeted for persecution because of ethnicised difference, they had to some extent to do. A field crossing history, anthropology, sociology and politics has debated how far twentieth-century notions of the relationship between ethnicity, language, territory and sovereignty would also have been held by inhabitants of the region in the medieval and early modern past, or even the late Ottoman and Habsburg periods (Fine 2006; Judson 2007; Blumi 2011b); used evidence about ethnopolitical conflict dynamics from the region for broader theory-building about nationalism and ethnicity (Brubaker 1996) or post-Cold-War international security (Posen 1993); investigated how alternative, multi-ethnic models of belonging were marginalised by Yugoslav constitutional logics, erased before and during the wars, and silenced again in post-conflict settlements (Dević 1997; Gagnon 2004; Hromadžić 2015); and shown how intersecting ideologies of gender, sexuality and nation turn bodies into symbolic battlegrounds and women and sexual minorities into material targets of ethnopolitical violence, across and within ethnicised boundaries (Mostov 2000; Žarkov 2007; Helms 2008).

Despite this literature's concern with legacies of historic violence in the present, however, it rarely opens the question that would connect the region with an element of belonging already recognised as inescapable and constitutive for so many other areas: how has 'race', a notion propagated to support European colonial power and domination, manifested in the Yugoslav region, where attachment to 'Europe' informs so many forms of collective identity and where historical memories of being imperial subjects not imperial rulers inform so many narratives of national pasts? The Bulgarian scholar Miglena Todorova, writing in 2006, could already argue south-east European studies was separating its region from the rest of the globe by concentrating only on 'ethnicity' while excluding 'race':

> Native and non-native scholarship on the history and culture of peoples in the region treats 'ethnicity' as the central category that has organized group and individual identities and social relations in the area. Political scientists and area studies scholars in the so called 'West' describe the Balkans as the embodiment of 'ethnic nationalism' and 'ethnic violence' while highlighting the democratic, pluralistic, civic and developed nature of a Western first world. From the perspective of this scholarship, 'race' has not played part in the historical, cultural and social experiences of peoples in Southeastern Europe. (Todorova 2006: 3)

So powerfully has this structured the field that even studies deconstructing or decentring ethnicity beyond realist frameworks of 'ethnic war' still hold their ethnicity and nationhood conversation largely outside race.

This is the case, moreover, even though south-east European cultural studies since the early 1990s has drawn heavily on postcolonial and subaltern theory, which, explaining the condition of the Middle East and India (Said 1978, 1993; Mohanty 1988; Spivak 1988; Bhabha 1994; Chakrabarty 2000), would not have had to exist were it not for the same European imperialism that spread modern ideas of 'race'. If 'the West' had defined itself for so long against (its own imagination of) 'the Orient', might 'Europe' not have been constructed against 'the Balkans' or 'eastern Europe', and how had the Balkans themselves internalised that? While Homi Bhabha's approach to cultural hybridity helped anthropologists of south-east Europe critique essentialist notions of ethnicity, the most influential work for south-east European studies has been Edward Said's *Orientalism*, which Milica Bakić-Hayden and Maria Todorova both used as a critical tool for understanding the imagination and representation of 'the Balkans' from inside and outside (Bakić-Hayden and Hayden 1992; Todorova 1994, 1997; Bakić-Hayden 1995). These critiques developed throughout the 1990s as tropes about 'the Balkans' multiplied through and around accounts of the Yugoslav wars (often, erroneously, called the 'Balkan' wars) (Todorova 1997; Goldsworthy 1998; Bjelić and Savić (eds) 2002). Bakić-Hayden's and Todorova's very terminology wove Said into their discipline: Bakić-Hayden (1995) wrote of 'nesting orientalisms' (e.g. Croatian narratives framing Croats as 'European' and Serbs, across a symbolic boundary of national identity, as 'Balkan', even as Slovenian identity narratives laid the European–Balkan boundary at the Slovenian–*Croatian* border, further west), and Todorova termed the whole discourse 'balkanism' (Todorova 1994: 453). Critical analysis of how 'symbolic geographies' (Bakić-Hayden and Hayden 1992) are based on civilisational hierarchies – the very model that, on a global scale, gives critical race theory its reading of the genesis of white supremacy (Mills 1997) – became and would remain foundational in south-east European studies.

Todorova's and Bakić-Hayden's own differences over whether balkanism existed within broader structures of orientalism (as Bakić-Hayden thought) or whether (as Todorova thought) it was separate and sometimes antagonistic had less impact than the lens into which their work combined. In disciplines from cultural studies to International Relations (IR) (or even where both overlap), the 'balkanism' literature's parallels between postcoloniality and the Balkans' own global structural position illuminate questions such as the exoticising pressures facing south-east European cultural producers on 'world' markets (Iordanova 2001), or the prejudices of Western peacekeepers and politicians whose stereotypes first provided rationales for not intervening against aggression during the Yugoslav wars (Hansen 2006), then for various levels of international tutelage over the successor states (Majstorović and Vučkovac 2016). Yet even then, it rarely interrogates the underlying history that made postcolonial thought necessary: the legacies of European imperialism and the 'global racial formations' (Collins 2011: 167; see Omi and Winant 1994) of thought, feeling and power that colonialism spread around the world. Outlasting decolonisation, structuring present-day settler societies and former metropoles, and circulating globally, either these formations must have passed through and been adapted into the region, or some distinctive aspect of historical experience must have immunised the region against them.

The notion that the Yugoslav region, the Balkans or eastern Europe could have entered the twenty-first century without exposure to the global dynamics of race is, this book argues, unsustainable, when these spaces have so often been defined in relation to 'Europe' and when the very association between Europeanness and modernity is, in critical race theory and decolonial thought (Mills 1997; Mignolo 2000), an inherently racialised logic. Such a notion would require the region to have been subject to utterly separate historical forces from those that shaped western Europe and the territories it colonised; and it weakens further once one views postcoloniality and postsocialism (i.e. the social–economic–political–cultural dislocations produced by the collapse of state socialism, often thought to distinguish contemporary eastern Europe as a region) not as analytics for separate parts of the world but as descriptions of two twentieth-century world-historical transformations which both had global reach. Sharad Chari and

Katherine Verdery, a geographer of capitalism and an anthropologist of postsocialism, respectively, termed this agenda 'thinking between the posts', urging scholars not to divide the globe into one sphere defined by the end of empire and another defined by the end of the Cold War; their 2009 article epitomised efforts in literary theory, social/ cultural history and gender studies to combine postcoloniality and postsocialism into one globally aware lens for understanding eastern Europe, including the Yugoslav region (Bondarenko et al. 2009; Chari and Verdery 2009; Owczarzak 2009; Gille 2010; Cervinkova 2012; Veličković 2012; Imre 2014; Koobak and Marling 2014). Recognising that the history of state socialism does not and should not isolate eastern Europe from the rest of the globe strengthens the presumption that identities in the region *have* been formed not just around ethnicity but also race.

Contemporary south-east European studies, while bracketing off race, engages much more critically with ethnicity. Dissatisfied with accounts in the 1990s attributing the Yugoslav wars to historic ethnic and religious schisms, scholars questioning why Yugoslavia experienced not just socio-economic shock but also ethnopolitical conflict when state socialism collapsed have deconstructed the hardening of ethnicised boundaries in late Yugoslav society, the escalation of collective narratives of victimhood, and the processes through which proponents of violence intimidated rivals seeking inter-ethnic coexistence or socio-political orders that were not based primarily on ethnic identity (Dević 1997; Gagnon 2004; Žarkov 2007). Some anthropologists of post-war Bosnia-Herzegovina have set the pace in decentring ethnicity altogether. Rather than seeing the Yugoslav region just as a post-conflict space, defined by the extent of inter-ethnic tension/reconciliation, they treat it as simultaneously post-conflict *and* postsocialist, structured by intertwined shocks of the collapse of socialism and the destruction of everyday socio-economic fabric through war (Bougarel, Helms and Duijzings (eds) 2007; Helms 2013; Hromadžić 2015). Even more recently, these two linked turns have inspired research into social inequalities in Yugoslavia which, by 'bringing class back in' (Archer, Duda and Stubbs

2016), seeks to understand the late Yugoslav crisis as Yugoslav officials, experts and the public perceived it, rather than assuming that the ethnicised frameworks which were made hegemonic *during* the 1980s crisis had necessarily structured Yugoslavs' perceptions so pervasively at the beginning.

Together, these moves to recover 'what nationalism has buried' (Dević 2016) – the social and political alternatives stifled by the manipulation of social grievances into ethnicised entitlement, the violence of ethnopolitical separation and the clientelism that still keeps wartime ethnonationalist elites in power – open more space for recognising race and whiteness, as well as ethnicity, as dimensions of identity construction in the region. This is not only because the social inequalities turn asks scholars to account for a wider range of experiences of marginalisation and how these intersected – some studies explicitly call their framework 'intersectional' (e.g. Žarkov 2011; Bonfiglioli 2012: 58; Bilić and Kajinić (eds) 2016b), others echo the diffusion of intersectional analysis into the social sciences in the 2010s – but also because among the very things nationalism buried were memories of Yugoslavia's global Non-Aligned entanglements and the idea of explaining Yugoslavia's role in the world through global connectivities not ethno-territorial antagonisms. Rhetorics of anti-colonial solidarity and histories of thousands of African and Asian students who travelled to Yugoslavia – hundreds who settled there – have been subsumed, as Vedrana Veličković (2012) notes, in the necessary but not all-encompassing work of explaining (post-) Yugoslav ethnopolitics. If today's Yugoslav region is both post-conflict and postsocialist, it is also – following Chari and Verdery (2009) – postcolonial. Yet we cannot explain the region's position(s) within those global legacies of colonialism and slavery if we exempt it from global formations of race.

Yet positioning it within them is still complicated by its position on what has, many times over, been constructed as a periphery of Europe. Gilroy's *The Black Atlantic*, a cornerstone of postcolonial cultural history, connects the transnational 'structures of feeling, producing, communicating and remembering' (1993: 3) within which black people in the Atlantic world were dispersed because of enslavement, imperialism and postcolonial migration. Given that the Yugoslav region was not a colonial power in the age of empires and was a subject not protagonist of imperial rule, what might arise from translating Gilroy's lens to south-east Europe and seeking a 'black Adriatic'? Instead, south-east European studies treats race with exceptionalism, sometimes through unease at applying it outside former imperial metropoles and settler colonial societies, sometimes through well-meaning reluctance to import Western analytical frameworks into the supposedly separate historical context of (post)socialism. Race is subsumed into ethnicity and nationhood – but it need not be.

Beyond exceptionalism: intersections of ethnicity, nationhood and race

Scholars in Black European Studies at locations including Germany, the Nordic countries and the Netherlands have had to confront exceptionalism in order for the mainstreams of their own area studies to hear them (Loftsdóttir and Jensen (eds) 2012b; Wekker 2016). Exceptionalism obscures the global pervasiveness of 'race' as a structure of thought by implying that race is not relevant for understanding somewhere because it was not directly involved in European colonialism; because it was colonised itself; or even, in the Dutch white liberal discourses that Gloria Wekker (2016) critiques, that its imperialism was benign compared with other powers'. The racial exceptionalism of south-east European, east European and Soviet studies lies not only in extricating these regions from globally connected historical analysis but also in conflating race with ethnicity on one hand while defining eastern Europe as a space where identities are defined by ethnicity *rather than* race on the other. The feminist media scholar Anikó Imre explained unequivocally in 2005 why she studied antiziganism (the marginalisation of Roma) as racism and how white Hungarians often reacted defensively:

> Race and racism continue to be considered concepts that belong exclusively to discourses of coloniality and imperialism, from which Eastern Europe, the deceased 'second world,' continues to be excluded, and from which East European nationalisms are eager to exclude themselves. (Imre 2005: 83)

Her interlocutors' insistence that US racial politics and eastern European ethnic-minority questions stem from separate, incomparable historical conditions is not too far from how white Dutch or Nordic progressives exempt their nations from reckoning with racism and whiteness: dividing the world into zones where racism and colonial violence are 'an issue' and zones where they are not. What drives postsocialist racial exceptionalism, Imre argued further in 2014 while calling for a 'postcolonial media studies in postsocialist Europe', is how ethnic-majority narratives of national identity blur ethnicity and race:

> In these narratives, *race* is generally occluded by *ethnicity*, a term used almost synonymously with *nationality* with reference to linguistic and cultural identity markers. While these identity markers are understood to be as powerful as genetic codes, *race* itself is not part of the vocabulary of nationalism. It has a hidden trajectory in Eastern Europe because the region's nations see themselves outside of colonial processes and thus exempt from post-decolonization struggles with racial mixing and prejudice. As a result, Eastern Europe may be the only, or the last, region on Earth where whiteness is seen as morally transparent, its alleged innocence preserved by a claim of exception to the history of imperialism. (Imre 2014: 130; emphasis original)

Although the Netherlands was an imperial power and eastern Europe was first under imperial domination then in state socialist geopolitics imagined as a site of global anti-imperial solidarity, the expressions of 'white innocence' (Ross 1990) against which Wekker and Imre both write suggest that, in racial exceptionalism and attachment to whiteness, the two regions are not so far apart. They share, at least, a European family resemblance transcending the west/east divisions constructed before and during the Cold War; recognising race as a systemically *global* structure (Mills 2015) makes them not just in parallel but connected.

Scholars of other eastern European countries and the USSR, not just the Yugoslav region, face the obstacle of reconciling the predominance of ethnicity and the invisibility of race. The fact that in Soviet ideology race was not a category applied to the Soviet population, but only a social problem that capitalist–imperialist America had brought on itself, often led post-Soviet scholars to insist that only contemporaneous categories of ethnicity (*narodnost*) and nationality (*natsional'nost*) mattered for understanding collective identities in (post-)Soviet space; yet Soviet thinking about those, Kesha Fikes and Alaina Lemon (2002: 515) argued, still contained a hierarchy of biological and cultural essentialism that did resemble race. The argument that '[w]e don't have races, we have ethnicities' – with which Miglena Todorova (2006: 168) summarises Marxist–Leninist and liberal racial exceptionalism in (post) socialist Bulgaria – epitomises the division of the globe into spaces 'with' and 'without' race even more succinctly. While state socialism co-operated in separating these by projecting racism on to the West in order to undermine interwar and Cold War Western claims to moral superiority, late-nineteenth- and twentieth-century nationalist thinkers had themselves projected contemporaneous European and American racial thought on to their own concepts of the ethnic nation (Todorova 2006; Turda and Weindling (eds) 2007; Bartulin 2013). Paradoxically, both the complete separation and the complete conflation of ethnicity and race have closed down opportunities to understand the interaction of both ideas in pre-socialist, socialist and postsocialist constructions of nationhood.

Even immensely significant works for understanding nationalism and social identities in eastern Europe, which could not have posed their questions if not for postcolonial scholarship, may struggle to separate race from ethnicity or race from nation. Susan Gal and Gail Kligman's *The Politics of Gender after Socialism*, a foundational work in postsocialist gender studies on reproductive politics and nationalism in eastern Europe, is informed by postcolonial studies of anti-colonial nationalist movements which, as Partha Chatterjee (1993) argued, cast women as bearers of tradition while letting men be 'unmarked, and rational, subjects of "modernity"', regulating sexualities, bodies and behaviour through gendered double standards (Gal and Kligman 2000: 26). Gal and Kligman, like Chatterjee, show how patriarchal control over women and reproduction (in postsocialist Poland restricting abortion, or in the then very recent history of mass sexualised–ethnicised violence during the Yugoslav wars) became 'a logical project of nationalism', fuelled by a 'focus on motherhood and women as "vessels of the nation/race"' (Gal and Kligman 2000: 26). The postsocialist nationalist projects, not the book, had conflated 'nation' and 'race'; the book still did not disentangle their relationship or historicise how global formations of 'race' might have influenced specific instances of 'nation' over the decades when nationhood in eastern Europe, including the Yugoslav region, became an organising principle of statehood and society.

Postsocialist feminism, acknowledging the mutually constitutive relationship of ethnonationalism and patriarchy as nationalist governments largely replaced state socialist regimes across eastern Europe after 1989, was not only at the forefront of questioning early 1990s liberal assumptions that the collapse of Communism would bring all east Europeans greater freedoms, but also of recognising interlocking systems of oppression in ways that did not then call themselves intersectional but might still have been compatible with intersectionality, or with a translation of it to east European settings. Feminists recognising the intersection of gender and ethnicity in sexualised ethnopolitical violence during the Yugoslav wars and in the patriarchal politics of postsocialist 'retraditionalisation' (Mostov 2000; Žarkov 2007) drew on Nira Yuval-Davis's *Gender and Nation*, a feminist intervention in nationalism theory; yet Yuval-Davis's earlier *Racialized Boundaries* with Floya Anthias, explicitly linking 'race, nation, gender, colour and class' and more grounded in the politics of anti-racist struggle in Britain, where the two authors taught (Anthias and Yuval-Davis 1993), has had far less influence in comparison. Yet can or should intersectionality, a theory developed by African-American women to explain their situation in the USA, be translated into feminism in Europe? A common critique of European feminist adaptations of intersectionality that address hinges of gender, class, nationhood and ethnicity but displace race 'beyond the national borders' is that they make 'the preoccupation with intersectionality ... an interesting theoretical puzzle' (Petzen 2012: 293–4).[2] Sirma Bilge, similarly, warns against a 'depoliticized', 'ornamental' and whitened intersectionality that, by naming intersecting identities without theorising what structures of power produce them, diminishes 'the constutive role of race' in intersectional feminism; she discerns 'a chronic avoidance of race' in white European feminist theory (Bilge 2013: 408, 412–13). How might east European gender and sexuality studies that frame themselves as intersectional take on board Bilge's critique?

Recent post-Yugoslav translations of intersectionality already, in fact, position themselves within a tradition originating in African-American feminism. Vera Kurtić, executive co-ordinator of Ženski prostor/Women Space in Niš, noted in 2013 that '[d]espite the growing acceptance of Intersectionality in the US and mainstream Western Liberal feminism, the idea of the intersection of different oppressions ... is rarely applied when it comes to Romani women in Serbia', far less to Romani lesbians, the position from/about which she was writing (Kurtić 2013: 6). Bojan Bilić and Sanja Kajinić, editing a volume on LGBT activist politics in Croatia and Serbia, grounded intersectionality in 1960s–80s African-American (and Chicana) traditions of feminist theory and activism, encouraging activists in the Yugoslav region to recognise their own structural positions through understanding how and why these thinkers theorised interlocking oppressions where they were (Bilić and Kajinić 2016a: 10–14). This book suggests that, alongside translating intersectional analyses from elsewhere to model interlocking oppressions in the region, intersectionality can and should also recognise the *global* formations of race that connect the USA, Britain, Germany, the Netherlands *and* former state socialist Europe – and the rest of the globe – into a deeper history of colonialism that has both made whiteness available as an identification within east European national identities and informed the frames through which it is disavowed.

The sensitivity of adapting intersectionality to local contexts without detaching it from its origins exemplifies the politics behind Walter Mignolo's decolonial revisiting of Said in *Local Histories/Global Designs*: 'what happens when theories travel through the colonial difference?' (Mignolo 2000: 173). Said's orientalism, Mignolo argues, captures the historical and cultural locations of India and the Middle East far more than the 'greatest and richest and oldest colonies' of Europe, the Caribbean and the Americas, where European colonial formations of race began; moreover, it exhibits 'enormous silence' about race (Mignolo 2000: 57). If Said offers postcoloniality without race, so too may theories based on him. These are directly relevant questions for the Yugoslav region's ambiguous position, but the region only appears in *Local Histories/ Global Designs* once, in a passing hint towards 1990s sectarian violence, as Mignolo explains that all scholars' knowledge production is shaped by where and when they have lived, and how colonial power has operated on their bodies and lives:

> As recent events in postpartition India, Ireland, and ex-Yugoslavia reveal, the sensibilities of geohistorical locations have to do with a sense of territoriality ... and includes language, food, smells, landscape, climate, and all those basic signs that link the body to one of several places.
> (Mignolo 2000: 191)

Mignolo's decoloniality would later engage more deeply with postsocialism in collaboration with the Russia-based feminist Madina Tlostanova, extending a decolonial 'thinking from the borders' – itself based on W. E. B. Du Bois's 'double consciousness' of African-American experience (Du Bois 1994 [1903]) – to historicise how simultaneous attachment-to-Europe and rejection-by-Europe have characterised national identities across the former Russian and Ottoman empires (Mignolo and Tlostanova 2006). *Local Histories/Global Designs* itself, however, did not suggest where amid the colonial difference the Yugoslav region might lie, showing once more that even global postcolonial thought in the 1990s viewed that region more as a space of ethnopolitical conflict than a former space of state socialism, Non-Alignment and global connectedness.

Nevertheless, theory that views 'race' as a global structure of power, thought and feeling, more than an identity category only relevant to nations directly implicated in or subjected to European overseas colonialism and the Atlantic slave trade, helps to connect the translations of postcoloniality and intersectionality that have helped theorists from the region and outside explain its geopolitical position(s) under state socialism and postsocialism.

'The Balkans' in global racial formations

Positing a 'black Adriatic' from Gilroy's 'black Atlantic', a device through which I encouraged listeners in Nottingham and Budapest to trace such connections in their own work at workshops in 2015–16, is to ask: what questions would south-east studies have to pose in determining what an equivalent of Gilroy's transnational approach to black intellectual history might be?[3] Gilroy both calls for a 'transcultural, international', non-nation-state-centric mode of black social, intellectual and cultural history inside and outside Europe (Gilroy 1993: 4) and emphasises that racialised hierarchies of belonging, the legacies of colonialism and slavery, are still circulating the globe in what many Americans and Europeans were then imagining as the supposedly cosmopolitan, multicultural and post-racial present (Gilroy 2004); moreover, his anti-essentialism towards race and racism harmonises with the deconstruction of ethnic identities in recent post-Yugoslav studies.

The critical race theorist Charles Mills, meanwhile, links race both to the violence of colonialism and slavery and to the construction of spatialised hierarchies of civilisation/backwardness around people(s) and territories, an insight that sets south-east European constructions of 'Europe' and the 'Balkans' within a global history of such formations. 'Race', for Mills, represents a 'moral cartography' that, on levels from colonial grand strategy to twenty-first-century urban micropolitics, divides the world's territory into civilised and modern spaces, populated by and belonging to people of white European descent, and the remaining 'wild and racialized' spaces, where people, territory, histories, cultures and knowledges are marked for permanent subordination, exploitability and disposability, exotically appealing and viscerally threatening at once (Mills 1997: 46). Racialised hierarchies of modernity, civilisation/wildness and Europeanness, in critical race theory, were embedded so systemically into modern intellectual and political history that they must be in the lineage of any symbolic geography invoking these concepts today (Winant 2001: 16; Gilroy 2004: 157; Goldberg 2009). Balkanism – as Miglena Todorova (2006: 39) already suggests for Bulgaria – is no exception.

By emphasising processes of 'racialisation', not ascriptions of race to pre-existing groups, critical race theory also fits with the turn in the 2000s towards studying ethnicity as process rather than fixed 'groupness' (Brubaker 2004: 4) in the history, anthropology and sociology of southeast Europe. Racialisation, like 'ethnicization' (Oberschall 2000: 984), describes the processes that reproduce these categories and structure the social world: chief among them, for race, are the violence and dehumanising tutelage that, as Frantz Fanon (1963, 1986 [1952]) showed, coerce people racialised as non-white to internalise the structures of white supremacy and their subordinate, contingent position within it (Mills 1997: 89). Another consequence of the construction of the racial order is the condition of 'whiteness' itself. 'Whiteness' encompasses the people, spaces, beliefs, aesthetics, histories and types of knowledge that enjoy full personhood and modernity within the racial order (Dyer 1997; Garner 2007). So deeply is it naturalised, indeed so deeply must it *be* naturalised, that those who uncontestedly fall into it have the privilege of not needing to recognise it (Frankenberg 1993; Ahmed 2007), a condition Mills (2015) calls 'white ignorance'.

The grounds for racialising people, symbols and spaces into categories have however varied at different historical moments (Winant 2001), and taken different forms across the globe (Goldberg 2009), making it more accurate to talk of multiple 'racisms' (Garner 2010) or 'racializations' (Bonnett, in press) than one unchanging 'racism'. In particular, what Howard Winant terms the mid-twentieth century's 'postwar racial break' of decolonisation and anti-racist struggle (which did involve state socialist

Europe) marked a 'transition to a new racial order' where racism still operated but more diffusely, less perceptibly (Winant 2001: 10, 14, 308). Post-Cold-War Europe, for instance, witnessed what were often termed forms of 'new racism' (Barker 1981) or 'cultural racism' (Taguieff 1990), with boundaries of collective identity based on cultural values rather than perceptions of inherent biological difference (Balibar and Wallerstein 1991); such racisms coexisted uneasily with myths that Europe in defeating fascism, relinquishing its colonies and acquiring multi-ethnic populations had become 'post-racial' (Lentin 2008: 497). This context, whether or not white nationals acknowledged it, informed any European society that had experienced mass migration and where racism was a named political issue (Gilroy 1987; Anthias and Yuval-Davis 1993; Lentin 2004; Fekete 2009).

While south-east (and eastern) Europe has seen less migration from outside Europe (and that is not the same as *no* migration), other bonds tie it into the global racial order. These include the fantasies and desires of colonial exoticism, legible in the region's contemporary and historic popular culture, and the transnational imaginative circuits along which globalised popular entertainment travels; histories of people of colour who travelled through and settled in the region, among them Africans enslaved under the Eastern Mediterranean slave trade, African students who travelled to Yugoslav universities and Chinese merchants traversing postsocialist Europe; south-east European states' and individuals' global entanglements, especially at world-historical moments such as the Cold War or the present refugee crisis; the adjustments migrants from south-east Europe make to their new home countries' racial formations and how they themselves are, often ambiguously, racialised there; and the racial ideologies that motivate anti-Semitism and antiziganism explicitly, other constructions of ethnic and national identity less so. They run through a region whose people often complain, with reason, that Eurocentrism placing the Balkans on the outside has targeted them, and yet where many expressions of national, urban and socio-economic identity enact identifications with Europe which might, or might not, be part of the Europe that imposed colonial domination on the world.

Here lies the ambiguity which the 1990s translations of Said's orientalism into balkanism could not resolve. Maria Todorova, in a reissued *Imagining the Balkans*, distanced herself from direct orientalism–balkanism parallels, the Ottoman Empire from 'empire' as European imperialism and the Balkans from postcoloniality at all:

> [T]he main difference between the two concepts is the geographic and historical concreteness of the Balkans versus the mostly metaphorical and symbolic nature of the Orient. The lack of a colonial predicament for the Balkans also distinguishes the two, as do questions of race, color, religion, language, and gender. […] Postcolonial studies are a critique of postcoloniality, the condition in areas of the world that were colonies. I do not believe the Ottoman Empire, whose legacy has defined the Balkans, can be treated as a late colonial empire. (Todorova 2009: 194–5)

Several scholars from south-east Europe who do view their work as postcolonial – including Dušan Bjelić, Konstantin Kilibarda and Miglena Todorova – view this as 'foreclosing' (Bjelić 2017: 4) the Balkans' place in global (post)coloniality. Bjelić lights particularly on Maria Todorova's remark that 'Balkanism conveniently exempted "the West" from charges of racism, colonialism, Eurocentrism and Christian intolerance: the Balkans, after all, are in Europe, they are white and they are predominantly Christian' (Todorova 1994: 455).[4] While this 'after all' was imaginary reported speech, Bjelić (2009) perceived an unexamined whiteness in Maria Todorova's own framework as he would in Julia Kristeva and Slavoj Žižek.[5] Kilibarda (2010: 41), meanwhile, argues directly that Todorova's 'coding of the Balkans as "white", "European", and "Christian" and thus, somehow, placed outside the realm of postcolonial critique' overlooks the role of 'whiteness' as a colonial legacy worldwide, including in this region.

Miglena Todorova, in 2006, had anticipated all these articles in arguing that *Imagining the Balkans* did not provide the necessary intersections for relating Western orientalism and balkanism in a wider post-Ottoman space (Todorova 2006: 60). Using critical race theory, she set balkanist discourses within a broader sphere, in which 'Western balkanist narratives shared properties because these narratives originated in the "transnational" culture of the "white Atlantic"' (Todorova 2006: 55) – an extrapolation of Gilroy's 'black Atlantic' towards the global circulation of whiteness as a subject position that anticipated Stam and Shohat (2012: xv) by six years.[6] The result is an explicitly connected history, explaining what *Imagining the Balkans* itself did not: that even as the book distanced the Balkans from postcoloniality, it furnished south-east European studies with a vernacular postcolonialism making it easier, not harder, to draw global connections.

Indeed, the Yugoslav region is already linked into transnational European racial formations by studies of antiziganism. For Kurtić, or the socio-legal scholar Julija Sardelić, post-Yugoslav structural discrimination against Roma proves that constructions of *racial* (phenotypical and cultural) difference, beyond just constructions of *ethnic* belonging, are inherent in such marginalisation. Sardelić (2014), for instance, draws on the Romani activist Valeriu Nicolae, plus Balibar, Gilroy, and Antonio Negri and Michael Hardt, in seeing Yugoslav/post-Yugoslav antiziganism as one expression of transnational European 'cultural racism' against visibly different, supposedly-unwilling-to-assimilate minorities. Some writers on European racisms had also used the region's inter-ethnic relations in arguments that late-twentieth-century racisms were becoming reoriented around constructed cultural difference not skin colour, with John Solomos (2003: 251) perceiving 'new types of cultural racism based on the construction of fixed religious and cultural boundaries' in the break-up of Yugoslavia. Even the fixing of ethnicised boundaries between South Slavs acquired racialised dimensions during the violence, when ethnicised myths of certain nations standing at the 'bulwark of Christianity' (*antemurale Christianitatis*) during European wars against the Ottoman Empire cast Muslim or 'Balkan' Others as the new threat from the East (Žanić 2005).

Post-Yugoslav scholars have linked the antemurale myth to race and whiteness most tightly for Slovenia, Yugoslavia's most prosperous republic. Slovenia was where independence supporters in the 1980s first contrasted their nation's identification with 'Europe' against the rest of Yugoslavia's supposed 'Balkanness' as a reason to separate (Croatian nationalism soon followed), and was the region's first EU candidate and member, integrated earliest into EU border security structures and ideologies (see Chapter 4). Maria Todorova calls the antemurale myth 'one of the most important European mental maps', portable around Europe as the imaginary front line against Islam shifted from the Spanish Reconquista to the Habsburg–Ottoman wars and even taken up by the USA after 9/11 (Todorova 2005a: 76). The antemurale myth predates both Atlantic slavery and the Spanish exclusion of indigenous people in the Americas from European humanity, Mills's and Mignolo's respective origin points for 'race'; yoking nationhood with Christianity, it was, once Europeans started dividing the globe into 'civilised' and 'uncivilised' territories according to inhabitants' skin colour, implicitly racialised long before today's West explicitly racialised Islam. The conflation of historical myths about defence against Islam with contemporary transnational security discourses about terrorism and migration was widespread in post-Yugoslav Slovenia and, as they too built relationships with EU border security structures, the other successor states (Mihelj 2005; Petrović 2009: 44–5).

Tomislav Longinović, writing on 1980s–90s Slovenian identifications with Western Catholicism/'Mitteleuropa' and on interwar Yugoslav ideas of a 'Dinaric race', already reads 'race' and whiteness as distinct from 'ethnicity' in Yugoslav national identity narratives (Longinović 2011). The 'Dinaric race' described by the Yugoslav anthropologist Vladimir Dvorniković had offered certain forms of interwar Yugoslavism a category that unified Bosnian Muslims, Croats, Serbs and Montenegrins but excluded Jews, Albanians and Roma. Slovenian attachment to 'Europe' in the 1980s did not use the language of race but for Longinović was simultaneously attachment to whiteness, marking the Balkans as a space on a fundamentally lower civilisational level and thus racialising the Serbs. Longinović describes the discursive separation of the Slovenian nation from Yugoslavia's south and east as involving a 'racism [which] was not immediately perceivable by Western observers, because whiteness, technological superiority, and universalist humanism have all been incorporated into the specter of Europe itself as the symbolic foundation of the West' (Longinović 2011: 90–1).

Although Longinović does not explore the racial politics of post-Yugoslav *Serb* identities (of those racialised by Slovenian nationalism), his explicit linking of symbolic geographies of Europeanness and modernity with race and whiteness shows that critical theories of global racial formations can combine with approaches to identity and nationhood in south-east Europe to create deeper understandings of the region's politics of belonging. Through naming such articulations as explicit not implicit, structural not coincidental and globally connected not regionally isolated, ideas about race and expressions of racism become recognisable as more than impossible-to-contextualise anomalies or 'scattered experiences' – and then one can discuss how often others have encountered them too (Ahmed 2015: 8). Indeed, scholars of every part of Europe beyond the 'core' countries in the history of race and imperialism have struggled against the exceptionalism of imagining other European nations as 'historically white' and viewed even those nations that did not have their own empires or were ruled by other empires through an explicitly postcolonial lens. Despite the political and economic disparities between the Nordic region and the ex-USSR, studies of both areas have insights for understanding race in the Yugoslav region.

Postcoloniality and whiteness in peripheralised Europe

Much scholarship on race, postcoloniality and whiteness on European peripheries is indebted to academics and activists in German Studies, including Afro-German women who started theorising their 'double oppression(s)' in white German society in collaboration with Audre Lorde (Obermeier 1989: 173; Campt 1993). The title of Sander Gilman's *On Blackness Without Blacks* (Gilman 1982) first summarised, then undid, the conceptual basis of German racial exceptionalism: that race was not relevant in German society or German Studies as it would be for Britain or France, because the German-speaking cultural area's population had until very late on been white (see, e.g., Sieg 2002; Campt 2004; El-Tayeb 2011). Germany resembles the Netherlands, Gloria Wekker's subject, in the levels of public and academic exceptionalism confronting scholars committed to Black European Studies and/or transnational postcolonial history. Both had large overseas empires, though the Netherlands' was two centuries older; indeed, contemporary queer of colour critique grounded in both countries often unites them as sites where recent celebration of white gay/lesbian identities combines with racialised stigmatisation of blackness and Islam in identifying the nation with a white, secular, sexually liberated 'Europe' (El-Tayeb 2011; Haritaworn 2015). As former imperial metropoles, however, they invite a common objection against extending conclusions about their racial formations to other areas where German literary–cultural traditions influenced the nineteenth-century production of national cultures: that 'race' did not matter in European nations without colonies. Yet postcolonial studies of the Nordic region have overcome this, showing striking similarities between former colonial powers and nations that were sometimes under their own neighbours' imperial rule.

Coalitions of white and Afro-Scandinavian scholars, working across national boundaries, have demonstrated that not only the assertive middle-ranking empires of Denmark and Sweden, but also national identity-making projects in Swedish-ruled Norway and Danish-ruled Iceland, were implicated in the systems of thought and power that constituted the racial project of colonialism. In Sweden and Denmark, dominant public narratives hold (as in the Netherlands) that Scandinavian imperialism was less exploitative than British or French and that racism is not a Scandinavian social problem (Pred 2000; Sawyer 2002). Yet Ylva Habel (2005: 125) still documents a 'longstanding fascination with the exotic' in Swedish national culture, using Fanon's understanding of the 'hypervisibility' of blackness to set Swedish reception of Josephine Baker's tours in the same structure of feeling and power as public fascination with 'blackamoor' pages brought to Sweden by eighteenth-century transatlantic trading companies. Kristín Loftsdóttir, studying fin-de-siècle

Icelandic textbooks and adventure narratives, argues meanwhile that Icelanders identified their nation with Europeanness, civilisational mastery, masculinity and whiteness, and enacted 'counter-identification' with Africa, through comparable racialised/gendered frameworks to those described by historians such as Ann Laura Stoler (1995, 2002) and Anne McClintock (1994, 1995) for western European imperial nations (Loftsdóttir 2009: 271). While Sweden had an empire and Icelanders could have viewed themselves as imperial subjects not colonisers, notions of whiteness and European civilisational advantage, constructed versus 'Africa', defined both nations.

Loftsdóttir and Lars Jensen, a scholar of postcolonial Denmark, collected similar studies from across the Nordic region to demonstrate that colonialism was 'a narrative with universal ramifications', beyond the areas imperial history usually sees. Despite the range of Nordic historical experiences 'from colonizing powers, to colonies themselves', the volume emphasised that the Nordic countries, 'while … certainly peripheral to the major [European] metropolitan cultures … generally participated actively in the production of Europe as the global centre and profited from this experience' (Loftsdóttir and Jensen 2012a: 1). They, like Habel, linked past with present by showing how perceptions that Nordic countries did not participate in European imperialism have informed contemporary national narratives of tolerance, innocence and cosmopolitanism while impeding public recognition of structural racism and obscuring global asymmetries of power in the humanitarian and peacekeeping projects that fed into Nordic states' geopolitical identities after 1945 (Habel 2012; Jensen 2012; Loftsdóttir and Björnsdóttir 2015). Nordic societies were involved in processes of colonialism even if most individuals producing it 'had never been to Africa nor participated directly in the colonial project' (Loftsdóttir 2010: 43): through Nordic scientists' contributions to racial theory; white Scandinavians' participation in settler colonialism in British dominions or the USA; popular cultural representations of Africa or Islam that invited past or present Icelanders, Swedes, Danes, Norwegians or Finns to share in racialised constructions of nationhood and whiteness, 'self' and 'Other'; and the impact of these legacies and their disavowal on present-day responses to migration and multicultural change.

South-east European studies can likewise ask how intellectuals and travellers from south-east Europe participated in these global processes, and what identity-work travel narratives and visual consumer cultures – familiar sources in imperial history – performed in the Habsburg South Slav lands, the post-Ottoman nation-states or unified Yugoslavia. These two peripheries of Europe nevertheless have different structural positions, with the economic gap widening during and after state socialism; moreover, the politics of 'ethnicity' in south-east Europe differ from Nordic (or Dutch) models. Whereas in the Netherlands only non-autochthonous people supposedly possess ethnicity, or in the USA 'ethnic' labels denote multiple non-Anglo-Saxon diasporic heritages with shifting relationships to conditional whiteness (Wekker 2016: 22), in south-east Europe the ethnicity–nationhood–territory nexus means autochthony *is* ethnicity. The only people without ethnicity in its dominant politicised sense are from outside the region – though, when racialised as black or Chinese, they certainly have 'race'. These might seem obstacles for Nordic/south-east European comparison – yet the postcolonial social/cultural history of Russia and the ex-USSR has addressed them already.

Integrating the USSR into transnational black history began with the thought of African-American intellectuals like Du Bois and Langston Hughes who travelled there, then continued through Allison Blakely's groundbreaking *Russia and the Negro* into a series of studies on Cold War racial politics, black Soviet histories, and Soviet concepts of 'race' and 'nationality' (Blakely 1986; Baldwin 2002; Fikes and Lemon 2002; Hirsch 2002; Matusevich (ed.) 2007; Roman 2012) plus the explicit post-Soviet hinge between Russian identity and 'privileged whiteness' (Zakharov 2015: 13).[7] These, on various scales, connect histories of Afro-Russians with the Cold War politics of Soviet internationalism and Soviet–US rivalry, answering what even most self-described studies of global racial formations leave unasked: how histories of state socialism and global raciality combine.

Blakely, Maxim Matusevich and others show that before state socialism – when exceptionalism would hold inhabitants of the Russian Empire had not encountered 'race' – encounters with race and coloniality were already part of imperial Russian life. Matusevich and his contributors to *Africa in Russia, Russia in Africa*, for instance, juxtaposed histories of Africans and African-Americans in Russia since the eighteenth century (from Pushkin's great-grandfather to African students' descendants in post-Soviet cities) with studies of Russian/Soviet assistance to African rulers and liberation movements before as well as during Soviet rule (Matusevich (ed.) 2007). The Soviet instrumentalisation of race in international relations that threw the oppression of enslavement and settler colonialism back at the USA, already well established in the 1920s, informed the racial politics of state socialist regimes in eastern Europe – including Yugoslavia's – after 1945 (Todorova 2006). For Russian/Soviet spaces as for northern and western Europe, studies of racialised European colonial imaginations in the everyday reveal that representations of race and whiteness were circulating well before late-twentieth-century contestations of European belonging and multiculturalism, even before state socialist ideology would inscribe the USSR and Communism in general into a zone of the globe where racial politics were supposedly irrelevant.

Two studies of Latvia exemplify this longer history of race. The literature scholar Irina Novikova researched constructions of blackness, whiteness and collective identity around popular music through Soviet reactions to jazz (Novikova 2004). Investigating the travelling 'Dahomey Amazon shows' (human zoos) that visited 1890s–1900s Moscow and Riga, she then showed that even though Russia and Latvia did not have their own African colonies their capitals were still implicated in the same racialised logic of fin-de-siècle colonialism, modernity and spectacle through which audiences in Britain, France, Germany, the Netherlands, Nordic countries and Austria-Hungary understood themselves as protagonists of a European civilising mission and Africans as inhabitants of an eternally primitive space (Novikova 2013). Latvia's colonial engagement had once been even more direct: in 1651–8, the Duchy of Courland, under a German-speaking aristocracy, had founded colonies in Tobago and what is now Kunta Kinteh Island, Gambia. The project of reconstructing an autonomous, non-Russian and demonstrably modern Latvian national past after independence from the USSR, Dace Dzenovska shows, has led contemporary Latvians to reappropriate the Tobago colony's history as 'a narrative of national historical presence' (Dzenovska 2013: 405). Explicitly linking identification with the colonial project to the politics of postsocialist nation-building, Dzenovska signals appreciating coloniality as well as nationalism in understanding the implications of the 'return to Europe' (see Petrović 2009) that many members of postsocialist nations in the 1990s sought.

For Ukraine, meanwhile, the work of Adriana Helbig (2014) on African migration and hip-hop makes the very connections between global translations of 'race' and postsocialist national identity-making that I did not perceive when I encountered their everyday manifestations in Croatia. Helbig, a Ukrainian-American ethnomusicologist, had 'thought of difference predominantly in terms of ethnicity' because of her own diasporic experience and disciplinary training but found that her 'research on global hip hop has forced me to crystallize my thinking on race' (Helbig 2014: 5). Helbig's *Hip Hop Ukraine* is based on ethnographic research with black Africans (often students, in Ukraine via routes established during the Cold War) and white Ukrainians in local hip-hop scenes or working elsewhere in Ukrainian popular music. It connects postcolonial Soviet studies with global translations of 'race' through the transnational routes of popular entertainment. These translations of 'race' include: legacies of state socialist ideologies about music, blackness and Soviet identity (deriving from Soviet interpretations of African-American experiences and Soviet displacement of racism on to America) in the context of post-Soviet Ukraine's migration history; functions of blackness and whiteness in contemporary Ukrainian identity narratives; white Ukrainians' fetishisation of black performers; and the agency of black musicians seeking to change white Ukrainians' frames of reference about race but constrained by an existing white Ukrainian gaze that essentialises an exotic, wild and tribal 'Africa' and expects every black rapper to be African-American. The space of Gilroy's conceptual 'black Atlantic', Helbig shows, reaches far beyond the spatial Atlantic to make these Ukrainian/Soviet experiences comprehensible (Helbig 2014: 164).

Helbig's recognition that identity discourses around as everyday a phenomenon as music reveal deeply embedded legacies of historical processes of racialisation, like Wekker's approach to studying race and whiteness before mass postcolonial migration, inspires the structure of this book, which begins where my own rethinking of race and the Yugoslav region began: with imaginations of blackness, African-Americanness and Africa in Yugoslav and post-Yugoslav popular music, and what they might reveal about how musicians and their public understood the region's own relationship to race (Chapter 1). So contradictory are these identifications that explaining them requires treating the region's history not through the lens of ethnopolitical conflict between settled nations but as a more complex historical contact zone: Chapter 2, therefore, suggests how often-neglected aspects of the history of ethnicity, nationhood and migration reveal connections that tie the region into the global history of race – and that explain the many different racial formations, before as well as during state socialism, that people in the Yugoslav region have translated into localised understandings of geopolitics and identity, self and Other (Chapter 3). With these histories explicit, it becomes possible to perceive what two and a half decades of research on the Yugoslav region have so rarely expressed: the *racialised* politics of post-Yugoslav postsocialism (Chapter 4). Beyond a mode of analogy that would simply liken ethnicised prejudice or international structural marginalisation in the Yugoslav region to racism or postcoloniality elsewhere, the Conclusion argues for a mode of connection that places the region, systematically, within global legacies of colonialism, slavery and 'race'.

In doing so, moreover, it demonstrates that tools already exist for fitting studies of other postsocialist societies, not just this region, into global histories of race and coloniality as well as European histories of nationalism and modernity. Indeed, critical race scholars emphasise that a European history of nationalism *is simultaneously* a global history of race. The 'postsocialism and postcoloniality' agenda, inspired by Chari and Verdery (2009), has already inspired scholars of eastern Europe as well as the USSR to trace connections between the 'Second World' and 'Third World' – a project that even as this book was being written was encouraging more and more historians to do so for Yugoslav state socialism. For south-east Europe, however, there are not only legacies of state socialism but also longer-term legacies of Ottoman rule in the configurations of memory, inequality and identity that structure constructions of nationhood, ethnicity, Europeanness and race; while Yugoslavia differed even from its Soviet-satellite neighbours in positioning itself as neither east nor west through its distinctive geopolitical narrative of Non-Alignment. All these factors complicate understanding how global racial formations have been adapted and translated into, across and through the Yugoslav region. None of them places the region outside the global history and politics of 'race' altogether.

Notes

1 See Dragović-Soso (2007); Baker (2015).
2 See, for instance, Jennifer Petzen's commentary on a 2009 German feminist intersectionality conference which invited white German feminists and well-known US and European feminists of colour to speak but no feminists of colour from Germany. This despite, for instance, 'Fatima El-Tayeb [being] probably one of the first people to write about gay racism in Germany' (Petzen 2012: 293).
3 The move of translating Gilroy's title to another ocean to emphasise transoceanic connections in the context of global histories of racism and anti-racism was already being made by Robbie Shilliam's *The Black Pacific*, which situates South Pacific indigenous activists, African diasporic struggles, and notions of blackness and Africanness within 'a global infrastructure' of anti-colonialism (Shilliam 2015: 10), while in Soviet studies Maxim Matusevich (2012) has argued directly for 'expanding the boundaries of the Black Atlantic' in proposing African students' travel to the USSR as a vector of modernity and globalisation into Soviet society. Robert Stam and Ella Shohat (2012: xv), meanwhile, name 'red' and 'white' as well as 'black' Atlantics (transnational ideas of indigenous radicalism and transnational ideas of whiteness) in their study of 'race in translation'.

4 The text Bjelić cites from Todorova's 1997 book is slightly reworked, but 'in Europe, they are white and they are predominantly Christian' appears in both (Todorova 1997: 188).
5 On Žižek and whiteness, see Conclusion.
6 This usage is worth distinguishing from David Armitage's reference to 'the white Atlantic' as the conventional, Eurocentric mode of Atlantic history, then being challenged by studies of the 'black Atlantic' and a 'red Atlantic' that for Armitage denoted radical labour not indigenous resistance (Armitage 2001: 479).
7 Cold War politics of race both prompted the USA to give African-American artists key roles in public diplomacy towards state socialist countries and, arguably, to grant greater civil rights at home (Dudziak 2000; Borstelmann 2001; Von Eschen 2006).

1

Popular music and the 'cultural archive'

This book began its Introduction, and begins its chapter structure, not in the mainstream of international affairs (the politics of state socialist Non-Alignment, or postsocialist European border control) but with what might seem a more distant topic: popular music. It does so because the everyday structures of feeling perceptible through popular music are a readily observable sign that ideas of race are part of identity-making in the Yugoslav region; proving this point opens the way to revisiting other open questions in the study of the region through the lens of 'race'. Both the transnational histories of popular music's globalised production and circulation, and the narratives and fantasies of identity revealed in its audiovisual and embodied dimensions, are encounters with and often reconstructions of global formations of race, where musicians, media workers and listeners–viewers respond to music from outside the region and participate in musical cultures grounded inside it. It is integral within what Gloria Wekker (2016: 2), showing how to study race and whiteness in societies where prevailing identity narratives position the nation 'outside' race, calls the 'cultural archive': the often everyday and ephemeral, but no less significant, sites that make explicit how deeply race has permeated constructions of individual and collective identity.

The cultural archive, alongside 'innocence' (neither knowing nor wanting to know about racism) and 'white Dutch self-representation' (in which the national self belongs to Europe while national Others do not and cannot), is one of Wekker's three central concepts in *White Innocence*, which builds on Said's reference to imperial fiction and poetry as a cultural archive via Ann Stoler's sense of the archive as a 'repository of memory' (Stoler 2009: 49 in Wekker 2016: 19) for everyday legacies of imperial rule in postcolonial metropoles. It is

> located in many things, in the way we think, do things, and look at the world, in what we find (sexually) attractive, in how our affective and rational economies are organized and intertwined. Most important, it is between our ears and in our hearts and souls. (Wekker 2016: 19)

Popular music is just such a repository; moreover, across south-east Europe ideas of 'popular music' are very often given meaning by relating them (by claims of continuity or performative distance) to folk traditions. South-east European folk music, in turn, has long been a symbolic resource in constructing collective cultural identities by ascribing or denying 'modernity' and 'Europeanness' to certain territorial–demographic spaces but not others (those 'non-European' ones are ascribed to 'the Balkans'). This characteristic of ethnonational and socio-economic identity-making in south-east Europe reveals both the music and the discourses as part of a common post-Ottoman space (Buchanan (ed.) 2007). The break-up of Yugoslavia, meanwhile, enmeshed popular music in the same political processes of ethnic separation and marginalisation of social alternatives that operated throughout post-Yugoslav public spheres (Čolović 1994; Pettan (ed.) 1998b; Gordy 1999). The powerful interventions in everyday public consciousness necessary to normalise the primacy of ethnic identity and polarisation against national Others placed popular entertainment, including music, in a continuum with phenomena more conventionally thought of as 'political' (Baker 2010), where one might often look for evidence about nationalism and race.

Wekker's search for the affective legacies of racialised colonial imagination in the 'cultural archive' reinforces Anikó Imre's argument that scholars of European media ought to apply the lens of east European postcoloniality to everyday popular culture as well as highbrow literature and cinema (Imre 2014). Indeed, south-east European studies uses the critique of balkanism to discern a common politics of representation and exotification – with many incentives for creators to internalise exoticising Western gazes on their region – affecting music, cinema and literature alike (Iordanova 2001; Baker 2008; Volčič 2013).[1] More than just a *parallel* to what Stuart Hall termed the 'spectacle of the "Other"' (Hall 1997) driving the construction of racial difference since imperial consumer and visual cultures were born, gazes that partition the globe into national cultures and expect essentialised representations of identity from each (but the most tradition-bound zones most of all) originate from the same fin-de-siècle international expositions (Bolin 2006) at which white Europeans as gazing audiences could form first-hand stereotypes of Africans and indigenous peoples (Pieterse 1992: 94–7; Blanchard, Boëtsch and Jacomijn Snoep 2011; Novikova 2013). The conclusion is more complex than saying the stereotypes the West projects on to eastern Europe racialise eastern Europeans as non-white, though in certain contexts they may (Longinović 2011; Fox, Moroşanu and Szilassy 2012); it also raises the uncomfortable, silenced, necessary question of what else eastern Europeans, identifying with 'Europe' and modernity, might be identifying with.

Popular music itself, meanwhile, belongs to a history of globalisation structured by the routes and legacies of colonialism and Atlantic slavery (Gilroy 1993; Erlmann 1999; Radano and Bohlman (eds) 2000; Weheliye 2005; Lipsitz 2007; Denning 2015). Gilroy's 'black Atlantic' as a transnational cultural space of struggle, communication, memory-work, history-making and political critique is constituted by soul, reggae, Afrobeat and hip-hop musicians as well as the poets, novelists and scholars who have expressed written black thought (Gilroy 1993). Their music takes its sonic and embodied forms because of the movements of people, capital, technologies and sounds that resulted from European colonialism, Africans' enslavement and what this violence left behind (Weheliye 2005). Simultaneously, it is part of a global consumer culture that commercialises racialised gazes and desires into exotica (Gilroy 2000) and of the complex global imagination of 'America': indeed, African-American music and musicians were important for US cultural diplomacy during the Cold War (Von Eschen 2006), towards Non-Aligned

Yugoslavia (Vučetić 2012) as well as the USSR. Sounds, songs, stars and genres deeply embedded in US racial politics, from jazz to Michael Jackson through Motown, were also cultural artefacts that entered Yugoslavia as symbols of Americanness, coolness and hipness, feeding into how vocalists, musicians and producers thought performers should sound and move; while black diasporic musics from Jamaica and Nigeria, from Britain and France and Germany, were also part of Yugoslav popular music cultures for at least some listeners, via multilateral and Non-Aligned routes of musical circulation as well as historic western European cultural entrepots.

Anglo-American popular music's influence on the Yugoslav region or anywhere else is not – as studies of global hip-hop, especially, emphasise (Mitchell (ed.) 2001; Alim, Ibrahim and Pennycook (eds) 2008) – one-way cultural homogenisation or 'Americanisation'. Rather, it is an active vernacularisation or 'cultural translation' (Stokes 2003: 298) interpreting the sound, style and content of foreign popular music through the lenses of existing local identity narratives (such as the modernity–Europe–West/tradition–Balkan–East narrative) and combining foreign musical elements with musical practices understood as belonging to a collective (national, urban, regional, ethnic) self. Foreign frames of reference for popular music in this region have included Anglo-American music, Italian and German light-entertainment traditions (peaking in the 1950s–70s), northern European pop–dance–rap (late 1980s–present) and music from the wider post-Ottoman space (Rasmussen 2002). For instance, one pan-south-east European genre with different national inflections, 'pop-folk', combines post-Ottoman elements of musical meaning and practice (such as vocal styles; instruments; rhythms; melody; lyrical devices), which themselves bridge ethno-linguistic boundaries and the greater symbolic boundary between 'Europe' and 'the Middle East', with elements from the Anglosphere and larger European centres of musical production (electric guitars; synthesisers; drum machines; hip-hop beats; rap; electronic dance music), in resonance and tension with ideologies of national and ethnic cultural identity (Buchanan (ed.) 2007; Samson 2013).

While ethnomusicologists of south-east Europe pay important attention – more than many other disciplines – to the politics of Romani identity and representation (Imre 2008; Pettan 2010; Silverman 2012), even they still rarely consider the racial politics of popular music in a *transnational* sense, or how expressions and signifiers of those politics are translated, recognised and reappropriated (or not) as music circulates. Every musical genre connected to the Anglosphere, however, exists within the Black Atlantic's racial formations – whether inherently and symbolically connected to black struggle, like hip-hop and soul; whether implicitly defined through whiteness, like country, metal or rock; or whether they have been racialised in changing ways as they gained popularity, as occurred in the history of rhythm-and-blues or rock'n'roll. The transnational circulation of popular music and its translation into local musical cultures, therefore, inherently bring 'a politics of race and power' (Gilroy 1993: 103) – acknowledged or not – as part of what musicians and listeners hear, see, interpret and transform. Popular music does not just reflect 'race in translation' (Stam and Shohat 2012); it *is* race in translation. Some of these translations exemplify as racialised a European colonial imagination as anything from Britain, France, the Netherlands or Germany; yet others have situated the region's national identities in genuine solidarity with the subjects of colonial oppression and the marginalisation of blackness. The puzzle of how the same collective identities could lend themselves to both positions is the subject of this book.

Translations of Black European dance music: national and racialised bodies

The most unambiguous identification of nationhood with Europeanness through an explicitly racialised geopolitical imagination in the region's popular music is perhaps the very musical movement with which this book began: Croatia's mid-1990s translation of 'Eurodance' music (a Dutch–German–Nordic format) into 'Cro-dance'. Cro-dance combined sung vocals in Croatian, and English-language rap, with adaptations of the sound and style of Eurodance acts like Dr Alban and 2 Unlimited, who were very often black Europeans. Cro-dance producers explicitly named the Western, modern identity they ascribed their music as evidence that Croats had a completely different cultural mentality from the Yugoslav state they had left (Baker 2013: 318). Cro-dance differed from Eurodance as an audiovisual spectacle both in its linguistic translation and the whiteness, rather than blackness, of its performers. Media presented Cro-dance acts as from a white, Croat ethnic background even if performers were Bosniak and/or Romani (which would have positioned them outside the nation in post-Yugoslav Croatian identities' hierarchical symbolic geography). Blackness as a signifier was nevertheless part of Cro-dance's symbolic language: in performances of African-American street style through dress, simulations of African-American Vernacular English in rap, and most visibly when directors placed black dancers alongside the white musicians in some videos that gave the genre an audiovisual identity.

One 1996 video featuring two Cro-dance singers who established longer pop careers than most, Nina Badrić and Emilija Kokić, for their song 'Ja sam vlak' ('I am a train'[2]), for instance, used graffiti-covered concrete urban sites to evoke the inner-city landscapes (racialised as African-American) of US hip-hop photography and video, and featured the two women flirting with a multiracial trio of shirtless men.[3] The central dancer was a black model who was a minor celebrity in mid-1990s Zagreb, whose one moment of agency was to contribute the (English) words 'Move it, move it, move it' to the soundtrack. Explaining why a mid-1990s Croatian director or viewer considered this an attractive and sexy way to direct a black male dancer goes back, through critical race theory, to the objectification and sexualisation of black male bodies through which, Fanon (1986 [1952]) argued, colonialism had removed black men's agency as political subjects.[4]

Cro-dance's sonic and visual presentation evoked blackness through 'African-American' urban space and fashion blended with images of a tribal, primitive and rhythmically ecstatic Africa. Ivana Banfić's first major hit, 'Šumica' ('Little forest'), in 1994, added exoticism with stamping and chanting sounds (repeating the invented word 'mumbayao') to its lyrics about swimming naked off what was probably (with red wine and olives) the Croatian coast.[5] Her 'Šumica 2', in 1995, repeated the formula with a faster beat.[6] Both songs' videos connoted primitivism through dancers shaking raised palms and performers wearing fluorescent costumes and body paint, blurring mid-1990s European rave aesthetics with evocations of a ritualistic, sexualised Africa on which rave's own 'tribal' and 'shamanistic' imaginaries (Hutson 1999) already played.[7]

'Afrika' itself was the title of a 1995 hit (voted 'Hit of the Year' and 'Best Arrangement' in Croatia's annual music awards) by Dino Dvornik, a Split-born funk musician crossing over into commercial dance. Croatian critics before and after his early death in 2008 regarded Dvornik as Croatian dance's most accomplished musician and as epitomising the irrepressible spirit Croatian place-myths commonly ascribe his home city. The song, in Split dialect, identified first its character, then 'the whole world' and 'the whole of Split', with love of Africa and its 'madman's rhythm'.[8] Its video's psychedelic computer graphics (again matching mid-1990s European rave culture) incorporated bongos, zebras, globes, African tricolours and a photograph of a black porter beside a white man in safari clothing, while Dvornik himself briefly appeared both in a pith-helmet (the white explorer's iconic headwear) and dancing with abstract paint-like patterns projected on his body – making shifting identifications with coloniser and colonised via 'Africa'.[9] Dijana Jelača (2014: 254) argues that such identifications should be seen 'not [as] a mere literal translation' of masculinity and whiteness into Yugoslav society but through the lens of local social issues at the time of reception. In Split, these included the whole country's difficult economic conditions at war's end, their acuteness in Split (a large port and naval base which had been on the front line) and the sense of lost future (often alleviated by heavy drug use) many young people felt in Split (Lalić 2003).[10]

In Serbia, meanwhile, mid-1990s 'turbo folk' also updated 1960s–80s practices of incorporating fashionable or newly possible sounds, instruments, rhythms and styles into Yugoslav 'newly-composed folk music' (see Rasmussen 2002) by adapting arrangements, style and movement from Eurodance and transatlantic commercial hip-hop. Serbian anti-nationalists and feminists criticised turbo folk for celebrating patriarchal masculinities and organised crime when paramilitaries and gangsters formed Milošević's social elite (Gordy 1999; Kronja 2001). The 1994 song later canonised as the beginning of turbo folk, Ivan Gavrilović's '200 na sat' (200 km/h), adapted 'No Limit' by the Dutch group 2 Unlimited, sonically localising 'Eurodance' into Serbian pop-folk by adding a traditional accordion break to the already familiar techno phrase.[11] These Serbian and Croatian movements were contemporaneous with many other global popular music cultures adapting hip-hop, rave and techno aesthetics, sounds and signifying practices into local settings, sometimes with outcomes that would be adapted elsewhere. These cultural translations, in the Yugoslav region as in globalised popular music around the world, were also translations of 'race' – but coexisted with other practices with direct colonial origins.

Blackface performance and the colonial imaginary

The most unambiguous examples of colonial racialised imaginaries in post-Yugoslav entertainment – even more so than Cro-dance's tribalism and primitivism – were occasional blackface performances on music television. Blackface, as a 'grotesque stereotyping and appropriation' by white entertainers impersonating black characters, had lasting effects on American and European imaginations of blackness and the body (Gubar 1997: xiv–xv; see also Lott 1993; Rogin 1998). In the Netherlands, indeed, its present-day persistence (in the traditional blackface carnival character, Zwarte Piet ('Black Pete')) is politically contentious, pitting Dutch people of colour and white anti-racists against white opponents contending the tradition is not racist (Wekker 2016).[12] Its uncontested, though occasional, presence in post-Yugoslav musical entertainment suggests either the endurance or the postsocialist appropriation of a racialised colonial imagination already pervading the German-speaking cultural area by the fin-de-siècle (Wipplinger 2011). In at least one case, however, it seemed intended as commentary on the region's post-Yugoslav geopolitical position rather than purely as spectacle – yet could not transcend the practice's colonial stereotypes.

The Serbian pop/hip-hop group Tap 011 were already well known when they played black/African bakers, in blackface, in the video for their 1995 song 'Pekara' ('Bakery'). This satirical fantasy of abundance, with the bakers handing a dancing queue of white Belgrade citizens large loaves of bread, appeared during widespread shortages and hyperinflation caused by UN sanctions against Milošević. In this context, their costume, the men's faux 'African' accents and the jealousy of the band's two women (Ivana Pavlović and Goca Tržan) when two white, blonde women dressed as blue-helmeted UN medics flirt with the men, could have implied the municipal and national 'we' were being treated 'like Africans', and/or played on a racialised Othering of Albanian bakery proprietors that had escalated since mid-1980s Serbian media had started provoking alarm over Serb–Albanian relations in Kosovo.[13] 'Pekara' the song had already revealed other global connectivities behind post-Yugoslav popular music, as an adaptation of Ini Kamoze's 'Here Comes the Hotstepper'. This Jamaican reggae hit, sampling several US soul and rap songs then appearing on the soundtrack of Robert Altman's *Pret A Porter* in 1994, exemplified how popular music circulates around and through the Black Atlantic (Alleyne 1998: 76). Tap 011's video, however, was trapped between expressing resentment at global structural inequalities (exacerbated by Milošević's actions) and the caricature used to communicate it.

Other songs about a post-Yugoslav state's international standing detached the device of the caricatured 'African' voice from bodies. The Bosnian rock band Zabranjeno Pušenje began their 2006 song 'Hag' ('The Hague'[14]) with heavy drums and chanting, then imagined a Rwandan man talking to the narrator in Zagreb about the Rwandan and Bosnian genocides. Even without visual impersonation, this was what Daphne Brooks (2010: 41) terms 'sonic' impersonation of blackness. Like 'Pekara', it clearly commented on post-Yugoslavs' (this time Bosnians') place in international affairs – yet for listeners to parse these visual and sonic strategies still required a certain imagination of the racialised structure of international affairs and post-Yugoslavs' deserved place there. Other examples of blackface beyond geopolitical commentary, however, suggest less ambiguously that the Yugoslav region does exist within formations of racialised caricature as entertainment that originated in European colonialism – a connection it is easier to make after recognising that the fin-de-siècle spectacle of colonial exhibitions and human zoos extended beyond Germany to late-nineteenth-century Austria-Hungary, that is, the north of the Yugoslav region.

German encounters with blackface minstrelsy and African-American entertainers in turn-of-the-century variety theatre already suggest in German history that racialised difference was a symbolic boundary in German identity construction before Germans met black Allied soldiers during and after the First World War (Wipplinger 2011: 458). The German-speaking linguistic–cultural area, extending into the Habsburg lands and Switzerland, placed Habsburg cities too on the fairs' itineraries. More historical research tracing translations of blackface, representations of Africa(ns) and other racialised modes of representation (such as operatic orientalism) from the Germanophone cultural area through Vienna and Budapest into 'South Slav' Habsburg lands, within the transnational history of European colonialism, is overdue – since determining how deeply embedded such fantasies were in Habsburg cultural politics (the intellectual milieu where Slovenian and Croatian nationalisms, and some forms of Yugoslavism, developed) would help demonstrate whether or not their post-Yugoslav echoes were novel to postsocialism.

Beyond the identification with an imagined African-American gangsta blackness through which one 1994–9 Montenegrin hip-hop duo named themselves 'Monteniggers' (referencing the 'blackness' of Montenegro's name across languages),[15] a routinized and very recent form of blackface characterises the celebrity talent-show *Tvoje lice zvuci poznato* (*Your Face Sounds Familiar*), produced in Serbia, Croatia and Slovenia since 2013–14. The franchise, developed by Dutch producers Endemol and the Spanish broadcaster Antena 3, has been sold to forty territories in Europe, the Americas and Asia since its Spanish launch in 2011. The first Serbian series was the most watched musical entertainment programme in both Serbia and Bosnia-Herzegovina in 2014 (Dokić Mrša and Miljević Jovanović 2015: 1115), when Croatian and Slovenian broadcasters also bought it. *TLZP*'s format challenges established musicians to re-enact well-known concert/video performances by domestic and foreign stars, across boundaries of age or gender or – in many countries, including those of the Yugoslav region – race.

TLZP offers viewers the spectacle of cross-gender drag, cross-racial drag or both, with contestants' skin colour routinely altered across what, to a gaze socialised in the UK or USA, would be racialised boundaries. Not only are the 'transformations' (as tabloids and online portals call them) part of the spectacle, but the very design of the 'international' star impersonations seems to be part of the franchise – the same blackface Stevie Wonder impersonation, with the 'blind' performer led on stage, has appeared in Croatia, Slovenia and Greece, and in France for an impersonation of Ray Charles. The narrative of continuity in African-American creativity and style that Will.i.am's 'Bang Bang' video might tell (in a speakeasy setting where its African-American performers might evoke the Harlem Renaissance) comes closer to reinterpreting 1920s minstrelsy if performed, as on Serbian *TLZP* less than six months later, by a white man such as the Serbian rapper Sky Wikluh, even more once his performance starts involving sexualised advances towards a white woman.[16]

Gloria Wekker (2016: 35), reading 'everyday racism' (Essed 1991) in Dutch popular entertainment juxtaposed with Zwarte Piet as evidence of 'white ignorance' about the legacies of colonialism in the Netherlands, argues that understanding the 'everyday, casual chains of signification' through which such representations make sense to Dutch onlookers requires tracing the 'shared racial and sexual fantasies' that inform them. Dutch participation in colonialism and slavery differs from the experiences of south-east Europe, much of which was under Ottoman rule while the Netherlands and Britain prospered through colonial trade and enslaving Africans. The casualness of blackface as spectacle in *TLZP* suggests similar racial and sexual fantasies are nevertheless shared in the Yugoslav region – and that the dependence of 'Europeanness' on whiteness extends beyond former imperial metropoles.

If embodied and sonic caricatures of blackness and Africanity in post-Yugoslav popular entertainment are more confusing than Dutch or American equivalents, part of the confusion stems from the region's more marginal geopolitical position. Some, though not all, such impersonations aimed to comment on how many inhabitants of the region perceived that their collective place in global structural hierarchies had been reversed after the collapse of Yugoslav state socialism, the end of Yugoslavia's self-appointed distinctive and prestigious place in global affairs, the Yugoslav wars, and the consequent reversal of Yugoslavs' expectations about living standards and international mobility (see Jansen 2009). Others could not even claim that intention. Whether they could or not, they relied on stereotypes of blackness with origins in colonial spectacles of domination. These showed unambiguously that those racial formations were present in the Yugoslav region – yet were not even the only way that the region participated in the embodied cultural politics of race.

The embodied cultural politics of global raciality

Popular music, a domain of gendered and racialised labour as well as a cultural text (Silverman 2012; Hofman 2015; Lordi 2016), stands alongside transnational sport and film as a major vector for an *embodied* transnational cultural politics of race, where what producers and audiences perceive through transnational media is adapted or vernacularised through their own perceptions of race and identity. This is already recognised, latently, in south-east European feminist media studies of female embodiment in pop-folk performance, which often comment on the vernacularisation of style, movement and sound from Anglo-American musics but much more rarely discuss how many of these practices at point of origin are racialised as black. Does it matter, in interpreting these performances, that their representations of aspirational excess using the visual language of hip-hop/R&B are racialised in their home context? Gilroy, again, can situate these politics of style within global, not just regional, formations: here is both unease about how 'the translocal glamour and attractiveness of African-American culture' becomes a commodity in contemporary media, and a problem of identity regarding the twenty-first-century global black diaspora's cultural achievements: 'Are they local or global forms? To whom, if anyone, do they belong?' (Gilroy 2000: 178, 346). Indeed, the question of exchange between non-Roma and Roma performers, especially in women's performance that (grounded in south-east European orientalisms) eroticises and exoticises post-Ottoman belly-dance and associated dress, would already start raising this issue.

The complex of orientalisms behind south-east European pop-folk combine some produced at national or intra-Balkan levels (Buchanan (ed.) 2007) with others circulating around globalised circuits. These latter were reinvigorated when the 'generalised, non-white, exotic "other"' (Railton and Watson 2012: 109) became a trope in the aesthetics of transatlantic female celebrity, available across some racialised boundaries to certain women (conventionally attractive to a male heterosexual gaze) who could have many different racial and ethnic identities (Latina; biracial; any spatialised ethnic origin 'from' Spanish 'to' Iranian; light-skinned but black; dark-haired but white; or not even stated). Pop sometimes signifies their 'erotic multiculturalism' (Mcgee 2012) sonically with 'oriental' strings. Many women from the Balkans might occupy this ambiguous category, where contemporary transnational glamour practices resonate with the resources of real or ascribed Roma ethnicity in south-east European folk celebrity; the sexuality of the light-skinned black R&B diva, as well as 'the athletic perfection' of the black male body, is part of the spectacle of embodiment and race that Gilroy argues has been 'recycled' from its imperial, nationalist and fascist origins so contemporary commerce can sell goods around the world (Gilroy 2000: 348).

The suggestion that south-east Europe lies outside US racial categories altogether, meanwhile, is dramatised literally in a 2009 song and video by the Kosovo Albanian pop-folk singer Genta Ismajli, 'Si panter i zi' ('Like a Black Panther'). Whereas its title indexes African-American liberation and white colonial fantasies of Africa at the same time, employing several layers of transnational racial symbolism already, its video places 'Albanian' alongside whiteness, blackness and Latinity as a thoroughly separate racialised category. Accompanying lyrics switching between Albanian and English, the video uses a common, transnational convention of pop/R&B video by blending sequences of the star dancing in different costumes and settings to express various aspects of sexuality and power.[17] The Albanian lyrics imply that rhythm has captured her body, entering an irrational, ecstatic, addictive state where she 'tremble[s] like a black panther' ('valvitem un si një panter i zi') and rhyme 'lives inside me' ('në mua jeton').[18] The English section attaches the video's four personas to different racialised identities: 'Now do it like a black girl' (her most revealing costume), 'now do it like a white girl' (her most subdued and businesslike); 'now do it like Latinas', with a castanet sound (in a red feathered dress, shaking hips); 'now do it like an Albanian girl' (with dress and movement evoking Albanian folk costume and dance). Three of these racialised personas belong to US categories; the fourth, here situated outside them, is an 'Albanian' ethnonational position, either racialised separately or outside 'race' altogether. Similar, though not identical, ambiguities end up ascribed to women with ethnic heritage from south-east Europe or the South Caucasus, such as Rita Ora or Kim Kardashian, working as celebrities in the Anglosphere.[19]

In Anglo-American music video, gendered and sexualised bodily performances clearly inhabit 'a genealogy of ... definitions of blackness and whiteness from the Victorian era to the present', including the construction of a hypersexualised, animalistic black female sexuality and a controlled, unobtainable or fragile white female equivalent (Railton and Watson 2012: 95). To what extent, however, do the complex of bodily practices that racialise performers in American or British gazes (such as movement, cosmetic skin tones, hair style and texture, and racialised–classed–gendered dress) also signify race when employed in south-east Europe – and would controversies over 'cultural appropriation' (Rodriquez 2006) of sonic, visual and embodied practices, or white people's extracting value from racialised people's cultural practices while perpetuating structural racism (what bell hooks (1992: 21) termed 'eating the Other'), also apply along this axis of exchange? In pursuing this further, feminist media studies would need to accommodate the longer history of (musical, visual and bodily) signifiers of Romani identity in pop-folk, attached to or detached from performers identifying themselves as Roma (Silverman 2012); the racialising elisions between Romani identity and blackness/African-Americanness already made in some white eastern European national identity narratives (see Todorova 2006); and the identifications and parallels Roma have drawn between their own experiences of marginalisation and anti-blackness in the USA (Imre 2006).

South-east European popular music has thus sometimes, as a site for gendered and ethnicised performances of style and identity, explicitly translated US racialised signifiers into its own sonic, visual and embodied representations. Sometimes it places its 'own' region (a 'self' that may slip between the ethnic nation, a more diffuse 'post-Yugoslav' space or 'the Balkans') outside those formations. Sometimes, especially in music claiming the 'etno' category in south-east European music-marketing (a mode of knowingly repackaging tradition to suit the 'world music' market's Westernising gaze), the 'self' performs modernity and Westernness by casting itself as consciously, strategically deploying 'tradition' (Čolović 2006) – a common tactic in several mid-2000s post-Yugoslav performances at the Eurovision Song Contest (Baker 2008), including two which subtly added Malian djembe to the performers' array of traditional Balkan instruments.[20] Both approaches externalise race as a phenomenon belonging to other regions (above all the USA) but alien to one's own space. Yet such externalisation was not new to postsocialism; it stood in continuity with state socialist geopolitical identity narratives that cast racism as 'a problem of Western capitalism' (Law 2012: 2) and a reason for the socialist bloc to appear morally superior.

Anti-colonial and anti-racist solidarities

The racial politics of Yugoslav state socialism, which identified Communism as an anti-imperialist ideology and linked capitalism intrinsically with imperialism, had many similarities with the Soviet bloc's (Todorova 2006; Slobodian (ed.) 2015c). Yugoslav Communists, like their Warsaw Pact counterparts, expressed solidarity with African and Asian anti-colonial resistance and implied that racial tensions in the USA, about which east European publics heard, were produced by capitalism. After Stalin ejected Yugoslavia from the Cominform in 1948, however, Yugoslav Communists responded by imagining Yugoslavia standing between East and West, without either bloc's social problems (Mihelj 2012: 97). This new geopolitics made racism and capitalist exploitation the failings of the West; repression the failing of the Soviet East.

Yugoslav popular music in the 1980s – the greatest decade of international anti-apartheid struggle – retold this idealised geopolitical narrative. The singer-songwriter Đorđe Balašević, whose 1980s music aimed at reconstructing an optimistic Yugoslav and socialist identity for his generation amid intensifying economic, constitutional and cultural crises, depicted it in his 1986 song 'Virovitica', named after a small Croatian town near the Hungarian border.[21] Its touring musician narrator, comparing the superpowers, concludes that despite appreciating their place-myths (California; Rostov; (Soviet) Georgia) and culture (Donald Duck; Dostoyevsky) he is afraid both of the USSR's lack of liberties and the beggars, junkies and Black Panthers he might find in America (plus a certain unpleasant 'Ronald', perhaps Reagan and/or McDonald). The song makes these sources of fear and disorder in the US, but not in unpressured Virovitica, where 'everyone lives peacefully, like hippies' ('i žive mirno svi, kao hipici').

Also in 1986, the Sarajevo-born pop/rock musician Dino Merlin released 'Cijela Juga jedna avlija' ('The whole of Yugoslavia [is] one courtyard'[22]), one of many Bosnian songs in the mid-to-late 1980s celebrating Yugoslavia's multi-ethnicity (and other foundations of Yugoslav socialism, like its Partisan heritage) during a heightening constitutional crisis with undertones of impending – yet still avoidable – ethnopolitical conflict (see Mišina 2013). Merlin's avlija, a fantasy many Yugoslavs still wanted to believe, contained 'Serbs, Bosnians, blacks and Albanians / [who have] never been foreigners in my city' ('Srbi, Bosanci, crnci i Albanci / nikad u mom gradu nisu bili stranci'). Dalibor Mišina (2010: 282) reads this as attempting to rearticulate a 'moral and ethical compass' for Yugoslavia. He does not directly discuss the inclusion of blacks alongside Serbs, Bosnians and Albanians, but could: the Yugoslavism of Merlin's narrator did not just build multi-ethnic bridges across *South Slav* identity boundaries but also epitomised, if not multi-raciality, at least the race-blindness that had characterised Non-Aligned anti-colonialism (Subotić and Vučetić 2016), soon to be marginalised by the open racism as well as xenophobia of the homogenous ethnonational narratives of national identity that were about to become hegemonic across the Yugoslav space. The translation of hip-hop into the region's professional and grassroots music scenes, at the turn of the 1980s/1990s, occurred at this moment of fracture.

Hip-hop, 'the most visible and widely disseminated conduit of U.S. black popular imagery globally' (Perry 2008: 635–6) since the late 1980s, undergoes at least four translations in eastern Europe: first, when Roma musicians narrate racialised and socio-economic marginalisation, and claim pride, through identification with African-American experiences (Imre 2008); secondly, when ethnic-majority rappers in their countries' economic and urban peripheries enact the same identification through style (dress and breakdance), with state socialist urban landscapes standing in for the 'ghetto' (Bosanac 2004); thirdly, as a reservoir of musical, visual and embodied style, adaptable into the wider entertainment industry; and fourthly, when US hip-hop and film become a source of public 'common sense' about blackness and race for local viewers (Todorova 2006; Helbig 2014). All four translations happen in the post-Yugoslav region. In Croatia, the most critically acclaimed Cro-dance group (Electro Team) emerged in 1990–1 from Zagreb's hip-hop underground; rap in post-Yugoslav Bosnia is centred on Tuzla, home of the FMJAM collective of politically engaged, anti-ethnonationalist rappers such as Edo Maajka (Edin Osmić) and Frenki (Adnan Hamidović) (Mujanović 2017).[23] Other rappers take anti-elite, oppositional patriotic stances, such as Shorty from Vinkovci in Croatia (Baker 2010: 118–20) or Beogradski Sindikat from Belgrade, while others yet take non-political stances and rap about urban youth life. Roma in the region, as in Hungary (see Imre 2006), have, meanwhile, explicitly identified their structural position with anti-black racism through hip-hop. They include the Serbian Roma rapper Muha Blackstazy (Muhamed Eljšani), who called his first recording in 2003 'Crni smo mi' ('We are Black'); Euro Black Nation, from the periphery of a town in Baranja, Croatia (Banić Grubišić 2011; Pavelić 2012); and Shutka Roma Rap from Šuto Orizari, a Roma settlement pushed to the edge of Skopje by Macedonian authorities (McGarry 2017: 147). These rappers typically perform at alternative cultural centres and human-rights festivals while continuing to work in their hometowns' low-paid and informal economies.

Similar translations of hip-hop as a visual, sonic and embodied language of both marginality and glamour have happened around the world. The complex of hip-hop music, fashion and dance in mid-1990s Japan, for instance, made one anthropologist ask: 'as hip-hop goes global, what happens to the cultural politics of race inherent in American hip-hop?' (Condry 2007: 638). This could equally be asked in south-east Europe. Ian Condry, drawing on Cornel West's 'new cultural politics of difference' (West 1990: 35 in Condry 2007: 639) to explain why some rappers questioned the homogeneity of Japanese ethnonational identity while corporate pressures encouraged others either to fetishise visible signifiers of blackness or de-emphasise hip-hop's black origins, called for 'a transnational cultural politics of race' without essentialising either one single African-American identity or one homogenous local/Japanese one. The constructed and contested nature of national, ethnic and racial identifications is equally important for understanding the politics of race in music from the Yugoslav region, where imagined solidarities between South Slavs and the people of the Third World based on shared histories of colonial exploitation underpinned state socialist geopolitics.

The history of black entertainers in the Yugoslav region did not begin under state socialism but acquired a new structural context within the global racial politics of the Cold War. The most transient, but often most spectacular, presence of black musicians came through foreign stars' tours: before US-sponsored visits by jazz musicians like Louis Armstrong in the 1950s–60s (Vučetić 2012: 170), there had been spectacles like Josephine Baker's 1929 tour, which Jovana Babović (2015) shows sparked contrasting reactions in Belgrade and Zagreb.[24] Reviews in both cities used imaginaries of race, sexuality and modernity to construct collective identities through discourses about what Belgrade/Zagreb audiences desired: but Belgrade's cultural elite hailed Baker's daring and sensuality as evidence the capital must be a modern metropolis (since she wanted to perform there), while their Zagreb counterparts, who had belonged to Austro-Hungarian intellectual milieus until 1918, took against what they viewed as licentious, uncivilised displays. Both these responses depended on contemporaneous European imaginations of black female sexuality, but drew contrasting aesthetic judgements about what kinds of performance their cities should contain.

More sustained black participation in Yugoslav popular music arose through Non-Aligned Yugoslavia's hosting of African students in the 1950s–80s. One Congolese student, Edi Dekeng, formed a band called Crni panteri ('The Black Panthers') with classmates in 1964–5, then became frontman of the Belgrade rock band Elipse, which started covering soul music not beat; he also recorded, in 1967, a duet called 'Bobi Smit' ('Bobby Smith') with the Serbian actor Dušan Golumbowski, calling on US soldiers to understand they were being sent to kill civilians in Vietnam. A Kenyan student, Djungo Chokwe, took the name Steven Hannington – suggesting Yugoslav as well as Soviet constructions of blackness as 'cool' condensed Africanity into African-Americanness – and recorded two disco and Afrobeat albums for the Zagreb label Jugoton in the 1980s. These recordings, and others by Africans in post-Yugoslav Serbia, were re-collected in the early 2010s by the (white) Belgrade rapper Bege Fank, reconstructing a history which – like the African student exchanges (Veličković 2012) – is rarely remembered in contemporary Serbia (Radinović 2014).

Today's grassroots digital economy, meanwhile, enables black musicians in the post-Yugoslav region, and white musicians from the region working with them, to express transnational solidarities across boundaries of 'postsocialist'/'postcolonial' space. The black British rapper and vlogger Smooth Deep (Nick Semwogerere), who co-founded a production company in Sarajevo, began filming rap videos with Bosnian producers in 2011: one sampled Halid Bešlić's classic newly composed folk song, 'Sarajevo, grade moj' ('Sarajevo, My City') (Hadžiahmetović 2011). The duo Crni Srbi (The Black Serbs), David Brkljač (a white Serb) and Jovan Crnović (an African-American who met Brkljač in his hometown, Novi Sad), began making YouTube comedy videos (in Serbian) about Serbian–US cultural encounters in 2013 after Brkljač moved to the USA, with Crnović playing a stereotypical ultra-patriotic Serb.[25] In 2016 they branched out into music video. 'Balkan Latino', filmed in Chicago with Joshua Lazu, blended Serbian and Puerto Rican Spanish lyrics, rap and salsa to celebrate Latin American and Balkan friendship.[26] 'Rintam' ('I'm Doing Hard Work') involved another post-Yugoslav black YouTube celebrity, Ron Holsey, whose videos of himself singing well-known newly composed folk songs in Serbian led to several tabloid interviews with headlines like, 'Here's what a guy from Los Angeles who sings folk songs [narodnjaci] has to say about Serbia!'[27]

'Rintam''s video depicts all three men in tiring manual occupations (Holsey, first, in a bakery), complaining about working conditions, resenting their older white bosses, and anticipating a weekend of partying, rakija and release.[28] Its caption, 'The story of my life!!! I work like a black and my wages are low', referenced the same Serbo-Croatian idiom the video seemed to dramatise: 'working like a black' ('raditi kao crnac'), a phrase that embeds the history of Atlantic slavery in many European languages (Giovannetti 2006: 5). One Croatian linguist argues 'crnac', when evoking hard physical work, expresses 'empathy for the oppressed and the exploited', and identification with the treatment of black slaves, rather than representing a slur (unlike saying someone was working 'like a Gypsy' ('kao Cigan')) (Ćupković 2015: 223–4). While her reading does not capture the colonial fantasies still projected on to black bodies in the region, 'Rintam''s interracial, class-based friendship hints at a horizontal, translocal solidarity closer to socialist internationalism than postsocialist identification with whiteness and 'Europe'.

Indeed, even though Serbian tabloids and internet portals create spectacle for white readers from the sight and sound of African-Americans performing Serbian language and song, Crni Srbi's own productions are further from the mass media's exoticism, nearer the expressions of brotherhood with African footballers, Black Power activists and West African miners in the 'left populism' of the Belgrade hip-hop collective Bombe Devedesetih (Bombs of the Nineties) (Papović and Pejović 2016: 118), who similarly communicate through social media not the mainstream media/recording industry: on the margins of commercial popular music but well within popular music as a mode of expression. The routes through which an African-American visits Novi Sad, a Serb from Novi Sad moves to Chicago and hip-hop's sound and style offers them a medium for commenting on youth precarity in contemporary Serbia are part of a Black Atlantic extending across Europe's interior, not just to its west coast. The imaginaries of race popular music reveals, therefore, are contradictory: if identifications with imperial Europe sustain racialised colonial imaginations even today, identifications with the subjects of colonial oppression have sustained genuinely felt anti-colonial solidarities, and both positions have their origins in the region's historical experience.

Conclusion

Evidence from popular music, sometimes (or especially) the most ephemeral, shows that the Yugoslav region just like other European countries – whether they were colonial powers or not – does possess a 'deep reservoir' (Wekker 2016: 2) of notions of modernity, morality, hierarchy and entitlement through which popular culture and everyday discourse mobilise meaning. Critical race scholarship emphasises it is through popular culture that racialised imaginaries and mythologies acquire what Mills (1997: 19) calls a 'virtual reality', reconfirmed every time they are encountered, to sustain the narratives and stereotypes behind public understandings of race. If the musicologists Ronald Radano and Tejumola Olaniyan (2016: 13) contend '[w]e can hear empire in the familiar orders of the here and now', the empire one can hear in the region's music is global, not just Ottoman. Moreover, the racialised and sexualised imaginations of the body that Fanon, hooks and Gilroy have all shown to be part of colonial power remind us that empire is simultaneously heard and seen.

Situating the region's popular culture within global imaginaries of race means recognising what specific identifications with or against race worked through any national identity at a given moment, establishing what localised translations exist(ed), and how people position(ed) their individual and collective selves in relation to them. By the millennium, Gilroy (2000: 13) argued, 'planetary traffic in the imagery of blackness' through media, celebrity and advertising had started making 'some degree of visible difference from an implicit white norm … highly prized as a sign of timeliness, vitality, inclusivity, and global reach' but without disrupting everyday racisms. Gilroy found this both a troubling form of commodification – with 'the fruits of alterity' often more desirable than 'the company of the people who harvested them' – and also a potential source for 'still-emergent means of living with and through difference' in spaces where counter-hegemonic interconnectedness might resist a depoliticising corporate multiculturalism (Gilroy 2000: 249–50).

Yet if Gilroy talks primarily about countries which saw the racialised structure of their population change significantly in the twentieth century through postcolonial migration, or Germany which experienced comparable change through recruiting guest-workers, how far must or can theory also account for regions such as ex-Yugoslavia which did not? The 'unequal power relations' that, Katrin Sieg (2002: 259) writes, 'cultural transactions are [both] framed by and reproduce' are not suddenly cut off when they reach the Balkans – as south-east European cultural theorists using postcolonial thought were first to see. Sieg also shows, however, that these transactions do not simply occur on one (asymmetric) scale between global centre and homogenous global margin: they follow multiple routes, between different 'margins' (sometimes asymmetric to each other) as well as towards 'centres' and out.

The cultural production of global racial formations through the Yugoslav region depends, therefore, on how people have watched, listened, identified with and desired through popular culture, including but not limited to that understood as 'black' – although the 'blackness' of popular musics from the global African diaspora is, Stuart Hall (1993: 111–12) emphasises, not one essentialised experience but the sum of diverse historical experiences and intersecting social identities.[29] The idea of 'racialized listening practices' (Stoever 2016: 33) – often simultaneously viewing practices – implies that music, voice and sound are heard through ears already attuned to contemporaneous racial imaginations, producing further understandings of race, blackness and whiteness based on what and how one hears. In the Yugoslav region and many other parts of Europe, the valences of 'sonic blackness' (Weheliye 2005: 5), of 'sounding black' or equally 'sounding white', were and are enmeshed with 'sounding American'. These everyday judgements form part of a 'popular geopolitics' (Dittmer 2010), informed by but outlasting the Cold War, where 'race' and the inequality and disorder caused by racism are problems of the US (and Western European cities that might appear to have become like it), but separated from the nation's or region's 'own' identity. Yet these geopolitics are unusually flexible in permitting shifting identifications with Europe, modernity and whiteness on the one hand, and with global structural marginalisation on the other, in terms always inflected but not fully determined by ethnonational identity; moreover, each position has some grounding in the Yugoslav region's historical experience. Understanding the puzzle of race in the Yugoslav region begins with revisiting a more comfortable concept for studies of this area – the idea of ethnicity – in a region which is often seen through the lens of ethnopolitical conflict between settled nations but is in fact a far more complex historical contact zone.

Notes

1 The Yugoslav region may also be better served than elsewhere in postsocialist Europe for studies of everyday popular culture because of the impact that 1990s cultural critiques of 'turbo folk' music and nationalism had on post-Yugoslav studies.
2 After I played this song during a workshop in 2016, one white American participant remarked on a translinguistic wordplay she had heard or imagined under its title: 'Ja sam black?'
3 'Nina Badrić & Emilija Kokić – Ja sam vlak', www.youtube.com/watch?v=u7Jbn4LSm78 (5 December 2008; accessed 8 September 2017).
4 With thanks to David Eldridge.
5 'Ivana Banfić (I Bee) Šumica (official music video)', www.youtube.com/watch?v=oeZVRLbnvgg (26 July 2010; accessed 8 September 2017).
6 'I Bee – Šumica 2 (spot)', www.youtube.com/watch?v=Tm2Lmx8F5cc (11 March 2016; accessed 8 September 2017).
7 The first few seconds of 'Šumica 2''s video showed a white woman with dark bobbed hair, like Banfić in 1994, watching a montage of (possibly black) dancers in a darkened room; after a close-up panning from her eye to her lips as she takes pleasure, the scene dissolves into the image Banfić debuted with 'Šumica 2' (sexually dominant, with cropped and bleached hair), implying that the pleasure of watching and listening to the music amounted to a temporary transformative identification with the primitive. Naked except for neon body paint, her character is both tracked by the ravers and, once found, leads their dance.
8 'Afrika, to je moj bit / Afrika voli cili svit' (or, in the last line, 'cili Split').
9 'Dino Dvornik – Afrika', www.youtube.com/watch?v=hmNMZPbAJbg (30 December 2008; accessed 8 September 2017). The Serbian novelist Dobrica Ćosić, accompanying Tito on a tour to West Africa in 1961, described his encounter with 'unknown, exciting ... threatening' Africa through 'listening to Radio Dakar ... that muffled, incomprehensible sound of tam-tam' (Hozić 2016). The trope of exoticism and drumming not only bridges state socialism and postsocialism but also what have been commonly opposed symbolic boundaries of ethnicity (Croat and Serb).
10 The title of the book cited here, *Split kontra Splita* (*Split against Split*) by the Croatian sociologist Dražen Lalić – from Split –plays on another well-known Dvornik song, 'Ništa kontra Splita' ('[I Won't Hear] Anything against Split', using a regional Italianism 'kontra' not the standard Croatian 'protiv' for 'against').
11 'Ivan Gavrilović – 200 na sat (HQ video 1994)', www.youtube.com/watch?v=3is49vWMwFI (9 January 2013; accessed 8 September 2017).
12 On the 'morčić', a blackface character in Rijeka carnival parades, see Chapter 3.
13 Many Kosovo Serbs leaving in the mid-1980s had claimed they suffered from ethnicised persecution by Albanians and institutionalised discrimination against

Serbs. Their grievances, relayed by Serbian media, inspired Milošević to adopt ethnicised populism in 1987.
14 Site of the International Criminal Tribunal for the Former Yugoslavia.
15 It is unclear if they had heard of the 1907–8 industrial dispute on the Mesabi Iron Range, Minnesota, where a mining company used Montenegrin Serb strikebreakers against striking socialist miners of Finnish, Slovenian, Italian and possibly Croatian origin; amid tensions between the Montenegrins and their Swedish overseers afterwards, the overseers, already identifying with US racial ideology, started calling the Montenegrins this same term (Lubotina 2015: 42) – while 'immigrants from Finland, Italy, and the Balkans also abused African Americans on the Mesabi Range to demonstrate their superiority over a more maligned race' (Lubotina 2015: 42, 54).
16 'Wikluh Sky kao Will I Am', www.youtube.com/watch?v=yj88lZ_E9MY (3 November 2013; accessed 8 September 2017).
17 'Genta – Si panter i zi', www.youtube.com/watch?v=MtY-hGkpHeo (25 December 2012; accessed 8 September 2017).
18 With thanks to Isabel Ströhle.
19 'Rita Ora's not black, but her hair sure thinks she is', wrote the African-American fashion writer Marjon Carlos (2015) on Ora's exploitation of gendered and racialised ambiguity after Ora photographed herself for Instagram wearing blonde box braids. Accidentally exemplifying a different ambiguity, the same article described her briefly as 'the British pop import by way of Bosnia,' not Kosovo or even Albania. On Kardashian, see Sastre (2014).
20 Željko Joksimović's performance of 'Lane moje' ('My Faun') representing Serbia in 2004, and Boris Novković's 'Vukovi umiru sami' ('Wolves Die Alone') representing Croatia in 2005 – though, in both, the djembe could easily be missed or mistaken for another Balkan instrument. Novković's djembe was played by Tomislav Tržan, who had supposedly given Ivana Banfić the idea for 'Šumica'. Viewing Novković's performance through the lenses of ethnic (but not racialised) symbolic boundary-markers and the symbolic geographies of balkanism (but not coloniality) in 2006–8, I had commented on his black frock-coat and the authentic costumes of his female vocalists from the folklore ensemble Lado (Baker 2008), but not Tržan's djembe – an unexpected symbol of Africanity in a performance so linked to national and European identity (Petrić 2015: 53). And yet, when I had already argued Novković had sought to embody a Mitteleuropean, pseudo-Habsburg bourgeois masculinity on stage (proof that he as the song's composer and the Croatian nation as its symbolic sender had the modernity and mastery necessary to package folk tradition for Europeans to enjoy as spectacle), Tržan's contribution to the mis-en-scene was as racialised a representation as the rave tribalism of 'Šumica'. It was not impossible to imagine the Habsburg gentleman visiting an exhibition of indigenous peoples in Vienna or Budapest; though not in Zagreb, which did not yet have a zoo (see Chapter 3). With thanks to Mojca Piškor for further discussions.
21 Balašević came from Novi Sad, the largest town in Vojvodina. This autonomous province of Serbia had, like northern Croatia, been part of the Hungarian

half of the Habsburg Empire until 1918; locating the song on the other side of the Serbian–Croatian border aligned Balašević with a form of everyday Yugoslavism where shared cultures and mentalities derived from common historical experience (especially the Danubian and Habsburg past) were more important to identity than ethnically bounded territorial claims. This remained a theme in his songwriting during and after the collapse of socialism and the Yugoslav wars, when the Croatian side of the Serbian–Croatian border became a front line.

22 'Juga' was a colloquial name for Yugoslavia; an 'avlija' is a front yard characteristic of the 'čaršija' ('marketplace') of Sarajevo and other towns built up during Ottoman rule.

23 Edo Maajka's 2004 song 'Legenda o Elvisu' ('The legend of Elvis'), set in a Tuzla where the US-led division of NATO's multinational peace enforcement force had had its headquarters since 1996, described an affair between a married Bosnian cleaner working on the US base and an African-American soldier, ending in a fantasy where their son (Elvis) grows up into a basketball star able to beat the Americans in a world championship final – a result that would have been in the grasp of socialist Yugoslavia's famous basketball teams (Perica 2001), but unimaginable for the fragmented basketball teams of the successor states. With thanks to Srđan Vučetić.

24 Compare, on Baker's reception in Stockholm, Habel (2005).

25 'Serbia coming to America ep 1 – Crni Srbi', www.youtube.com/watch?v=PkvektlQo6A (1 November 2013; accessed 8 September 2017).

26 'Balkan Latino', www.youtube.com/watch?v=pWEnRnPDIv0 (4 July 2016; accessed 8 September 2017).

27 'Kad Amerikanac uvija sarmu: pogledajte šta momak iz Los Anđelesa koji peva narodnjake kaže o Srbiji!', *Blic*, 16 December 2015 (www.blic.rs/zabava/vesti/kad-amerikanac-uvija-sarmu-pogledajte-sta-momak-iz-los-andelesa-koji-peva-narodnjake/3pfm4mc; accessed 8 September 2017) – a headline that (like other tabloid reports about Holsey or Crni Srbi) posits the singing of narodnjaci and the embodiment of African-American identity as a fixed boundary that it is remarkable to cross.

28 'Rintam', www.youtube.com/watch?v=tUcBWqzwN1k (18 August 2016; accessed 8 September 2017). With thanks to Dario Brentin and Astrea Pejović.

29 With thanks to Elizabeth Dauphinée.

2

Histories of ethnicity, nation and migration

Nationhood, ethnicity and migration have been linked in south-east Europe, including the Yugoslav region, since the descendants of Slav clans who migrated there from Central Asia in the sixth to eighth centuries CE and others living there who came to share their collective identity started to understand themselves as nations – however long ago or recently that might be (Fine 2006). Ottoman rule in south-east Europe, moreover, both represented and caused further migration. The region's nineteenth- and twentieth-century history, however, is (in the prevailing paradigm) primarily a history of (what are constructed as) settled mono-ethnic nations forming states and engaging in territorial disputes which have often led to forced migration when perpetrators of ethnicised violence purge those they identify as minorities from what they intend as homogenous national territories, but which are rarely viewed in the context of migration around the globe.

Histories of 'race', however, are always and already migration histories. White Europeans' transoceanic movements, their conquest and acquisition of indigenous peoples' lands in the Americas, and their transportation of millions of enslaved Africans across the Atlantic are the acts of violence which 'race', in demarcating fully human and sovereign populations from those who were not, was constructed to enable and explain (Gilroy 1993). Outside postcolonial studies and anti-racist activism, white scholars are not used to calling these processes by names they use all the time to talk about collective violence in eastern Europe: displacement, forced migration, genocide.[1] Transnational feminist histories of race and empire meanwhile reveal the everyday, intimate politics of global racial formations, where racialised ideologies of gender, sexuality and bodies circulated between colonised territories and metropoles, indeed into any society that even aspired to the modernity of European civilisational superiority (McClintock 1995; Young 1995; Stoler 2002). 'Race' simultaneously structures new experiences of migration, informing states' classifications of who may cross borders or settle more freely or less so, and shaping everyday experiences of belonging in old and new homes (Silverstein 2005; Yuval-Davis 2011).

Just as ethnicity has been more central than race in south-east European studies, certain migrations – those necessary to understand majority ethnic identities, their forced migrations and diasporas – have been more central than others, which do not need to be explained to tell the history of majoritarian ethnicity but are integral to understanding the place of 'race'. Indeed, even the ethnopolitical violence responsible for forced migrations within and away from the region has often involved translating ethnicity and nationhood through 'race' to more effectively dehumanise the subjects of violence and harden the symbolic boundaries of ethnic difference to their extreme. The established categories of inter-ethnic relations represent significant social realities in the region but do not account for all the migration histories in which the region has appeared. Establishing the area as a global, not just regional, 'contact zone' (Pratt 2008: 2) conversely widens the lens of which migrations might seem to be at the centre of south-east European studies (Chang and Rucker-Chang (eds) 2013), revealing connections that tie it into the global history of race.

Ottoman imperial rule and transnational histories of empire

For many historians, the centrality of migration to nation formation is what distinguishes the Balkans *as* a region (Mazower 2002: 53). Many south-east European national mythologies, as articulated since the nineteenth century, date ethnogenesis to the sixth to eighth centuries for South Slavs, or the ninth for Magyars; Greek origin myths meanwhile connect today's nation with pre-Roman city-states, Albanian myths to pre-Roman 'Illyrians' and Romanian myths either to pre-Roman 'Dacians' alone or intermingled with Roman legionaries. The shifting borders of the area's pre-Ottoman kingdoms left competing national claims to territory, history and heritage once Ottoman decline and Habsburg politics created conditions for nineteenth-century national movements to aspire to unify their nation-states.

Ottoman incorporation of south-east Europe into administrative, political and religious structures, from the late fourteenth century, shaped its migration history in many ways (Sugar 1977; Hoare 2007; Wachtel 2008). Authorities directly settled Anatolian Turkish cavalrymen on conquered land as 'timariots' who taxed local peasants and raised troops, while Ottoman trade-routes developed towns like Sarajevo and Thessaloniki into provincial capitals, refuges for many Sephardic Jews expelled from Spain in 1492. The Ottoman politics of conversion to Islam, necessary for South Slavs and other Catholic/Orthodox Christians seeking bureaucratic advancement in an empire stratifying access to power around religion not ethnicity or race, created a new Muslim South Slav ethno-religious identity among these men's descendants. 'Bosnian Muslim' identity, with South Slav linguistic heritage but Islamic religious identity/traditions, increasingly paralleled Serb (Orthodox) and Croat (Catholic) ethno-national identities during the twentieth century, even if it had first indexed a class/religion intersection; Tito's Yugoslavia institutionalised Muslim ethnicity by including it as a census 'nation' (nacija) in 1971 (Markowitz 2010: 79).

South-east Europe, peripheral in an Istanbul/Anatolia-centred empire but the frontline of Ottoman–Habsburg–Venetian imperial–territorial competition, experienced new outward migrations imposed by, or adapting to, Ottoman rule. The 'devširme'/'devşirme' system, until the mid-seventeenth century, made Balkan and Anatolian rural communities provide annual levies of Christian boys for training as an administrative and military corps loyal only to the Sultan not Anatolian nobility. These often retained links to their birthplace, like Grand Vizier

Mehmed Paša Sokolović/Sokollu Mehmed Paša, who financed a historic bridge in his hometown Višegrad in 1577 (Kunt 1974: 235). Serb, Croat and Montenegrin national narratives, and interwar Yugoslavist novelists like Ivo Andrić, remember the devširme as a painful tool of Ottoman imperial oppression (Longinović 2011: 127–9). Another Ottoman social institution, the 'dragoman' role (interpreter–mediators for foreign embassies in Istanbul), was semi-hereditary, structured both by Ottoman elite apprenticeship practices and Venetian patrician kinship traditions (Rothman 2009: 773). Many dragomans had Greek or Albanian backgrounds, but others came from then-Venetian eastern Adriatic ports, independent Ragusa (now Dubrovnik) or Venetian Istria. Historical subjects like the dragomans are illegible to majoritarian ethnic histories but become visible through reframing history around notions such as Mary Louise Pratt's imperial 'contact zones' (Rothman 2015: 4; see Pratt 2008: 7), decentring ethnonational conflict and opening more complex connected histories of the Ottoman–Habsburg–Venetian past.

Some migrations caused by decades of Habsburg–Ottoman, Venetian–Ottoman and sometimes Habsburg–Venetian war (with land- and sea-based raiding and banditry between wars) decisively affected long-term inter-ethnic relations. To the extent that Serb–Croat relations defined the region's twentieth-century political history (Djokić 2007), the most significant was the depopulation of the Dalmatian hinterland and central Bosnia and their repopulation through alternating integration into Habsburg and Ottoman frontier governance structures. In 1522, the Habsburg Empire first established a 'Military Frontier', under direct military administration and outside any existing province's control, along its southern border. This eventually stretched from Varaždin, in central Croatia, to today's Serbia–Hungary–Romania border in the southern Banat. Initially garrisoned by mercenaries, by 1630 it was taking most of its military strength from households of displaced Catholic and Orthodox Christians from further south. The Frontier accommodated them and their descendants as reservist-settlers, obliging men to join the Habsburg forces during war.

The largest migration, in 1690-1, saw tens of thousands of Serbs flee Kosovo and southern Serbia when Ottoman forces retook territory the Habsburgs had temporarily held in 1686-90. Orthodox Christian settlers, often 'Vlachs' in seventeenth-century Habsburg sources, were identified and addressed by their Church and the nineteenth-century Serbian national movement as Serbs, fixing their collective identity along religious and ethnic lines. With programmes for Croat national unification (the Kingdom of Croatia, an autonomous part of Hungary, plus other Habsburg provinces inhabited by South Slavs), and wider South Slav ('Yugoslav') unification, also articulated from the 1830s-60s, the descendants of these Orthodox Christians and others would become geopolitically significant concentrated Serb minorities near Croatia's border with Bosnia and Serbia; this dispute-in-the-waiting between separate ethnonational projects could be managed or even erased by forming a Yugoslavia. This twentieth-century demographic impasse was, in longer view, a product of imperial competition.

Since these Ottoman and Habsburg projects occurred at the same time that settler colonialism and Atlantic slavery began, and European trading companies (not only the best known, like the British and Dutch East India Companies, but also those as short-lived as Courland's (Dzenovska 2013)) were expanding colonial power, a comparative history of empire might ask how far Habsburg or Ottoman imperialisms were informed by the notions fuelling Spanish, Portuguese, British, French, Dutch, Danish or Swedish colonial power overseas. Such questions, essential for decolonial longue-durée perspectives on south-east Europe, are only beginning to be pursued, with more emphasis on late Ottoman and Habsburg imperialism (Deringil 2003; Sauer 2012; Gökay and Hamourtziadou 2016) than the fifteenth to seventeenth centuries, which to Mignolo (2000) represent the origin of colonial formations of race.

Much better discussed is the Ottoman Empire's collapse and the wars to establish and expand Bulgarian, Greek, Romanian and Serbian (and eventually Albanian) nation-states, subjecting south-east Europe to the geopolitical logic of nationalism as a principle of international order (Gagnon 2004). Nationalism predicated sovereignty claims determining people's and places' ethnic identity, calculating majorities and minorities, and basing national borders on the resultant ethnic maps (White 2000). Before and after these nation-states gained full independence from Ottoman rule in 1878, they used churches, schools and language/naming policy to 'fix' ambiguous subjects' ethnic identity and increase their ostensible majorities against competing claims; during war and political instability, minorities could be targeted directly. The Habsburg protectorate over Bosnia-Herzegovina, agreed in the same 1878 settlement, directly expressed a European imperial 'civilising mission', with which authorities sought to temper Balkan/Muslim nationalism, backwardness and poor hygiene (Okey 2007). Discourses and technologies of imperialism circulating through the region between the 1870s and the Paris Peace Conference underlay the ethnicity–nationhood–territory relationships behind ethnopolitical violence even as the region's long-term economic marginalisation as an agricultural periphery of both empires motivated hundreds of thousands of people to take advantage of the opportunities settler-colonial societies offered to migrants who – however conditionally – could be racialised as white.

Ethnopolitical violence, forced migration and the racial 'Other'

In 1878–1918 – the moment when political elites fused 'state' and 'nation' into a conjunction that still structures international politics, and the height of European identification with direct colonial mastery – Habsburg and Serbian territorial projects competed over the Yugoslav region: how far could and should the Kingdom of Serbia expand south and east, and should the Empire's South Slavs owe loyalty to Belgrade or Vienna? For Serbian political and military leaders, especially the Kingdom's longest-serving prime minister Nikola Pašić, Serbia's historical mission was unifying all Serbs into one state. The conception of ethnicity/territory Serbia shared with its neighbours required determining Serb territorial majorities in the present and also establishing historic Serb identity (often symbolised by Serbian Orthodox monasteries) for any non-Serb-majority territory the Kingdom claimed. For sociologists like Đorđe Stefanović and Dušan Bjelić, reassessing these ideologies, the biological essentialism that architects of the Serbian national programme applied to national Others (Muslims, Turks, Albanians) then used to justify their expulsion suggests European ideas of 'race' and coloniality already permeated south-east European ethnonationalism (Stefanović 2005; Bjelić 2009).

Habsburg control of Bosnia-Herzegovina, tightened through annexation in 1908, made expansion into remaining Ottoman territory more feasible for Serbia than challenging Habsburg power. Serbian forces' expulsion of 49,000 Albanians and 22,000 other Muslims in 1878 from Toplica and Kosanica (areas near Kosovo awarded to Serbia at the Congress of Berlin) showed the state did not foresee a future for Ottoman Muslim landholders, or Albanians in general, within the Serbian nation. Up to 150,000 Serbs from Ottoman-governed Kosovo and Sandžak meanwhile fled into Serbia from disorder caused by armed Albanian groups. Serb proponents of expelling Albanians, like the politician and historian Vladan Đorđević (who called Albanians both 'European Indians' and 'lazy savages' in 1913 (Stefanović 2005: 472; see also Todorova 2005b: 156–7)), thought this necessary to revert the land to an authentically 'Serb' character erased under Ottoman rule. Such ethnicisation of territory, projecting historical symbolism on to land and then expelling those who became 'minorities', could justify expansion into strategically and economically valuable territory where demography would not support the 'unification' claim (Stefanović 2005: 476).

Serbia incorporated larger territorial gains after the 1912–13 Balkan Wars even more systematically by settling veterans to farm land from which Muslims, Albanians and Bulgarians had been displaced. Post-1918 Yugoslavia, under Pašić, rolled this into its promised land reform. The Serbian and Yugoslav states, and at least more ideologically committed settlers, viewed this as 'strengthening the national element' of liberated land; it could simultaneously be called 'internal colonization' through settlement (Newman 2015: 92–3), and Albanians readily identified their situation with other colonised peoples' (Malcolm 1998: xlvi). Figures like Đorđević casting Albanians as threats to Serbs in Kosovo evoked tropes of savagery and tribalism, identifying Serbs in the Balkans with white Europeans in America and Africa by suggesting they enjoyed civilisational superiority over yet were threatened by the subordinate Albanians. The Serbian academician Vasa Čubrilović, directly arguing for 'the expulsion of the Albanians' ('isterivanje Arnauta') in 1937, both advocated ethnopolitical separation and exemplified 'colonizing projects' that aligned Serbs (and maybe other Christian Yugoslavs) with the colonial Europeanness and whiteness of the former protectorates over Bosnia and Albania (Rexhepi 2016: 148), even as balkanist discourses made Serbs 'Others' to 'Europe'.

Viewing the 'colonisation' programme through an ethnopolitical conflict lens emphasises questions of territory, identity, aggression and victimhood. Among these are whether its expansionism should be considered aggression; how many non-Serbs were directly displaced through violence by Serbian forces and self-organised paramilitaries;[2] whether Serbia/Yugoslavia could legitimately settle Serb farmers on such lands; how well founded were competing Bulgarian/Macedonian/Albanian ethnonational claims; and how direct was continuity between this Serbian programme or its supporters' xenophobia with eliminationist positions in Serb political discourse during the 1990s. Comparative European history would place south-east European national expansionism within the same norms by which Piedmont and Prussia justified wars of national (Italian/German) unification in the 1860s–70s.[3] South-east European ethnopolitics and European geopolitics, however, both existed within a deeper framework of global coloniality in a fin-de-siècle when, Dušan Bjelić (2009: 286) observes, south-east European intellectual elites routinely attended the universities of their 'geopolitical allies'. European colonial imagination directly entered south-east European politics through these routes, translated through whatever identified one's own nation with 'Europe'.

Bjelić, indeed, arguably does most to set early-twentieth-century south-east European politics of identity in global not just European context. Bjelić's work on First World War colonial soldiers, often used in roles with even higher death-rates than white European troops', leads him to argue that a 'racial genealogy' of the Great War ought to replace the 'national paradigm' in European First World War histories that has erased the 'constitutive violence' of bringing almost a million black and Asian colonial soldiers to fight on European fronts (Bjelić 2014); this involved not just the Western Front but others, including the Salonika Front, where French African divisions fought in autumn 1918 (Bjelić 2016). Elsewhere, researching emigration from south-east Europe beyond the most-studied destinations of Europe and the Anglosphere, he traces Bulgarian Zionists' participation in colonising Palestine to directly connect – not just compare/contrast – south-east European history and the colonial history of the Middle East (Bjelić 2017). Prevailing approaches in the region's historiography could not even frame the question of where the Serbian national project or Yugoslav unification would fit into a 'racial genealogy' of the First World War – and yet the black soldiers on the Salonika Front, even alone, would show the region was not *outside* that genealogy (Bjelić 2016). The Great War is as much a part of the history of race and the Yugoslav region as the theme on which the most explicit discussions of race in the region have turned – the racialisation of ethnonational and religious boundaries that facilitated genocidal expressions of Serb and Croat ethnonationalism during the Second World War.

Scientific racism and ethnonationalism before and during the Second World War

Interwar Yugoslavia, more than any other period, saw national identity construction in the Yugoslav region dependent on explicitly as well as implicitly evoking 'race'. This Yugoslavia's identity was caught between Serb/Croat/Slovene ethnopolitical identities separate enough to be included (until 1929) in the unified Kingdom's first official name and the state's need for a unifying collective ideology around 'South Slav' ethno-linguistic commonalities (Albanians and other non-South Slavs were beyond the nation-state's majority community). 'Race' itself, and 'racial theory' dividing the world's peoples into named races with identifiable physical characteristics and equally immutable psychological ones, were demonstrably known in interwar Yugoslavia within the context of European scientific racism (Bartulin 2009), just as in neighbouring Bulgaria (Todorova 2006) and, indeed, in the US ethno-cartographic inquiry into south-east Europe that informed negotiations at the 1919–20 Paris Peace Conference (Crampton 2006). In Yugoslavia, however, race did not just signify the majority nation's global position but also mediated how separate South Slav identities related to overarching 'Yugoslav' identity.

Ideas of unifying all South Slavs (not just Serbs) had existed since the 1830s, in tension with Serbian unification and several different Habsburg approaches to the 'South Slav question' (Djokić (ed.) 2003).[4] Throughout the First World War, Pašić and Habsburg South Slav leaders had quarrelled over the constitutional balance between Serbs and other South Slavs, and Serbian and Habsburg state structures. After December 1918, when 'National Councils' in Zagreb and independent Montenegro unified with Serbia, the 'Yugoslav idea' – whatever it meant – had to become not only a concrete constitutional settlement but also an ideology of national cultural expression (Wachtel 1998).

The 'Dinaric race' named by the interwar Yugoslav anthropologist Vladimir Dvorniković in 1939 mediated these contradictions, Tomislav Longinović (2011) argues, through a culturalist definition of Yugoslav identity that distanced Yugoslavs, as a recently liberated nation, from imperial modernities. The Dinaric highland place-myth, and an ethnological imagination centred on Bosnia/southern Serbia/Macedonia, allowed Dvorniković to term South Slavs one 'Dinaric race'. This shared experiences of domination by foreign empires (not dominating other peoples) and a melancholic mentality expressed through Bosnian, southern Serbian and Macedonian – but explicitly not Roma – folk-song; it encompassed groups that ethnonational Serb/Muslim or (if Croats could accommodate Dinaric Balkanness) Serb/

Croat antagonisms separated. And yet 'non-Slavic peoples', including Albanians, Roma and Jews, only appeared 'as a negative against which the Slavic folk genius had been imagined' (Longinović 2011: 101). Even in its own terms, this historically subordinated, now-liberated Yugoslav race contained a racialised hierarchy, one of many 'intra-European racism[s]' (Robinson 1983: 67; Jahoda 2009) in anthropology at the time.

Interwar Yugoslav adaptations of scientific racism and eugenics indeed linked biological racial essentialism to existing Yugoslav ethnonational identity hierarchies. One Serbian doctor, Svetislav Stefanović, purported he could differentiate the peoples of 'Europe' from 'African and Asian peoples' by blood-type, that inhabitants of Yugoslav regions 'where ... the forces of state creation have been most prominent' (Serbia, Montenegro, the Adriatic coast) had 'the highest European blood index', and that 'the higher degree of mixture between foreign racial qualities' produced lower European blood indices in Croatia, Slovenia and Bosnia (Petrović (ed.) 2015: 508).[5] His racial thinking clearly suggested Serb political and cultural superiority over other South Slavs, implicitly justifying Serb predominance in Yugoslavia: scientific racism was thus applied to ethnonational differences between South Slavs even as it became a foundation for antiziganism and anti-Semitism.

Yugoslav anti-Semitism, as elsewhere, involved notions of 'race' that, even if 'unclear' (Sekelj 1988: 160), still strictly separated majorities from Jews. Croat students in Zagreb first demanded a maximum quota (numerus clausus) of Jewish students in 1920, when Hungary passed one; such demands intensified in Croatia's 1930s Catholic press, while other theologians like Andrija Živković denounced racism (Živković in 1938 condemned 'racists [who] consider the interests of race and blood ... the measure of good and evil' (Goldstein 2003: 122–5)). The last Yugoslav government before the Axis invasion introduced a numerus clausus, and banned Jewish military officers reaching high ranks, in 1940; the governor of Croatia, granted extensive autonomy in 1939, refused to implement it, arguing it interfered with Croatia's autonomy in education (Sekelj 1988: 169).

In March–April 1941, the Axis occupied Yugoslavia, installing puppet regimes in an enlarged Croatia and rump Serbia; both applied ideologies of racial purity, anti-Semitism and eugenics to the ethnic nation. Milan Nedić's 'Government of National Salvation', formed at Wehrmacht invitation in August 1941, established a 'Committee for the Protection of Serbian Blood' to pass eugenics laws for national cultural regeneration (Ramet and Lazić 2011: 28); its commander of paramilitary volunteers, Dimitrije Ljotić, had founded the fascist movement Zbor in 1935 and believed Jews, Bolsheviks, Freemasons and Western capitalists were conspiring 'to subjugate the "white" race', including Serbs (Sekelj 1988: 167). The 'Independent State of Croatia' (NDH), in power between April 1941 and May 1945, had even longer to implement its ideology, collaborating with the Nazi extermination of Jews and organising its own genocide against Jews, Roma and Serbs.

NDH ideology derived from the Ustaše ('Insurgents'), the Croat revolutionary–fascist movement founded in 1928 by Ante Pavelić, 'Poglavnik' ('Duce'/'Führer') of the NDH. It looked back to the nineteenth-century writer Ante Starčević, who (against emerging Yugoslavism) had believed Serbs, after long servitude under the Ottomans, lacked Croats' cultural advancement and state-building capacity. Croat nationalists of the 1920s had used racialised categories to posit Croats and Serbs had different histories of ethnic mixing (Serbs intermarrying more with Vlachs and Roma, Croats having more Nordic and Aryan blood) and oppose the unitarist idea of Yugoslavs as a homogenous race (Bartulin 2008: 84–5). Pavelić went further, arguing that Croats were not even Slavs but had separate Iranian, and therefore Aryan, descent (Bartulin 2008: 88). NDH racial laws, closely following German and Italian models (including a 'Law on the Protection of the Aryan Blood and Honour of the Croat People'), based membership of the national community on being 'Aryan', that is, 'having ancestors who were members of the European racial community or who descend from branches of that community outside Europe' (Blažević and Alijagić 2010: 905–6).

NDH racial ideology specified Jews and Roma as non-Aryan (Biondich 2002: 34), treated Bosnian Muslims as Aryans and Islamicised

Croats (Kisić-Kolanović 2015), and ostensibly offered Orthodox Serbs conditional belonging if they became Catholic yet in practice directed 'racial purification' against Serbs, Jews and Roma alike (Yeomans 2015: 22). Serbs, while not non-Aryan to the NDH (it classified them religiously as 'grčkoistočnjački' or 'Greek-Eastern'), were 'portrayed as … racially similar to Jews and Gypsies' because of miscegenation, and many discriminatory decrees still targeted them (Bartulin 2008: 91–3). NDH anti-Communist propaganda was also racialised: one 1944 pamphlet warned of 'the hordes of … the dark, uncultured barbarian East, that have today rushed towards Europe', and described Soviet soldiers behaving with Croat prisoners' keepsakes 'as if they were wild black men' (Erdeljac 2015: 78). The 'Ustaša terror' against Jews, Roma and Serbs, beginning with property confiscation and revocations of civil rights, became a mass extermination programme that claimed the lives of more than 75 per cent of Jews, 'and probably an equivalent proportion of the Roma', in the NDH (Dulić 2006: 273). More than half the victims at the NDH concentration camp at Jasenovac, opened in August 1941, were Serbs (Kolstø 2011: 225);[6] indeed, the NDH's first interior minister, Andrija Artuković, reportedly said the Ustaše 'had killed the black Gypsies [Roma], and all that was left was to kill the white Gypsies [Serbs]' (Reinhartz 1999: 86), indicating this genocidal ideology's racialised slippages.

While most studies of the NDH imply it imported racial theory from Nazi Germany, the historian Nevenko Bartulin argues racial theory was a Croatian and Yugoslav, not just a German, phenomenon: NDH ideologues also knew how interwar struggles over South Slav ethnopolitical identities had been framed around race by adapting German scientific racism (Bartulin 2013, 2014).[7] Hans Günther's six physically distinguishable European racial subgroups had included a 'Dinaric' race (alongside Nordic, Mediterranean, Alpine, East Baltic and Phalian) on which definitions of Yugoslav and single-nation identities would draw (Bartulin 2009: 199–213).[8] The NDH defined its ideal Croat as a 'Nordic–Dinaric' racial type, tall, fair-haired warrior heroes from the Croatian/Bosnian highlands, and accommodated Muslims by arguing that Islamicisation had not diluted their bloodline, Croatian language, or fair skin and hair (Kisić-Kolanović 2015: 194–5). Interwar and wartime Croatian ethnic belonging discourses contained transnational racial formations that historians would miss if they conflated race and ethnicity completely. For Gilroy, meanwhile, Pavelić's myth of 'descent from heroic Aryan sources' alongside the primordialist colonial separation of Hutu/Tutsi identities in Rwanda shows '[t]he specific force of *modern* racist discourse' (Gilroy 2000: 300; emphasis original) carried well beyond western Europe, where fascism is most studied. Reading Bartulin and Gilroy together emphasises the adaptive formation of race in Second World War Croatia, appropriating transnational racial formations into eliminatory ethnicised nationalism. These exclusionary identity discourses acquire fresh global contexts in a transnational history of 'race'; yet so do the discourses of mixing and hybridity, often held up in south-east European identity discourses as the opposite of ethnonationalism, which became an ingredient of post-1945 regional identities in the Eastern Adriatic.

Ethnicity and the silences of 'hybridity' in Istria

Within literature on ethnicity in the Yugoslav region, Istrian regional identities, with their historical narratives of everyday multilingualism and Italian–Yugoslav/Italian–Slovenian–Croatian border-crossing, often exemplify multi-ethnic alternatives to ethnonationalism. Both the inhabitants of ex-Habsburg Trieste, assigned to Italy in 1945–54, and post-Yugoslav residents of Croatian Istria resisting state-level ethnicised homogeneity in the 1990s (Kalapoš 2002; Bellamy 2003), imagined Istria as historically 'hybrid' – allowing Homi Bhabha's work on identity and hybridity (see Bhabha 1994) to be translated into theories of south-east European ethnicity – and cosmopolitan. Yet both narratives, the anthropologist Pamela Ballinger (2004) argued, still depended on essentialised ideas of ethnicity–modernity–territory. While Trieste's own identity myth still concealed earlier Venetian, irredentist and Fascist perceptions of Slavs as less modern, the myth of 'successful … ethnic *convivenza*' in post-Yugoslav Istrian regionalism also reflected a 'nesting orientalism' (Bakić-Hayden 1995) contrasting Istrians against nationalistic, violent Balkan peoples (including other Croats) responsible for the wars (Ballinger 2004: 36, 41–2). Moreover, 'authentic' Istrian hybridity still seemed not to accommodate 'nonautochthonous' residents (Ballinger 2004: 42) – including the Croatian, Bosnians and Albanian migrants Ballinger mentioned, and indeed racialised migrants from outside Europe who, in smaller numbers, belonged to Istrian social reality as well. Deep in the silences of Istrianity, did Istria's admixture of Italian heritage and even blood supposedly explain its differences?

Ballinger's deconstruction of Istrian place-myths contributes to the history of racisms in Europe from the often-neglected perspective of ethnicities in the eastern Adriatic – by proposing Triestine exiles' post-1943–5 racialisation of 'Slavo-Communists' as an antecedent of '[t]he elision of biologically ascribed race and culturally given national identity' in late-twentieth-century European cultural racism (Ballinger 2004: 36). Her warning not to romanticise hybridity uses postcolonial scholars including Gilroy, Robert Young and Anne McClintock to suggest that, if ideas of hybridity still depended on historic ideas of mixture, purity and race, Istrian hybridity discourse still possessed 'an inherent link to the very categories of classification that it claims to oppose' (Ballinger 2004: 34). Indeed, echoing Said's reservations about 'traveling theory', Ballinger also perceived a parallel with 'elite appropriations' of hybridity and mestizaje critiqued by anthropologists like Charles Hale (1999) in Guatemala and elsewhere (Ballinger 2004: 49).

The Ballinger–Hale reading of mestizaje was closer to some Latin American states' hegemonic nation-building ideology (Wade 2004) than the counter-hegemonic postcolonial and intersectional consciousness built by Chicana feminists and other feminists of colour around mestizaje's meaning to Gloria Anzaldúa (Tuhkanen 2009; Collins and Bilge 2016: 71–2). Anzaldúa's expression of a working-class Chicana lesbian consciousness, within global racial formations, inhabited a different race/class/sexuality intersection to anti-black elite 'whitening' of nationhood in Mexico or Brazil (Goldberg 2009: 218–36). Her balance between marginality and essentialisation – locating 'every identity ... in a culture, a language, a history' and naming their junctions – invites a 'politics of articulation' (Yarbro-Bejarano 1994: 10) that helps theory not just to travel but to connect. Such a connection for Istrian hybridity and Chicana mestizaje might ask: where is the Italo-Yugoslav borderland, as a legacy of Italian irredentism and South Slav nation-building, in relation to the US–Mexico borderland as a legacy of settler colonialism? Anna Agathangelou (2004a), in postcolonial and feminist International Relations, comes closest, reading the militarisation of the US–Mexico border and post-Yugoslav women's mobilisation in support of 1990s ethnonational wars as two facets of the transnational reconstruction of a capitalist patriarchy – a deeper superstructure behind both 'contact zones', in which even the internal migrations of socialist Yugoslavia deserve to be linked to global dynamics of border control and class.

Social inequalities and migration during and after state socialism

Extensive internal migration in socialist Yugoslavia, where hundreds of thousands of people moved in the 1950s–60s from rural/highland regions to urban centres for factory work or towards more fertile agricultural land, took place in a structure of property ownership shaped by the expropriations of the Holocaust, the Ustaša terror and the Communist expulsion of Germans in 1945, just as earlier settlements of Serb farmers in southern Serbia, Macedonia and Kosovo had been intrinsically linked to displacements of Albanians and South Slav Muslims. This migration – from the poorest south-eastern republics to the richest north-western ones, but also within republics from peripheries to centres – affected both urban and national identities. In large cities, established urban social strata complained new city-dwellers were bringing village mentalities into the metropolis, intensifying the 'urban/rural' clash in European-versus-Balkan hierarchies of modernity. Between Yugoslav republics, inhabitants of Slovenia and Croatia in particular perceived levels of cultural difference within their cities increasing (Dragićević-Šešić 1994; Archer, Duda and Stubbs 2016). The internal migrants most exposed to racialised practices of Othering that resembled Western European cultural racism were Albanians and Roma.

Albanians and Roma experienced similar, but not identical, marginalisations in socialist Yugoslavia. Security-minded state institutions viewed Albanians as a subversive minority because their ethnic kin-state, Albania, had a rival territorial claim; Roma suffered from their identity having no 'homeland' attached at all (McGarry 2017). During the Yugoslav wars, this would leave Roma caught 'in between' programmes of ethnopolitical violence in a way that, for Julija Sardelić (2015: 163), makes Bhabha's 'in-betweenness' more appropriate than 'Othering' to describe their position. Socialist Yugoslav media were ambivalent about whether Roma were a social underclass or an ethnic minority – but in agreeing that Roma were marginalised because of their own backwardness, they still made arguments that resembled Western European cultural racism, showing those discourses did not just appear as part of a *post*socialist resurgence of nationalism (Sardelić 2016: 102). Albanians in the late 1980s, meanwhile, were simultaneously labelled as fundamentalist Muslims in Serb nationalist media and treated as a semi-racialised, culturally and ethnically distinct underclass in Slovenia and Croatia.

These articulations of socio-economic inequality and ethnicised difference all allowed long-standing balkanist discourses of separating the national self from Ottoman cultural space to fuse with identification with late-twentieth-century meanings of 'Europe' informed by transnational cultural racism (Mihelj 2005; Longinović 2011; Sardelić 2016). The presence of 'race', in many facets, within the Yugoslav region's history of ethnicity puts the region within global formations of whiteness, 'Europeanness' and modernity well before the 1990s. And yet even broadening the history of ethnicity is not enough: migrations that do not fit this dominant theme so easily, and that are often therefore neglected, reveal a global past and present where encounters with blackness, indigeneity and other racialised constructions of difference ground the Yugoslav region even more tightly in transnational formations of race.

Microhistories of race and empire: the 'blacks of Ulcinj' and the explorers of Karlovac

Calls for globalised 'connected histories' of race, gender and empire, using lenses such as microhistory, translocality and intimate politics (Subrahmanyam 1997; Ballantyne and Burton (eds) 2005; Burton 2007; Bhambra 2014: 4; Potter and Saha 2015), suggest that quantitatively small migrations still reveal important underlying connections between regions. One such, for south-east Europe, is the history of biracial Afro-Montenegrin/Afro-Albanian families in Ulcinj, occasionally 'rediscovered' by anthropologists and journalists since the mid-twentieth century. A legacy of Ulcinj's place as a node in the Eastern Mediterranean slave trade, this migration probably involved fewer than a hundred households, but is evidence of a literal 'Black Adriatic': that is, the Adriatic just like the Atlantic is indeed a direct site of African diasporic history.[9]

Ulcinj, conquered by Montenegro from the Ottoman Empire in 1878, did not have as large a role as Tripoli or Benghazi in the Eastern Mediterranean slave trade, which 'affected the entire geography of Africa' while transporting slaves to south-east Europe and the Caucasus (Fikes and Lemon 2002: 498). A subsidiary slave port under Ottoman rule, it remained implicated in enslavement of Africans when Ulcinj-based merchant captains brought back slaves they had bought at sea for their own households or for sale to others. Although a few (Albanian) captains emigrated in 1878, at least two captains (Tahir Šurla and Hasan Šepeteja) at the beginning of the twentieth century still brought slaves to Ulcinj. These slaves had been captured aged 'from two to three up to 16 years old' (Lopashich 1958: 169) in Sudan, perhaps in Bagirmi, then taken along established caravan routes to North African ports. Aboard ship, they were given their captains' surnames, though many also acquired the surname 'Arap' (Turkish, Serbo-Croatian and Albanian for 'Arab'). Ulcinj might have had a hundred black families in the earlier nineteenth century (Lopashich 1958: 169), but this had declined to approximately fifty families (150 people) by 1878. Enslaved Africans in Ulcinj could marry each other but nobody else, though once freed some married into local Albanian and Montenegrin families, founding Ulcinj's small biracial community (Canka 2013).[10]

The anthropologist Alexander Lopašić, visiting Ulcinj in 1956, viewed this community through a racialising European ethnographic gaze. One family, he wrote, 'have retained their racial characteristics, a very dark and almost black skin, the typical curly hair, thick lips and physical strength'; another man 'possesses all the Negro characteristics, but his skin is somewhat lighter and he has an elongated skull' (Lopashich 1958: 173). Lopašić also recorded several family trees, and songs/dances with likely Arab or Bagirmi origins. His essentialised account of the 'Negroes' temperament was consistent with European and colonial formations of blackness:

> Though known for their kindheartedness, they were also much feared when in a bad temper … In spite of the new environment and a different social atmosphere, the Ulcinj Negroes succeeded in retaining some of their characteristics, such as lightheartedness, fondness of music, rhythm and fun, love of family life and a certain amount of personal attractiveness. (Lopashich 1958: 171)

Beyond acknowledging a movement of people and capital so marginalised in most Montenegrin/Yugoslav history as to be invisible, this said very little about the Africans' experiences of enslavement, or their visibly racialised descendants' experiences.

Another Yugoslav anthropologist, Đurđica Petrović (1972), and several Yugoslav/Montegrin journalists, have revisited the history of black families (often condensed to the Šurla family) in Ulcinj. In 1986, the photographer Rizo Šurla (who had been born in 1922, fought as a Partisan in the Second World War and joined the League of Communists (SKJ) in 1959) described life as a black man in Yugoslavia to *RTV Revija* in terms identifying with Yugoslavia's geopolitical position:

> I've never had any problems. I've always felt like a Yugoslav, a Montenegrin, I was born here, in this multi-national community […] Our country is,

in terms of equality, probably unique in the world and I'm proud to have been born in it and live in it. […]

Unfortunately, I've never been to Africa, my ancestors' birthplace, and I don't know what it's like there, but from what I've seen on television or in films – I don't think I could live there.

Look what's happening in South Africa.

I believe that many Blacks would envy me if they knew what kind of country I lived in. (Predić 1986)

This imagined Yugoslavia – unlike South Africa, a year into its state of emergency – was free from both racial prejudice and racialised/ethnicised violence, something Communists had consistently feared.[11] Šurla even narrated his own biography into the Communist state-building narrative: according to his war story, a well-known Montenegrin Partisan, Mitar Bakić, asked his identity during a parade. When Šurla answered, 'I am a fighter, a Partisan, Rizo Šurla, a Montenegrin from Ulcinj', Bakić apparently replied in dialect, 'I know we Montenegrins are black, but, brother, you're really pushing it! [ti ga, brate, prećera!]' (Predić 1986). The anecdote remained in the family – though the commander became another Montenegrin general, Savo Burić – when the Montenegrin newspaper *Vijesti* interviewed Šurla's son and grandson in 2013 (here, Burić supposedly said 'God, I knew we were black, but not like this!'). *Vijesti* also drew on Lopašić and Petrović's anthropological writing to describe the community's assimilation into Ulcinj:

> Ethnologists have also stated the blacks of Ulcinj [ulcinjski crnci] were well-built and powerful people, brave and bold. However, children from mixed marriages, as Petrović writes, had softer [ublažene] physical characteristics of blacks as well as lighter skin tone. Despite their new environment and living conditions, they retained their authentic characteristics such as lightheartedness, fondness of music, rhythm and fun, and love of family life. (Adrović 2013)

Indeed, the end of the extract from *Vijesti* follows Lopašić so closely that the racialising gaze of a British anthropological journal and Viennese-trained anthropologist in 1958 could still be reproduced in 2013, indeed more than in 1986 – except that the 'certain amount of personal attractiveness' with which Lopašić eroticised his subjects had disappeared.

Behind Ulcinj's local narratives are multiple dimensions of raciality, from the very question of Montenegrins' relationships to 'blackness' (South Slav languages, and Italian, all call Montenegro 'Black Mountain') to the longer history of Eastern Adriatic/Mediterranean slavery. In the early Middle Ages, Slavs from the coast and hinterland were enslaved and sold in the Middle East, North Africa, northern Italy and Spain, with Korčula and especially Dubrovnik as hubs. Europeans' direct enslavement of Africans from the mid-fifteenth century (forcing them to work sugar plantations in Madeira and the Canary Islands even before the colonisation of the Americas) reoriented Mediterranean slavery so that '[i]n Ragusa, where so many Slavs had been collected and registered for sale beyond the seas, now black "Slavs" arrived from beyond the seas' (Evans 1985: 52–3). This line, undeveloped in a conclusion yet implicating an Adriatic port directly in European domination of Africa, points to an article on 'Black slaves in old Dubrovnik (1400–1600)' by the historian Vuk Vinaver in the Belgrade Historical Institute's journal, *Istorijski časopiš*, in 1955. These connections are not completely unresearched; but rarely are they carried forward.

Based on the etymology of 'Slav' and the history of the region's national movements resisting imperial rule, some South Slavs have suggested a shared history of enslavement could be a basis for fraternity between Africans and Slavs (Jović Humphrey 2014: 1137–8). This direct equation of blackness/Balkanness, not unlike Yugoslav Non-Aligned identification with anti-colonialism, mediates some identifications with Africa in (post-)Yugoslav arts and culture. However, although the history of chattel slavery and transnational anti-blackness has occurred on the same globe and within the same networks of ideology and capital as the history of Eastern Mediterranean slavery and the marginalisation (sometimes amounting to racialisation) of the Balkans, they are still not reducible to each other. Moreover, the Yugoslav region's history of enslavement and coloniality would also include South Slavs' involvement in structures of European colonial rule: although the Habsburg Empire did not extend overseas, inhabitants of its lands – including South Slavs – still participated in other European countries' imperial projects.

The histories of South Slav explorers and colonial officials are told primarily through investigating collections of papers and objects they brought home. The town of Karlovac connected several late-nineteenth-century Croatian travellers to Africa, such as the cartographers Mirko and Stevo Seljan (who assisted Emperor Menelik II in Ethiopia during the late 1890s, and later helped map the Amazon) and the explorer Dragutin Lerman, who joined the Stanley expedition to Congo in 1882 and spent ten of the next fourteen years as a Belgian provincial official there (Kočevar 2012). The Seljans, Lerman and another Karlovac man who accompanied him (Janko Mikić-Bojkamenski) were all subjects of a 2013 exhibition on 'Karlovčani in Africa', curated by Sanda Kočevar, at the Karlovac City Museum. A Rijeka-based historical geographer, Mirela Slukan-Altić, has published several book chapters on the Seljans, Mikić and Croatian missionaries in Spain's Spanish colonisation of the Americas (Slukan-Altić 2003, 2008, 2012).[12] Yugoslav anthropologists researched some of these figures in the 1970s (Lopašić 1971; Lazarević 1975), with a collaborative article on Slovene, Croat and Serb explorers in Africa possibly the most complete overview (Šmitek, Lazarević and Petrović 1993) – but, published in French during the Yugoslav wars, it was unlikely to inspire a new direction for Yugoslav history.

The Karlovac explorers' mobilities show that South Slavs, as aspiring imperial subjects, could participate in exercising European colonial power and domination. If these are not grounds for collective guilt, neither can they be grounds for collective exculpation. Indeed, life histories from the region were entangled with global histories of empire and race well before the nineteenth century. Even if, like Mignolo (2000, 2008; Greer, Mignolo and Quilligan 2007), one traces 'race' to Spanish theologians' classifications of civilised and savage peoples during the conquest of the Americas, here too the region is present: we find the Korčulan-born Dominican, Vinko Paletin or Vicente Palatino/Paletino (1508–73), whose writings justified Spanish warfare against the 'Indians' in 1557–8 and rejected Bartolomé de las Casas's case for peaceful conversion (Hanke 1964: 294). Paletin, raised in the Venetian Adriatic when Ottoman–Venetian proxy warfare through piracy and banditry was at its height around islands like Korčula, had himself sailed and fought in Francisco de Montejo's 1535–41 conquest of the Yucatán (Bošković 1997: 202–3). One can only speculate how the younger or older Paletin translated his observations of Indians and the Americas through his knowledge of Adriatic warfare; but if the Yugoslav region is written, as it should be, into the European 'republic of letters' (Bracewell 2011), it cannot be written out of the coloniality that permeated that republic, as contested as the region's status within 'Europe' remained. The region's past interconnected histories of raciality thus turn new lenses on migrations in the present.

Postsocialist, post-conflict and postcolonial migrations

Migrations into the region, compared with migrations around or out, are marginal for most studies of the present-day Yugoslav region, even those that already join two explanatory paradigms by accounting for social inequalities as well as ethnicised conflicts. By the late 1990s, however, Slovenian polemics over 'asylum-seekers' (Mihelj 2004; see Chapter 4) were already showing that the post-Yugoslav region was not only a migration origin-point but also a destination. While most migrants were outside local categories of ethnic difference, many (through combinations of skin colour, religion, nationality and economic marginality) fell into local categories of racialised Otherness, with specific locations in the postsocialist/post-conflict economy.

One distinctive pattern of postsocialist/post-conflict inward migration has involved the travel of women from post-Soviet states as sex-workers, whose clients and sometimes even traffickers include the extensive foreign military and civilian workforce of international intervention in Bosnia-Herzegovina and Kosovo. These circuits, including (but not solely) coercive operations by organised criminals and some private security contractors, are global networks connecting sex-workers' home countries with south-east Europe and other zones of neoliberal enclosure such as the Emirates' spectacular hubs of capital and south-east Asian cities' business districts (Harrington 2005; Suchland 2015). Many post-Soviet sex-workers are fair-skinned, and the blonde, Russian, passionate 'Natasha' stereotype is a vector of desire (Gülçür and İlkkaracan 2002: 414). Their socio-economic marginality and the marginality of eastern Europe/Russia in 'Western' imaginations produces a racialised, exoticised category that Anna Agathangelou (2004b: 88) (after research in Cyprus) calls 'white but not quite', subordinated and available for exploitation by Western men and as exoticised 'object[s] of ultimate masculine "desire"'. Ethnic-majority members in Cyprus, Greece and Turkey can assert their group's own Europeanness and whiteness, in the face of semi-racialised formations projected by the West on to the post-Ottoman space, by signalling these women's marginality (Gülçür and İlkkaracan 2002; Agathangelou 2004b). The post-Yugoslav trope of the post-Soviet sex-worker, constructed as symbols of postsocialist crisis, might within the semi-racialised formations of Othering and balkanism projected across the post-Ottoman space facilitate a similar assertion.

Another 'symbolic' postsocialist migration involves Chinese traders. Many 'Chinese shops' ('kineške prodavnice') have opened since the mid-1990s selling cheap clothing and household goods from storefronts that closed during the wars, or marketplaces or urban peripheries like New Belgrade's 'Blok 70'. These have represented a new form of visible racialised difference in urban space and, for many post-Yugoslavs, another symbol in public discourse of how the collapse of socialism has altered life and the economy beyond recognition – while adding a new stereotype to how 'Chinese' is racialised (Blagojević 2009). Beyond urban myths in Milošević-era Belgrade, implausibly holding that Milošević offered tens of thousands of Chinese migrants visa-free residency in return for votes before the contested 1996 election – when Serbia did liberalise its visa regime with China to encourage investment (Korać 2013a: 229) – Chinese migration into Serbia and other post-Yugoslav states is just one dimension of a globalised economic expansion into economically depressed areas (including West Africa) that Western investors have not prioritised (Chang 2013b: 138–9). Felix Chang and Sunnie Rucker-Chang's 2013 edited volume on Chinese migration in Russia, Central Asia and eastern Europe is one of few studies of postsocialism with racialised migrants at the centre, not the margins. The very concept of 'Chinese migrants', Chang establishes, in fact hides many positions within the formal and informal economy, plus much more specific translocal dynamics of economic chain migration (Chang 2013b: 142).[13]

Chang's difficulties obtaining official data about Chinese migration (beyond those of counting undocumented migrants and those who do not interact with census-taking) indicate statistical practices in Serbia and other post-Yugoslav states are more geared towards existing frames of ethnopolitics rather than recording new multicultural and multiracial categories in society: Serbia's Chinese population, estimated by Chang at 20,000–30,000 – similar to recorded numbers of Macedonians (25,847) or Bulgarians (20,497), and larger than the traditional Slovene, Ukrainian or Czech minorities of 2,000–5,000 – was invisible within the twenty-two categories of 'national belonging' or ethnic identity inherited from Yugoslavia (Chang 2013a: 155–6). The Department of Foreigners, which collected passport nationality data, meanwhile recorded 4,947 Chinese nationals in 2009 (Korać 2013b: 247) – while Serbian media quoted up to 100,000 (Blagojević 2009: 48). This statistical lack arguably prevented Chinese litigants proving that police demanded bribes more often from them than Serbian traders, since they would have had to rely on enforcement figures which were not broken down into specific enough ethnic or racial categories to prove disparate treatment of Chinese traders as a group (Chang 2013a: 169–76). Race was even more invisible beyond categories of historic ethnopolitical territorial competition in Bosnia-Herzegovina.[14] There, the Dayton Peace Agreement of December 1995 jettisoned most Yugoslav ethnonational categories, a post-war reduction of ethnic complexity to the Bosniak–Serb–Croat triangle. The state thus only collected data on these three categories plus 'Others', not even the country's largest minorities of Jews or Roma (Markowitz 2010).[15]

Chinese presence is, however, recognised in post-Yugoslav film (Rucker-Chang 2013). In particular, the early-2000s wave of Slovenian,

Croatian, Bosnian and Serbian films framed as commentaries on the extent of post-Yugoslav socio-economic change often contained storylines about Chinese traders, restaurateurs and undocumented migrants. Only in Serbia, however, did film-makers represent their country as the destination not the transit point. The other films, with plots about human trafficking, used Chinese migrants as a device to illustrate Slovenian hierarchies of xenophobia (with Middle Eastern and Chinese migrants more external and less knowable 'Others' than ex-Yugoslav migrants); to dramatise Croatian small-town intolerance (towards a single mother's biracial white/Chinese child) as a departure from idealised European values, albeit one that needs the audience to share a 'visceral reaction' to the child's visible difference; or to comment on post-war Bosnia's lack of future (Rucker-Chang 2013: 205, 210) – all, in other words, to be 'a proxy for unrecognizable change' in narratives about post-Yugoslav 'transition' while still appearing 'wholly outside the *historically* defined Other' (Rucker-Chang 2013: 201; emphasis added) of Roma, Jews and ethnonational enemies. Post-Yugoslav public culture makes Chinese and other racialised migrants symbols not subjects of postsocialism – whereas migrants *from* the region remain protagonists of post-Yugoslav studies even on the far side of the globe.

Confronting race and whiteness in diaspora

The Yugoslav region's worldwide diaspora communities, whether place-of-origin-based ('zavičajni'), ethnonational or (post-)Yugoslav, encounter destination countries' formations of race and whiteness even as they reconfigure identities they know. Some destinations, like the USA, have unmissable, everyday racial politics, where migrants must try to understand the balance of interracial relations and determine how they, individually and collectively, might desire to be racialised or are racialised by others. In others (like Sweden or the Netherlands), where the historical whiteness of national identity is so hegemonic that – for white people – racial politics are less perceptible, late-twentieth-century migrants were caught between identifications with Europeanness and whiteness that might have been common sense in Yugoslavia and cultural racism in the majority nation that might classify them, alongside Somalis, Rwandans and others fleeing 1990s conflict zones, as social problems. The migration of Roma, racialised into a specific category in Europe while subject to more diffuse discrimination in the USA, is an even more complex translation of individual experiences of racialisation along transnational migration routes – yet if race is an undeniable category of analysis for Romani migration, so is it for the region's ethnic majorities.

Bulgarian and Macedonian Roma in the US, for instance, often discover that stigmatised markers of Romani identity in south-east Europe are either less recognisable as Romani in the US (language, dress, skin colour) or do not exist because of different settlement patterns (Silverman 2012): the racialised categories for differentiating US urban districts do not include 'Romani', while in south-east Europe 'Romani' is the primary category for demarcating and racialising urban space (Kilibarda 2011). While their skin colour exposes them to racist profiling and microaggressions, they are not so readily racialised *as Roma* in the US, and therefore have more passing strategies (like describing themselves as Turkish) – and sometimes contrast Americans' 'ignorance' about Roma with 'blatant discrimination back home' when explaining why they left (Silverman 2012: 67, 69). The antiziganism of western *and* eastern Europe still confronts south-east European Roma living in France or Britain but is less tangible in the USA.

Studies of South Slav diasporas – which consist of several waves, formed for different prevailing reasons during economic depressions, regime changes and war (Pryke 2003; Cederberg 2005; Colic-Peisker 2008) – have also started asking how migrants interpret their new countries' configurations of race. Hariz Halilovich's translocal ethnography of Bosniak refugees from Prijedor and Srebrenica, for instance, suggested Bosnians in St Louis and Melbourne understood their own racialised position differently because of different US and Australian discourses of race. Bosnians in St Louis had internalised 'race ... as the source of their newly discovered white identity' (perceptible when they discussed the segregation of 'white' and 'African-American' neighbourhoods) more than Bosnians in Melbourne, who seemed 'much less attached to the colour of their skin and ... more ready to engage critically in deconstructing racial identities and prejudices against which they have not been completely immune' (Halilovich 2013: 228–9). These are translocal even more than transnational translations of race, with cities' immediate racial politics forming the everyday knowledge through which new Bosnian immigrants learned to racially position themselves – as events in Missouri after police killed Mike Brown would show (Croegaert 2015).

The Kosovo War, meanwhile, created new Albanian diasporas in countries like Britain, and enlarged existing ones (e.g. in Germany, the Netherlands, Sweden, the USA), just as migration studies was consolidating as a discipline, inspiring many studies of identities among their adolescent second and '1.5' generations (e.g. King and Mai 2008; Vathi 2015). These young people's everyday experiences were shaped by accommodating to the racial politics of multicultural London, Florence or Gothenburg (Vathi 2015: 105–8). Young Albanians in Britain, for instance, encountered the first wave of racialisation of 'east European' migrants which after 2004 would extend to Poles and other workers from new EU member states (see Fox, Moroşanu and Szilassy 2012). Albanians' location within racial formations in Italy illustrates Anthias and Yuval-Davis's argument (1993) that racism can take any 'biological, cultural, linguistic or religious' signifier as a boundary-marking symbol of difference, not just skin colour (King and Mai 2008: 4). While these diasporas do not contain people who any official Yugoslav ideology regarded as Yugoslavs, they overlap with the notion of 'diasporas from the Yugoslav region' in containing migrants from Yugoslavia's southern republics and their descendants, therefore should not be invisible in an argument about that notion. Moreover, the Kosovo War's sudden effect on how Kosovars and other Albanians in Europe were racialised also demonstrates how contingently people from the Yugoslav region fit into formations of 'race' elsewhere – an even more pressing question for Bosniaks and other Muslims after 9/11.

Bosniak ethnicity, after 9/11, stood at a specific intersection of identity and marginalisation. While Bosniaks' skin colour would racialise them as white-but-'ethnic' in the US, and white-but-linguistically-visible-as-eastern-European in Europe, their religious heritage positioned them in the racialised, stigmatised and securitised category of 'Muslim'. One outcome of this intersection, outside and inside Bosnia-Herzegovina, was presentation of Bosniak religious identity as a European Islam, a 'positive cultural exception' to other, non-tolerant and non-European Islams ascribed both to Islamic societies outside Europe and even to brown and black Muslim immigrants inside it (Bougarel 2007: 97). Another became identification with a transnational Muslim ummah. The Bosnian conflict itself popularised this idea among some Western Muslims, and as the War on Terror, state surveillance of Muslims and the distributed organisation of Islamist political violence intensified in the twenty-first century it would inspire small numbers of Bosniak and Kosovar youth (from the region and the diaspora) to 'make hijra' and join armed jihadist groups including ISIS (Chapter 4). A further intersection of religion, race and ethnicity with class – that many more rural Bosniaks practised religious tradition, while many urban Bosniaks' grand narratives of state socialism, modernity and the urban/rural divide associated religious practice with unmodernity – was common sense in south-east European identity discourses but little known outside diasporas in the countries where refugees moved (Al-Ali 2002).

Post-9/11 politics, Halilovich suggests, compelled Bosniaks in St Louis to identify with whiteness, anti-blackness and US performative patriotism (displaying flags outside houses) in order not 'to stand out as a minority' (Halilovich 2013: 218) – a decade after being persecuted in their home country for their ethnicity and religion – and to distance themselves from the threatening, racialised Muslim Other being 'cast out' (Razack 2008) from political communities across the West. Halilovich's book appeared a year before St Louis became a focus of African-American struggle – the site of Black Lives Matter's first street protest – in August 2014 when police in nearby Ferguson shot dead the black teenager Mike Brown. Racialised violence in St Louis affected Bosnians directly that November, when four African-American and Latino teenagers killed a Bosniak, Zemir Begić. Bosniaks' reaction, however, was more complex than a blanket identification with whiteness to explain the attack: while that did occur, young Bosniak women in particular viewed African-American experiences 'in relation to their own experiences with state violence, and lack of postwar justice, in Bosnia' and through online activism articulated intersectional solidarities with African-Americans and Black Lives Matter (Croegaert 2015: 75). Young women's activism in this '1.5 generation' suggested Bosniaks' identification with whiteness was not predetermined; instead, Ana Croegaert (2015: 64) wrote, it showed how Bosnians could 'reject "whiteness" in favor of interracial solidarity informed by shared experiences with injustice, viewed through the lens of imperialism and empire' – another anti-imperialist identification grounded in the region's global history.

Bosniaks' racialisation, and other south-east European immigrants', since the 1990s has thus been a contingent process, not predetermined by their ethnicity and nationality. Indeed, this is no post-9/11 phenomenon, but has long been the case in settler colonial societies' migration history and labour history. A whole literature now asks how immigrants from Europe were racialised on arrival, how ascriptions of their racialised identity changed, and when and how they themselves understood their new countries' racial formations and their place(s) within them, with David Roediger (2005) influentially suggesting eastern Europeans did not know whiteness as a dimension of identity before needing to assimilate into it in the USA. Another well-known title, Noel Ignatiev's *How the Irish Became White* (Ignatiev 1995), encapsulates the idea that immigrants arriving from European peripheries (the Mediterranean, Ireland and central Europe as well as the Balkans), against nativist opposition, only gained gradual access to whiteness in the early twentieth century, and gained it by participating in structures of racialised oppression. This paradigm, of south and east Europeans arriving without consciousness of 'race' and acquiring whiteness by rejecting some solidarities and pursuing others, is migration history's prevailing mode of connecting eastern European identities and race under settler colonialism.

White Anglophones at the 'centre' of their nations in Australia and New Zealand also equated whiteness with potential to assimilate. In the 1990s, Australian authorities attributed Bosnian refugees, including Muslims (who unlike Croats and Serbs were not joining an established diaspora), higher 'settlement potential' than non-white refugees, whom they perceived as 'culturally distant' – hence Val Colic-Peisker's telling quote, 'At least you're the right colour' (Colic-Peisker 2005: 618–19). Colic-Peisker (2005: 622) suggests identification with Europeanness as well as whiteness offered Bosnians 'emotional compensation for the loss of status' they experienced as refugees, restricted by linguistic and educational barriers from accessing skilled employment and fulfilling the 'settlement potential' that Australian racialised hierarchies of refugee resettlement had ascribed them.

In New Zealand, a century before, Dalmatian Croat labourers working on gumfields in the 1860s–1920s encountered a British imperial equivalent of the Ignatiev–Roediger pattern: core whiteness was Britishness, further whiteness was ascribed to ethnic groups in proportion to perceived assimilability, and the Croats themselves were racialised as socially and sexually disruptive to white morality, liable to be described as invasive 'locusts' just like Māori (Bozic-Vrbancic 2006: 186–7). By the mid-twentieth century, Croats' economic success in winemaking had opened whiteness up to them, while Māoris were campaigning to reconfigure national identity around Pākehā–Māori biculturalism. Biracial Māori–Croat children in the gumfields – possibly even the majority of children subjected to Native Schools' 'civilizing' mission (Timutimu, Simon and Matthews 1998: 111) there – experienced conditional identifications with both Māori and Pākehā culture and with a Dalmatia to which they often retained ties, while the advent of state socialism in Yugoslavia further complicated how they perceived the closeness or foreignness of this joint homeland (Bozic-Vrbancic 2005). Late-nineteenth-century South Africa, meanwhile, probably (the census recorded migrants by origin country, not ethnicity) had some 2,000–2,500 Croats, including 400–500 miners at Kimberley. More than 400 Croats identifying themselves as 'traders, miners and all kinds of artisan' petitioned Vienna in 1899 to open a Pretoria consulate (Laušić 2003: 241–2). A comparative history of class, ethnicity and race is necessary to link these petitioners in South Africa, the gumfield labourers in New Zealand and the miners of the Mesabi Range in Minnesota – all present in the historical record (Laušić 2003; Bozic-Vrbancic 2005; Lubotina 2015) – plus others from the Yugoslav region into the global history of empire and labour.

Studies of other destinations also show how South Slav migrants, stratified by both ethnicity and class, have been accommodated within and altered those countries' formations of race. They did so as refugees in Nordic countries negotiating boundaries of whiteness, autochthony and immigration status (Cederberg 2005; Grünenberg 2005; Huttunen 2009; Valenta and Strabac 2011); as guest-workers in 1960s–70s West Germany, socio-economically similar to Turks and Kurds but racialised by white Germans somewhat differently (Molnar 2014);[16] as migrants negotiating bourgeois belonging, whiteness, blackness and creoleness in turn-of-the-century Argentina;[17] or as Zionists or Muslims migrating from south-east Europe to Palestine, movements through which both Dušan Bjelić (2017) and Darryl Li (2015b) revisit the history of 'Balkan postcoloniality'.

Li and Bjelić both produce 'connected histories' of two regions usually treated as separate by illustrating wider historical contexts through migration. Bjelić reads the 48,000 Bulgarian Jews who moved to Palestine in 1944–8 as 'agents of a double colonization', 'subjects of internal colonization' in Bulgaria who then came as 'colonizers' to Palestine; the implication is that 'the continuity of a single history over two geographies' is more accurate than Maria Todorova's separation of balkanism from orientalism (Bjelić 2017: 1–2). Li, meanwhile, translates and introduces a 1981 article by the anthropologist Nina Seferović about a hundred Muslim mujahir families who emigrated from Herzegovina to Caesarea after Bosnia-Herzegovina became an Austro-Hungarian protectorate in 1878. Their descendants, known as the Bushnaqs (from 'bošnjak' or 'Bosniak'), were displaced from Caesarea during the Nakba in February 1948, when 'their village ceased to exist' (Seferović 2015 [1981]: 77);

the site became 'an affluent suburb' of Haifa, 'hosting Israel's only full-size golf course' (Li 2015b: 69). The (relatively light-skinned) Bushnaqs' migration history, reconstructed by Seferović, not only spotlights intra-Palestinian dynamics of race and ethnicity but also, Li (2015b: 71) argues, illustrates an interpretive lens that faded after the break-up of Yugoslavia: while since the 1990s Bosnia and Palestine have usually been treated as separate but comparable, Seferović views them and Li revisits them as part of a single history with ties lasting across time.

The most sustained treatment of global raciality and migration from south-east Europe is, however, Miglena Todorova's study of the twentieth-century circulation of people, media and racial formations between Bulgaria, the USA and the USSR. Todorova challenges the assumption that Bulgarian immigrants only learned identification with whiteness through living in the USA; instead, active translations of US biological and cultural racial thinking were already forming interpretive frames in Bulgaria for white Bulgarians' perceptions of Roma (Todorova 2006: 6–7). Bulgarian Communists also worked Stalinist notions of racialised differentials in modernity, then Cold War state socialist views of race, culture and development, into their racial formations. These translations of racialisation and whiteness thus did not only reach Bulgarians on migrating to the USA, as mainstream US labour/migration histories would suggest, nor did they travel solely around Atlantic coasts, as studies of race in translation (Goldberg 2009; Stam and Shohat 2012) usually emphasise; as asymmetric and contingent as they were, they certainly flowed in more than one direction. So too for the Yugoslav region.

Conclusion

Ethnicity and migration, two central topics for studies of the Yugoslav region, have been and are intimately linked to race: in the incorporation of racial theory into ethnonationalism, the hierarchies of belonging still present in cosmopolitanism or the adjustments that migrants from the region make to different racial politics abroad. All, moreover, exist within global, transnational and translocal frameworks shaped by European colonial domination. The lands of the Yugoslav region were not an imperial metropole, indeed were ruled for centuries by multiple imperial powers without extensive transoceanic colonies, and one such power – the Ottoman Empire – was itself 'non-European' in spatialised hierarchies of Europeanness, modernity and Christendom. Yet, even though the region's nations as political formations were not protagonists of colonial expansion, its people, businesses and capital from the region were still implicated, asymmetrically, in these structures, and as Tanja Petrović (2009: 55) observes: even 'representatives of states with no colonial legacy can also shape colonialist discourses'. The Yugoslav region, and south-east Europe as a whole, is not beyond the remit of translocal imperial and colonial history, nor outside the global history of race.

Nevertheless, race as distinct from ethnicity has rarely, in south-east European studies, provided the kind of lens that might lead to longue-durée histories like Peter Fryer's *Staying Power*, on black people in Britain (Fryer 1984), or, for a spatially closer comparison, Allison Blakely's *Russia and the Negro* (Blakely 1986), published at a similar time and also intervening in public narratives about race, history and nation. Such histories are overdue. And yet Kesha Fikes and Alaina Lemon's important interpretive questions about identifying, determining and naming 'African presence' in the USSR would also apply here. By noticing the Soviet system had not offered territorialised identities to formerly enslaved Africans in the Caucasus but did recognise 'other formerly enslaved, likewise mobile – but "non-African" populations' as ethnonational groups with theoretical rights over territory, Fikes and Lemon identified an immediate racialised differential in Soviet nationalities policy, specific to Soviet and Transcaucasian history, that would refute claims that race was simply irrelevant for understanding Soviet Communism (Fikes and Lemon 2002: 500) – yet faced the problem of how to research race without further essentialising its boundaries.

Their solution, though written for the USSR, also helps integrate race into anti-essentialist studies of ethnicity in other regions. First, they reject the 'conceptual distancing' and exoticism of stating as an initial premise that Russia and Africa were 'hardly ... farther apart', and prefer to integrate these histories into the region's historical mainstream, altering how its centre is conceived in the process. Secondly, drawing on Gilroy (2000), Jacqueline Nassy Brown (the geographer of 'black Liverpool' (Brown 2009)) and Pratt, they argue the search for histories of black presence should begin, not with biologically predetermined concepts of blackness, but 'the social productions that make race recognizable'; diasporas, in turn, become 'meaningful "contact sites" that constitute power, place, and difference' rather than pre-set groups (Fikes and Lemon 2002: 498, 502). This resonates with a similar turn in the history and anthropology of south-east/central Europe towards studying the social production of ethnicity and nationhood. Moreover, it returns to the 'contact zones' with which this chapter began. The Yugoslav region, as glimpses of its 'cultural archive' show, has been such a zone for different nations, imperial projects and world-historical processes, the preconditions for its shifting identifications towards race. Indeed, we shall now see, the very range of racial formations that have circulated through it – from Venetian to German, from Soviet to Non-Aligned – are all ingredients for how those identifications are made.

Notes

1 On the Cold War politics of the US Civil Rights Commission naming past and present racialised violence against African-Americans as 'genocide' in petitioning the UN in 1951, see Martin (1997).
2 The term 'Četniks' for Serb paramilitaries derives from these 'čete' (bands), and was revived by Draža Mihailović's Serbian/Yugoslav royalist army in 1941–5, then during the Yugoslav Wars by paramilitaries who accompanied the Yugoslav People's Army, Army of the Bosnian Serb Republic (VRS) and Army of Yugoslavia (VJ) to attack non-Serb communities in Croatia, Bosnia-Herzegovina and Kosovo.
3 Serbian newspapers had already compared Serbia to Piedmont in 1861; the newspaper of the 'Ujedinjenje ili smrt' ('Unification or Death') society, founded in 1911, made 'Piedmont' an even bigger trope in narrating Serbia's geopolitical position and destiny (Mackenzie 1984: 174–5).
4 Habsburg visions included anational imperial identity (the Emperor); enforcing Magyar assimilationist policies on Croats and Serbs (Hungarian nationalists);

and, shortly before 1914, constitutional reform involving a third, South Slav national unit (some South Slavs, plus Archduke Franz Ferdinand).
5 For a similar Bulgarian example, see Todorova (2006: 96–7).
6 A Jasenovac Memorial Centre list of 72,193 named victims identified 40,251 as Serbs (Kolstø 2011: 225). The 85,000–100,000 figure triangulates earlier demographic studies including unnamed victims (Dulić 2006: 271–3).
7 Bartulin's chief Croatian critic argues that the Ustaša blood descent principles expressed nationalism and showed no 'indication of racialist teaching or racism' (Jonjić 2012: 241).
8 Contemporaneous US racialisations of ethnicity meanwhile separated the 'Slavic' race, including Serbs and Croats, from the 'Mediterranean', including Greeks, Italians and Sicilians.
9 Forthcoming research by Sunnie Rucker-Chang on 'blackness' in Yugoslavia will cover the histories of black people in Ulcinj, African students in Yugoslavia (Chapter 3) and post-Yugoslav Roma.
10 With thanks to Florian Bieber.
11 Soviet media reported similarly on once-enslaved Africans in the Caucasus (Fikes and Lemon 2002: 513–15).
12 On the Seljans, see also Molvaer (2011) (the author is a retired Norwegian aid-worker). The Karlovac group were connected to Rijeka through descendants of Laval Nugent von Westmeath, an Irish-born Habsburg general awarded a castle there in 1826 whose ancestors had fled Ireland after the 1690 Battle of the Boyne; Laval's adoptive cousin branched the family out into Antigua.
13 For example, most operators of 'Chinese shops' come from two parts of Zheijang province (Qingtian County and Wenzhou); few Zheijangese work in other sectors; and most individuals stay only a few years, though a community persisting over time.
14 Bosnia-Herzegovina's Chinese population is approximately 10,000–12,000, according to a study of migrant communities' visibility in urban space that connects a Bosnian market in St Louis, a Chinese market in Rajlovac (a periphery of Sarajevo) and a street of ex-Yugoslav cafes in Vienna (Sirbegović 2011).
15 The Dayton system, with ethnic quotas for major political posts, thus excluded both groups (Jews and Roma), newer migrants like the Chinese and older migrant minorities from full political participation. Benjamin Markin, a Ghanaian–Bosnian surgeon who came to Yugoslavia as a student, called himself 'the first "Sejdić-Finci" in BiH [Bosnia-Herzegovina]' – referring to a case two Bosnian Jewish and Romani activists had brought at the European Court of Human Rights – when interviewed as Bosnia-Herzegovina's new ambassador to Japan: 'Dr. Markin: ja sam prvi "Sejdić–Finci" u BiH', *24sata. info*, 16 October 2013 (http://24sata.info/vijesti/bosna-i-hercegovina/166650-d r-markin-ja-sam-prvi-sejdic-finci-u-bih.html; accessed 11 September 2017).
16 Molnar argues that race did not determine Yugoslav guest-workers' experiences (because they were white, and perceptions of their difference from Germans were more linked to Cold War politics); yet that ascription of whiteness was still part of West German formations of race.

17 Migration from the region to Argentina, like South Africa, is under-researched compared with migration to North America or even Australasia – yet entailed no less complex and no less unique translations of race. See, for instance, the surprising appearance of Korčula's Moreška dance (see Chapter 3) in the Argentinian newspaper *La Prensa*'s carnival reviews: in the 1901 Buenos Aires carnival, a troupe called Perla del Plata from the immigrant district of La Boca 'dressed as *montenegrinos* (people from Montenegro) and danced with "great precision and elegance" a "moorish dance," which *La Prensa* understood to be "from the epoch in which the Republic of Genova, owner (sic) of a great portion of Greece and the coasts of Africa, held this dance in high regard"' (Siegel 2000: 70). Many such performances involved blackface (Siegel 2000: 69). Here is not only a(nother) conflation of Africanity and Montenegrin identity through 'black'-ness, but elisions of Genoa/Venice and the northern/southern Mediterranean – at least as reported to these readers in Buenos Aires.

3

Transnational formations of race before and during Yugoslav state socialism

In domains from the history of popular entertainment to that of ethnicity and migration, ideas of race, as well as ethnicity and religion, have demonstrably formed part of how people from the Yugoslav region have understood their place in Europe and the world. The region's history during, and after, the era of direct European colonialism differed from the USA's, France's or Brazil's; but this did not exclude it from the networks of 'race in translation' (Stam and Shohat 2012) which ran and run across the whole globe, not just around the postcolonial Atlantic. Among the political, social and cultural 'legacies' that the Bulgarian historian Maria Todorova (2005a: 69) argues give regions like the Balkans their intellectual coherence are, therefore, formations of racialised difference in areas to which the Yugoslav region has historical connections – even though Todorova's own work on Balkan history is ambivalent about the utility of race.

Perceptions that south-east Europe is distinct enough to be 'a region' arise, for Todorova, when historical experiences associated with specific regimes (and their collapse) intersect with constructions of territory. 'The Balkans', one such region-as-legacy, depends on the idea that the legacy of Ottoman rule in Europe still explains something about it; 'Eastern Europe' often stands for the perceived legacy of the collapse of multi-national long-nineteenth-century but was really, Todorova suggested, based on perceptions of the legacy of state socialism (2005a: 69–73). These perceptions themselves have often, wrongly, been bases for treating eastern Europe as inherently lagging behind the West – and yet it is precisely the history of fin-de-siècle European scientific racism, she hints briefly in a reading of the racialised hatred of Albanians that Vladan Đorđević expressed in 1913 (see Chapter 2), that should place south-east Europe 'in a common European or global space and in the proper comparative perspective', not 'ghettoiz[ed] ... in a diachronic and spatial Balkans continuity' (Todorova 2005b: 156–7).[1]

The emphasis on *plural* formations and imaginaries, rather than one globalised homogenous regime of thought, in theories of global raciality opens further possibilities for understanding 'race' in peripheralised regions like south-east Europe. Another Bulgarian scholar, Miglena Todorova, has demonstrated how scientists, politicians, cultural producers and the public in Bulgaria adapted not one but many foreign discourses on race to Bulgarian social realities: with northern European biological and scientific racism; the cultural racism that had manifested alongside it by the 1930s; US racialised imaginaries of African primitivity then, later, African-American physicality, musicality and criminality; and Soviet imaginaries of state socialist Europe at the vanguard of a new humanitarian civilising mission to develop and modernise postcolonial Africa all contributing (Todorova 2006). Equivalent sources for the Yugoslav region's translations of 'race' would be similar but – because of its pre-unification history as well as the geopolitics of socialist Non-Alignment – not the same.

Yugoslavia's participation in the Non-Aligned Movement (NAM) has very recently come into view in scholarship 'between the posts' (Chari and Verdery 2009) of postsocialism and postcolonialism as an explanation for its ambiguities within global raciality. The autonomous foreign policy and Marxist ideology that Yugoslav Communists sought after the 1948 Tito–Stalin split led Yugoslavia to become a founder member of this self-declared geopolitical third force that emerged from the 1955 Bandung conference of anti-imperialist African and Asian states. Recovering Non-Alignment as a topic of Yugoslav history creates much-needed space to recognise race in the region. Yet, even before Yugoslav unification, the region already occupied a distinctive conjunction of racial formations, with Venetian and Habsburg rule positioning different parts in Italian-speaking and German-speaking cultural areas; though

South Slav national movements viewed both Italians and Germans as dominators, they still translated Italian and German identity discourses on to themselves. Italian and German imaginaries of race have rarely been related to the Yugoslav region beyond the debate in Second World War historiography about how far Fascism and Nazism influenced the NDH (Kallis 2015); they still laid foundations that would transform again as the Yugoslav region negotiated the geopolitics of the Cold War.

Venetian formations of race

In October 2015, the Croatian football club HNK Rijeka, nicknamed 'Bijeli' ('Whites') for their all-white home strip, wore an unusual fourth kit against nearby Opatija: a purple shirt half-covered by a black-skinned, turbaned head, with prominent red lips and gold-rimmed eyes.[2] Rijeka's sporting director, hailing the team as 'world-class' for being the first Croatian club with a fourth kit, hoped that 'Rijeka is a touristic city and these strips ... could comfortably stand as tourist souvenirs' (Benčić 2015b). Rijekans, Opatijans, and Croatians more widely would have recognised the figure as the 'morčić' ('little Moor'), a traditional Rijeka carnival character wearing blackface and an ornate costume evoking Ottoman elite dress which decorates earrings, necklaces and tourist souvenirs. Viewed through transnational histories of race, however, its appearance, carnival associations and supposed Moorish origin resonate uncomfortably with 'Zwarte Piet', the black-faced servant in Dutch Christmas traditions, whom Dutch people of colour and anti-racists have been protesting against since the 1960s (see Wekker 2016: 139–67). The morčić attracts no comparable protests, either during carnival or in Rijeka's tourist promotion. It is mostly viewed as a quirky, unproblematic memento of the Venetian Adriatic (when Venice ruled much of the Istrian and Dalmatian coast, though not Rijeka). Yet Venetian racial imaginaries, constructed against Venice's Ottoman rivals and 'the Moor', may even have been the first racialising discourses 'translated' into at least this part of the Yugoslav region – leaving the morčić and Zwarte Piet not so far apart.

Venetian racialisation of Turks as black, with 'stereotypical black African physiognomies' in painting and sculpture, dates to the late fifteenth century and peaked during the Venetian–Ottoman wars (Kaplan 2011: 41). The trope, which inspired Shakespeare's Othello (leading to much more literature about this representation of race in early modern Venice than the history of race in early modern Venice itself), probably originated from existing traditions of painting Muslims and Egyptians as black Africans (Kaplan 2011: 47–9). Though Rijeka was Habsburg (Hungarian Croatia's main port) not Venetian, Italianate heritage is part of its contemporary identity. Other Moorish characters and blackface customs appear in Dalmatian/Croatian folk traditions further south, including Dubrovnik/Ragusa (independent until annexed by Napoleon in 1808) and the islands of Korčula (Venetian 1420–1797) and Lastovo (Ragusan until 1808).

Dubrovnik and Korčula folk traditions both include the 'moreška', a sword-dance where two kings fight over a symbolic princess, which ethnologists have compared to Spanish 'moros y cristianos' ('Moors and Christians') customs, Venetian mock factional battles and English morris dancing. Its contest between a Black King, who has abducted the princess and whose dancers traditionally (though rarely today) wear black faces or masks, and a White King, who in Korčula has the Turkish name Osman, has been interpreted as Christians against Moors and also as Moors against Turks.[3] One reading of the Korčula moreška, which emerged under Venetian rule, finds both a public narrative of Christian–Muslim combat and a resistive 'hidden transcript', accessible to Korčulans but not their rulers, where the Black side could be Korčulans, the Whites Venice and the princess the violated land (Harris and Feldman 2003: 312).[4] Lastovo's carnival meanwhile centres around making and burning a brown-faced effigy, wearing a fez and moustache, called 'the Turk'; traditionally, this simultaneously represents one of a band of Catalan pirates who unsuccessfully attacked Lastovo in 1483 or 1571 and the culprit for every misfortune suffered there since the previous spring (Oroz 2009).

What, however, do the morčić or Turk, or vestiges of whiteness and blackness in moreška, signify today? Since Venice was an imperial ruler, with its eighteenth-century travel writer Alberto Fortis exoticising Dalmatian highland Slavs and Vlachs into the orientalised, at least partially racialised 'Morlachs' (Woolf 2002), the direction of power is different from the Netherlands, where white Dutch people were the colonisers and enslavers of the black Africans stereotyped by Zwarte Piet. Yet just because eastern Adriatic national and regional identities developed in reaction against Venetian rule and Italian irredentism does not mean they formed in isolation from Venetian and Italian imaginaries of race (Ballinger 2004). Indeed, when the Dalmatian writer Giovanni Lovrich wrote back against Fortis to argue that the Morlachs could still be enlightened once lifted out of Turkish rule, he did so by refuting Fortis's rumour that Morlach women had the Hottentots' pendulous breasts (Bracewell 2011) – meaning Lovrich's reader still had to share the racialised stereotype of Hottentot women (a key trope in Europeans' construction of 'Europeanness' against racialised and sexualised imaginaries of African bodies) to understand what Lovrich was distancing the Morlachs from.[5] Moreover, when anthropologists hold that folk/carnival customs re-narrate the present around traditional symbols rather than simply re-enacting historical events, one can and should accept that contemporary racial formations will be among these traditions' undertones of meaning now even if they were not before. Yet the morčić and the Lastovo Turk do not elicit protest like Zwarte Piet, and anti-racist activism in Rijeka has other pressing priorities (fighting antiziganism and anti-Serb chauvinism, and migrant solidarity). Whether future Croatian social movements will frame carnival traditions as anti-blackness remains to be seen.

Race in the German-speaking cultural area and the Habsburg Empire

If Venetian imaginaries of race are part of the Yugoslav region's 'translation' even though Venetian rule there ended during the Napoleonic Wars, even more significant would be those from a cultural space to which the north and west of the region were connected for centuries as Habsburg peripheries: the German linguistic–cultural area, which overspilled from Germany – the most-researched country after Britain and France in Black European Studies (see Gilman 1982; Campt 2004) – into the Habsburg Empire. German-language literary, visual and consumer culture was part of the Habsburg South Slav everyday, as Pamela Ballinger (2004: 35) and Maria Todorova (2005b: 157) both hint when suggesting the aesthetics of whiteness, blackness and race-as-blood in Germany described by Uli Linke (1999) might have been disseminated to their regions of interest. Just as scholars trace the production of whiteness through 'cultural archive[s]' (Wekker 2016: 2) of advertising material, travel literature, schoolbook representations and visual ephemera for fin-de-siècle northern European countries (Zantop 1997; Loftsdóttir and Jensen (eds) 2012b; Wekker 2016), formations of race would become explicit if scholars of the ex-Habsburg lands did the same.

Late Habsburg cultural history has surprisingly rarely addressed race and anti-blackness in consumer and leisure culture, far less across the wider empire outside metropolitan, majority- German-speaking Vienna. Transnational studies also pass over it. In 1989–90, Amsterdam Tropical Museum's 'Negrophilia' exhibition – the basis of Jan Nederveen Pieterse's study of images of Africa and blackness in Western popular culture (Pieterse 1992: 15) – collected US, British, German, French and Dutch representations, with its transatlantic and transnational scope hailed as innovative (Pieterse 1992: 15), yet its 'Europe' went no further east than Imperial Germany (and no further south than the Pyrenees). Coloniality and race, in this end-of-the-Cold-War exhibition, was not a lens applicable to eastern Europe, conceptually the 'Second World' for forty years. Two decades later, a Louvre exhibition on 'human zoos' (which used to draw European spectators into an imperial gaze in person by beholding people of colour in exoticised tableaus) traced them 'through western Europe' into the USA and Japan (Blanchard, Boëtsch and Snoep 2011: 28). Yet, besides one brief reference to 'travelling village[s]' being exported to 'other northern and eastern European countries, though ... less visible' in the latter (Lemaire et al. 2011: 292), and counting Vienna among the zoos that hosted them (Schneider 2011: 131), these transnational studies rarely synthesise as far as eastern Europe – despite evidence that they should (Novikova 2013).

Yet 'commodity racism' (McClintock 1994: 130), the mass production of racialised narratives/visualisations of modernity and primitivism around commodities extracted from colonised land, permeated as a transnational, implicitly 'European' mode of representation far beyond the largest metropoles into smaller northern European countries like Switzerland and Iceland (Loftsdóttir 2010; Purtschert and Fischer-Tiné (eds) 2015). Inner Austria, indeed, is already within the scope of studies of German advertising, race and empire, since Austrian firms manufactured and designed for both German and Habsburg markets within a cross-border consumer culture (Ciarlo 2011: 9–11). Austria and Hungary were both nodes in the 'human zoo' tradition that emanated across Europe from Germany, and Vienna and Budapest regularly hosted touring anthropological spectacles in the 1890s–1900s, including exhibits of Australian Aborigines, Buffalo Bill's Wild West show (with dozens of Native Americans) and an Ashanti village, plus shows by the leading human-zoo entrepreneur, Carl Hagenbeck (Scott 1997; Hund 2013: 46; Rydell 2013: 97).

Marilyn Scott (1997: 51) suggests that, in increasingly multi-ethnic industrialising Vienna, this European colonial imagination offered a route for 'assimilation' across ethno-linguistic boundaries, where Europeanness and whiteness gave the multi-ethnic Habsburg imperial identity extra connective tissue. Indeed, invitations to participate in this gaze extended beyond the Habsburg capitals. Touring 'Dahomean' and 'Ashanti' villages came twice to Prague in the 1890s, just when the 1885 Berlin Conference, the 1889–94 Franco-Dahomean Wars and the 1895–6 British occupation of the Ashanti Empire were making these very territories' and peoples' colonisation a European geopolitical fascination (Herza 2016: 97). What impressions did the travelling villages leave in Zagreb, or other soon-to-be-Yugoslav cities? Zagreb did not have its own zoo until 1925, after unification, and more research is needed on what exhibitions might have passed through other sites; yet illustrated media reports and postcards from other cities' exhibitions (see Deroo and Fournié 2011) would nevertheless have disseminated these anthropological aesthetics further into Habsburg visual culture, including to Zagreb.

Nostalgic notions of 'peaceful and unambitious' (Bach 2016: 22) Habsburg imperialism, outside the European colonial mainstream, fall down against evidence of how nineteenth-century Habsburg officials and writers imagined a civilising mission in south-east Europe comparable to other powers in Africa and Asia (Fuchs 2011), and of Habsburg entanglements in colonialism overseas (Sauer 2012). Habsburg authorities in Bosnia-Herzegovina, for instance, tackled what they perceived as an Ottoman legacy of endemic backwardness through extensive public health programmes. The Czech-, Russian- and Polish-speaking, Swiss-trained women physicians they hired to visit Muslim women in 'the harems' (as per one 1903 public health report) took British women doctors' work in the gender-segregated Indian 'zenana' as a model, making Bosnia-Herzegovina 'the object of a characteristically colonial discourse' (Fuchs 2011: 76, 85; see Burton 1996). Habsburg distinctions between 'historic' peoples (Germans, Magyars, Italians) and peoples without history (Slavs, Romanians) (Glajar 2001: 19) juxtaposed the same temporalities with which Europeans divided places and peoples into civilised and backward zones (Mignolo 2000). Viewing European colonial dominance beyond just the direct colonisation of territory overseas meanwhile reveals multiple dimensions of Austro-Hungarian implication in global coloniality: from the travels of expatriate missionaries, doctors, agents and freelance 'explorers' (Chapter 2), to short-lived Indian Ocean fortresses supporting the empire's eighteenth-century trade, several failed plans to colonise the Nicobar or Solomon Islands in the nineteenth century, or the 1873 North Pole expedition (Sauer 2012). Since the Yugoslav region obtained many of its racial imaginaries from the empires that ruled it, studies of racial thought at the Habsburg imperial centre (e.g. Sluga 2001; Ruthner 2002; Turda 2014) are also part of the context for historicising 'race' there.

The afterlife of German imaginations of indigeneity, still meaningful in late-twentieth-century Yugoslavia, shows how everyday German-language racialised imaginaries in the region could remain. German fascination with Native Americans, ignited by Karl May's Winnetou novels (1875–1910), inspired hobbyist re-enactment groups and many popular films, and arguably represented a certain racial exceptionalism itself (May's white German protagonist, allied with Natives against villainous Americans, embodied a brotherhood with the Indian hero that distanced the nation from its own colonialism) (Sieg 2002). This fascination was directly accessible in Yugoslav popular culture, with May's books translated and well known. The Croatian musician Alka Vuica, for instance, said she started writing verse 'aged around 12, when I fell in love with Winnetou after reading Karl May's trilogy' (Car 2015), and named her debut album *Alka Vu Winnetou* in 1993; another Istrian musician, Franci Blašković, formed a band called Gori Ussi Winnetou in 1986. Through film production, moreover, German fascination with Native Americans simultaneously incorporated Yugoslavia into the material and financial circuits of a transnationally produced and disseminated imaginary.

Both West Germany's ten Winnetou films (1962–8) and the East German 'Indianerfilme' (1966–77) – with very different ideological frames around settler–Native relations – were filmed in Yugoslavia, making the Dalmatian hinterland's dusty valleys the backdrop for both Germanies' imagined Wild Wests (Goral 2014: 8). Local extras and stuntmen played most Native characters (Goral 2014: 84). Jadran Film, one of Yugoslavia's largest studios, co-produced the Winnetou cycle, while a Yugoslav actor, Gojko Mitić, became arguably East Germany's first film star as the lead in Indianerfilme (Goral 2014: 1, 67). Mitić remained in East German film and television, and in 1991, post-reunification, started performing live as Winnetou himself at the annual Winnetou festival held since 1952 in Schleswig-Holstein. Katrin Sieg (2002: 105) suggests casting the olive-skinned, well-built Mitić epitomised the 'exotic virility' and 'racial fetishism' gradually attached to Winnetou – another example of the ambiguous racialised identifications often available to south-east European entertainers.

The subject positions that these cultural translations of 'the Wild West' offered East German or Yugoslav spectators, conversely, distanced both nations from the whiteness of settler colonialism. The official historical narrative in Indianerfilme, reflected in one of Mitić's interviews while making the first (*Die Sohne der grossen Bärin* (*Sons of the Great She-Bear*), 1966[6]) was of a USA founded on racialised theft and conquest, as Mitić stated in his interview: 'The white people invaded the land of the Indians and wanted to take away their habitat because they wanted to live here too … basically, the whites ended up taking over the country' (Goral 2014: 91). State socialist subjects, taking up identification with Natives not settlers, implicitly belonged to a different geopolitical tradition. In late socialist Yugoslavia, the Western's tropes arguably underwent even more 're-appropriation' (Jelača 2014: 250): in Dijana Jelača's reading of a 1985 song by the rock band Haustor about the famous character Shane, his 'normative, silent, White Western outcast masculinity' became 'a fantasy echo of escape from one's own cultural and societal confinement', rejecting rather than reiterating hegemonic ideology. This fantasy about escaping the cultural stagnation of late socialism might become, in the 1990s, a fantasy of escaping the violent imposition of ethnicised borders in which listening to a pre-war band singing about the dream of identification with Shane would not have been an identification with masculinist militarised nationalism but an escape from it (Jelača 2014: 254). Even within the expanding history of state socialism and race, the impact of the 1990s wars on memory and identity set the Yugoslav region apart; yet the geopolitics of Non-Alignment had already distinguished Yugoslavia during the Cold War.

State socialism, postcoloniality and 'connected histories' of the USSR and eastern Europe

Historians already acknowledge the Cold War politics of envisioning state socialist space as a moral identity opposed to imperialism and capitalism, versus a USA built on racialised oppression, as a geopolitics of race. US policymakers partially realised, and Soviet diplomats exploited, the contradictions of advocating 'freedom' internationally while the Civil Rights and Black Power movements showed African-Americans were still far from free (Dudziak 2000; Borstelmann 2001). Keen to persuade foreign observers that the USA originated from a history of colonialism and white supremacy, the USSR offered African-Americans a performative welcome, and under Lenin had declared an intention to unite the world's racialised peoples against imperialism (Baldwin 2002; Roman 2012). After 1945, competing with the USA for influence in decolonised Africa, Khrushchev targeted the 'Third World' with cultural diplomacy, propaganda and student exchanges, and later Soviet leaders equipped and trained southern African armed liberation movements (Westad 2005; Matusevich (ed.) 2007; Bradley 2010). US and Soviet geopolitics of race evolved in interaction, in mainstream diplomacy and even the gendered structures of feeling and domesticity through which both powers constituted themselves against each other (Baldwin 2016). Permanent, as opposed to temporary, black and African presence was nevertheless erased in a Soviet racial politics that 'productively link[ed] Russianness to whiteness' (Fikes and Lemon 2002: 517) abroad.

Soviet racial formations influenced, but did not fully overwrite, constructions of race, whiteness and modernity in state socialist eastern Europe: adaptation to Soviet ideology was less an exercise in unthinking conformity, more an uneasy balance between responding to domestic factors and averting the coercion awaiting (as Hungary 1956 and Czechoslovakia 1968 reminded Communists elsewhere) a Party deviating too far from Soviet objectives. Without eastern Europe having any acknowledged history of implication in European colonialism, exceptionalism compounded by the whiteness of the Western academy has made race appear of little relevance for understanding this area. As recent studies of the Cold War trace material, political and intellectual links between the so-called 'Second' and 'Third Worlds' in order to unmake the conceptual borders that generally separate the histories of state socialism and decolonisation, however, they lay foundations that make questions about 'race' and whiteness in state socialist Europe both easier and more necessary to conceive.

Within the entangled histories of state socialism and decolonisation, east European states as well as the USSR offered development assistance to newly independent African and Asian countries, hosted foreign students, organised public anti-colonial solidarity campaigns, and participated in bilateral and multilateral internationalism. Race, in these activities, was discursively invisible behind state socialist rhetoric of internationalism and class. Quinn Slobodian, introducing a volume on East German engagements with the Global South, poses questions one could ask across the region:

> What was the status of race in a socialist world view that deemed class to be the medium that dissolved all other differences? How did race and racialized thinking operate in a socialist society like East Germany that had decreed racism out of existence? What alliances were created across ethnic lines in the German project of state socialism that had not, and could not, have existed before? (Slobodian 2015a: 1)

East German topics have taken the lead in studies of race and state socialism because Afro-German scholarship and activism and the social politics of post-unification racism and anti-racism after 1989 have made race a (relatively) more important theme in German Studies than east European studies; moreover, politics of academic knowledge production privileging larger countries at the Western 'centre' make studies of Germany relatively more likely to be published. Slobodian's *Comrades of Color* came shortly after monographs on Mozambican students educated in East Germany (Müller 2014) and East and West German humanitarianism towards the Third World (Hong 2015). All combined microhistories of people of colour moving temporarily or permanently to state socialist countries with analysis of constructions of race that – however race-blind state socialist rhetoric and the international discourses of cultural diversity that had been shaped through UNESCO both were (Shilliam 2013: 153; Subotić and Vučetić, forthcoming) – had still been formed through white east Europeans' engagements with and travel to postcolonial states. Indeed, Miglena Todorova on twentieth-century Bulgaria anticipated much of the transnational turn in Cold War history by centring race as part of identity under state socialism.

'European' scientific ideas of race as biology, 'American' sociological ideas of race as culture and Soviet racial thought were all being adapted by thinkers who positioned themselves within the Bulgarian ethnonation to explain and racialise socio-economic conditions, especially Romani poverty, even before 1945. State socialism did not make race disappear. Bulgarian Communism used categories of nationality not race, and applied an enlightened, race-blind internationalism to geopolitics, yet still possessed a racialised ideology (Todorova 2006: 216–17). Antiziganism persisted, though expressed in ostensibly anti-racist terms; discourses about Communist successes in modernising Africa had 'civilising mission' overtones; and teaching materials including biology textbooks still provided 'common-sense' knowledge about biologically defined race.

Todorova argues, similarly to Gloria Wekker (2016) that 'Bulgarian students learned … their own whiteness' through these textbooks, which showed white Europeanoid, yellow Mongoloid and black Negroid races while clearly distancing the latter two from Bulgaria (Todorova 2006: 198–9). In the mid-1980s, when a relaxation in cultural policy made more US film, television and popular music available, white Bulgarians viewed African-Americans through what they already knew about Roma, tightening the ascribed identification between the two groups (Todorova 2006: 292–4). Marxism–Leninism and liberalism, though opposites in the Cold War ideological–spatial binary, ultimately appeared to agree on race: both belonged to 'a modern epistemological world defined by whiteness and Eurocentric culture' and both envisaged futures where particularist racial, cultural and religious identities would be subsumed into a universalist society that could reform the globe (Todorova 2006: 176). This synthesis of critical race scholarship and south-east European social theory resonates beyond Bulgaria. Valuable throughout the Yugoslav region's history, it helps above all to unpick the complexities of foreign policy, internationalism and race within Yugoslavia's geopolitical identification with the Non-Aligned Movement of states defining themselves as developing and postcolonial, part of distinguishing Yugoslav from Soviet Communism.

Yugoslavia, the NAM and race

The NAM, positioned between US capitalism and Soviet state socialism, has for that very reason often been Eurocentrically discounted in Cold War historiography as irrelevant to the grand narrative of superpower relations. In the history of decolonisation, however, it represents the next stage of the Afro-Asian and anti-colonial Bandung conference movement, which gathered thirty mostly African and Asian states at the first Asia–Africa Conference in 1955.[7] Their grouping exemplified the post-war 'racial break' (Winant 2001: 143), framed by Gilroy (2000: 273) as a 'post-Bandung' planetary racial politics. Tito cultivated links with powerful Bandung leaders, including Ethiopia's Haile Selassie – whose 1954 visit to Yugoslavia anticipated Tito's later spectacles of Non-Alignment (Orlović 2012) – India's Jawaharlal Nehru and the post-Suez Egyptian president Gamal Abdel Nasser. Tito's meeting with Nehru and Nasser in July 1956 on Brioni, where Tito famously invited leaders and celebrities from both superpower blocs and beyond, laid groundwork for the first Non-Aligned conference in Belgrade in 1961.[8]

Yugoslavia, usually considered a NAM founding member alongside Egypt, Ghana, India and Indonesia, was a greater ambiguity or outlier in the movement's anti-colonial orientation and Afro-Asian-centred geopolitics than any participant at Bandung. Bandung's only European participants were Cyprus and (simultaneously in Europe and Asia if the Bosphorus represents their border) Turkey. Neither ascribed itself the role that Tito would write into Yugoslavia's official ideological and geopolitical identity. Yugoslavia was a European power in a region (the Balkans) perceived in Western discourses of modernity as European and not-European simultaneously; on territory formerly subject to one empire centred in central Europe and another centred in west Asia; where members of majority ethnonational groups (including their diasporas) were usually racialised as white but whose whiteness had still been conditional or 'white, but not quite' (Alcoff 1998: 9) to northern European and North American gazes in living memory;[9] and where ethnonational identities already, before and after unification in 1918 (and Communist-led reunification in 1943–5) incorporated adaptations of racial thought.

Yugoslavia's geopolitical non-alignment was a global restatement of the ideological belonging and distancing that Yugoslav Communism had been performing since the early 1950s, after the 1948 Tito–Stalin split (Mišković, Fischer-Tiné and Boskovska (eds) 2014; Životić and Čavoski 2016). Distinctive elements of Yugoslav Communism included a socio-economic ideology of 'workers' self-management' (experimentally extended into politics by 1974); aspirations to produce more consumer goods and offer higher living standards than Soviet-style planned economies could provide; a cultural policy which was (uneasily) more open than Warsaw Pact regimes to capitalist countries' artefacts and aesthetics; and a foreign policy that played both blocs against each other in trade yet feared invasion by either superpower, not just one. Within Europe, Tito's Yugoslavia has often been described as demonstratively standing 'between East and West', outside the Cold War binary (Kulić 2009). Decentring this binary, an aim of global Cold War history and indeed NAM, requires treating the East–West axis as only one of the historical–geopolitical hierarchies in play during the Cold War.

Common descriptions of Tito as one of the NAM 'founding fathers' (Adebajo 2016: 1192) alongside Nehru and Nasser not only suggest how power and leadership were gendered masculine in NAM diplomacy but also call for answers about how Yugoslavs reconciled attachments to Europeanness and whiteness with the logic of NAM (Kilibarda 2010). Yugoslavia's geopolitical realignment began with bilateral relations with India, expressed through the first joint Nehru–Tito statement in December 1954. This stated both countries had 'emerged as independent nations, through powerful movements of national liberation', with strong 'similarities of historic background and social and economic conditions' (Mišković 2009: 186). Yugoslavia's role in NAM implied its closest geopolitical counterparts were outside Europe but facing shared challenges of modernisation after liberation from imperial rule. Indeed, the United Nations Conference on Trade and Development – where Yugoslavia was heavily involved – assigned Yugoslavia to Group A (African/Asian states) rather than Group D (eastern Europe), or for that matter B or C (developed market economies and Latin American/Caribbean states respectively) (Alden, Morphet and Vieira 2010: 53–4).[10]

Non-Alignment made Yugoslavia's geopolitical and racialised identities even more ambiguous than the Soviet bloc's. Was Yugoslavia positioning itself outside Europe, or outside the coloniality with which postcolonial thought and critical race theory make Europe synonymous? Where did its ideology position South Slavs within (or outside) whiteness and 'race' – or was the UNESCO era's very race-blindness a precondition for predominantly-yet-contingently-white Yugoslavia to even be able to enter this self-declared subaltern coalition, and to claim parity with territories robbed of resources, wealth and people by white Europeans? Mao maintained Yugoslavia could do neither of those things, and spoke for Afro-Asianism not the expanded NAM (Byrne 2015: 921); yet many African leaders welcomed Tito. Besides a diplomatic grouping, the NAM was also, at least theoretically, a 'structure of feeling' connecting people with a space larger than the nation (or the alliance of nations Yugoslavia was supposed to be) (Gupta 1992: 64). How, then, did Yugoslavs experience Non-Alignment in practice, and did their state and leader's participation in the global movement change how they perceived their individual and collective places in the world?

Aimé Césaire, the Martinican writer and theorist of Négritude, encountered the complexity of Yugoslavia's relationship to Europeanness and coloniality after befriending the Croatian and Yugoslav linguist Petar Guberina when both studied in Paris – then 'a marketplace for the global spread of anticolonialism' (Goebel 2016: 1444) – in 1934. Césaire began 'arguably the foundational text of the Negritude movement' (Stromberg Childers 2016: 76), *Cahier d'un retour au pays natal* (*Notebook of a Return to the Native Land*) while visiting Guberina's hometown Šibenik in 1935 – inspired by seeing a small Dalmatian shore, reminiscent of his own Martinique, and learning it had the equivalent name Martinska (Kelley 1999: 6). Guberina founded the Institute for African Studies in Zagreb and co-organised, in 1956, the First Congress of Black Writers and Artists in Paris. Writing for *Naše teme*, the journal of the Croatian SKJ's mass youth organisation, in the early 1960s, he both promoted the study of African languages and critiqued the politics of translation and essentialism that structured whether and how Yugoslavs, Europeans and Americans encountered African art and poetry (Guberina 1961). The Négritude movement he knew so well coexisted in *Naše teme* with the 'African Personality' thesis of the Ghanaian president Kwame Nkrumah as modes for conceptualising 'African cultures' (Cvjetičanin 1979).

Césaire and Guberina were reunited by the Kenya-born director Lawrence Kiiru, who settled in Zagreb after studying at the Academy of Dramatic Arts, for a 1990 documentary, *Martinska–Martinique*.[11] Amid their interlinguistic performances of fraternity, Césaire called both Martinique and Yugoslavia '"handicapped," "underdeveloped," and "colonized"' societies (Jović Humphrey 2014: 1132). Césaire's suggestion that colonised peoples creating their new societies might look to Soviet models, Anja Jović Humphrey suggests, contained 'awareness that there exist two Europes … it was not the colonizer's Europe to which Césaire wanted to turn' (Jović Humphrey 2014: 1133). The Césaire–Guberina friendship, and the Afro-Yugoslav amity Guberina nurtured, represented a nexus between two projects of revising Marxism (Kelley 1999: 4; Césaire 2000 [1972]), but also a nexus between Yugoslavness and blackness permitting some Yugoslavs to identify Yugoslavia with Africa. Jović Humphrey goes as far as to suggest that identification between Slavs and black Africans could rest not only on shared histories of being racialised by German philosophers but even on shared histories of enslavement itself (Jović Humphrey 2014: 1140–1). Yet the Yugoslav region was also one from where South Slavs (like the explorers who joined Stanley in the Congo, or the captains bringing slaves to Ulcinj) had departed to participate in colonising Africa and enslaving Africans – contradicting socialist Yugoslavia's self-image. This tension pervaded the everyday geopolitics of Non-Alignment.

Everyday Non-Alignment and race in socialist Yugoslavia

Non-Alignment built identification with global anti-colonial struggle into the narrative of Yugoslavia's state identity – and, implicitly, into Yugoslav Communism's spatial–historical narratives about the South Slav nations (as struggling against their own imperialist rulers, including the interwar Yugoslav monarchy, before pooling their self-determination into socialist Yugoslavia). In February 1961, after the assassination of the Congolese prime minister Patrice Lumumba, the SKJ called a rally in Belgrade attended by 150,000, with a breakaway demonstration of 30,000 occupying the Belgian embassy and clashing with police (Kilibarda 2010: 33; Robertson 2015: 112). Tito, meanwhile, espoused race-blind anti-colonialism: meeting Algeria's Ahmed Ben Bella in 1964, minutes record, he 'railed against the suggestion that "all blacks are good and all whites bad" and [stated that] "the wrongheaded idea of divisions according to race merits the strongest censure"' (Byrne 2015: 924). *Naše teme*, which published two special issues on Africa in 1961 and 1979, described its hopes for Africa's future in the 1960s and its explanations for those dashed hopes in the 1970s through the Marxist paradigm of exploitation, dependency, and neo-colonialism – a term theorised in 1961–5 by Tito's Non-Aligned ally Nkrumah (Young 2016: 46–9). With colonialism described as a '*Western* European' imposition (Švob-Đokić 1979: 802; emphasis added), racism as a sin of, above all, the white regimes in South Africa and Rhodesia (Vukadinović 1979: 539) and 'the Black question' as what punctured the myth of America (Lisinski 1964: 2005), Yugoslavia seemed outside any of these things. If Miglena Todorova (2006: 205) believes state socialist Bulgaria still constructed identity around 'whiteness and civilization', continuing to attach symbols of cultural difference and backwardness to African and Asian spaces and bodies, was this less likely with Yugoslavia because it did not have membership of the Soviet bloc to perform?

The evidence is not so plain. Yugoslav diplomatic texts like Leo Mates's 1970 book on non-aligned theory and practice could, Konstantin

Kilibarda argues, display 'Eurocentric' tendencies: Mates, via Nehru's *The Discovery of India* and US developmental science, praised Indian anti-colonial movements' development of Non-Alignment and identified Yugoslavia more with 'Afro-Asian countries' than 'Europe', yet believed anti-colonial liberation movements had needed European revolutionary thought's 'platform and ... spirit' to mature and considered modernisation projects were still struggling with Africa's 'primitive social structures' (Kilibarda 2010: 39).[12] Representations of travel mediated Yugoslav Communists' and writers' encounters with Africa to the public. Authors of 1960s travelogues often expressed shame or guilt at their whiteness, considered themselves better able to understand Africa than Westerners, or even, like Oskar Davičo, wrote of wanting to renounce their white skin (Radonjić 2015). The Serbian historical novelist Dobrica Ćosić, accompanying Tito's 1961 yacht-borne West Africa visit, wrote instead about uncomfortable encounters with climactic and sonic difference that left him feeling more white and European, while Tito and his hosts co-operated to stage spectacles of white-uniformed Tito receiving prestigious hospitality that resembled colonial photography (Hozić 2016; Vučetić 2016).

Encounters with racialised difference and blackness were, meanwhile, an unusual yet everyday part of life for inhabitants of university cities where thousands of students from Non-Aligned countries studied. As in the Soviet bloc (Matusevich (ed.) 2007; Carew 2015; Slobodian (ed.) 2015c), Yugoslavia educated these students as the future engineering, technical and medical cadres of their newly liberated countries' journey towards modernisation – where Yugoslavs (again as in the Soviet bloc) believed they had an important pedagogical role (Kilibarda 2010: 39).[13] Though most returned, dozens founded interracial families, becoming a longer part of the region's still-largely-silenced history of people of colour. One, Peter Bossman from Ghana, became postsocialist Europe's first black mayor when elected in Piran in 2010 (Intihar 2013). Another was David Bangoura, father of the Croatian TV presenter Hamid, who recalled in 2007:

I came to Zagreb aged 20, as one of 30 Guineans who were coming to study here. We were the first Africans who ever came to former Yugoslavia. Before that most of us studied in Paris, but when Guinea gained independence in 1958, the French sent us home. The first president of Guinea, Sékou Touré, was a friend of Tito, so after we came back from Paris they quickly sent us to Zagreb. When before Zagreb we landed in Belgrade, we were the first Africans the people there had seen live. They looked at us, they followed us in the street, and some even touched us to see whether our skin colour would rub off on their hands. They thought we were covered in paint. (Simić, Biluš and Pavić 2007)

Bangoura hints at the exoticism with which these Belgraders had learned to perceive African bodies and blackness in 1958, but also at how disconnected this region's black history has been. The Guineans were certainly among the very first African students welcomed in Yugoslavia, but, enslaved Africans' history in Ulcinj shows, certainly not the first Africans in the region – and yet that very history would have complicated socialist Yugoslavia's performances of postcoloniality.

Peter Wright's work on 'the ambivalence of socialist anti-racism' (Wright 2016) in Communist officials' responses to African students' complaints (about living conditions and racist abuse from Yugoslav students) indeed shows Yugoslavs displaying what studies of Western anti-racism call 'white fragility' (DiAngelo 2011): when public ideology and Yugoslav socialist identity were so committed to anti-colonialism and anti-racism, how could Yugoslavs be racist? Yet Africans experienced racism. A dynamic so characteristic of twentieth- and twenty-first-century Western anti-racism (Lentin 2004) also existed in socialist Yugoslavia, another commonality across the supposed East–West divide.

Other Non-Aligned migration routes suggest further ambiguities of the region's position in the global racialised order. Yugoslavs faced fewer visa requirements when travelling abroad than citizens of either superpower bloc, a freedom of travel that was always conditional on income and political standing but greatly exceeded the visa restrictions Western states would place on ex-Yugoslavs during the 1990s wars (Chapter 4). Guest-worker programmes relieved Yugoslavia's unemployment programmes until host states officially ceased them after the 1973 oil crisis (Shonick 2009). Approximately 600,000 workers (1.3 million people including dependants), most from economically disadvantaged agricultural regions like the Dalmatian hinterland, Herzegovina and Macedonia, became 'Gastarbeiters' (supposedly temporary labour migrants) in north-west European states filling labour shortages from the Northern and Southern Mediterranean (Daniel 2007: 280).[14] The history of race in West Germany, which hosted the most Yugoslav guest-workers, therefore includes how authorities racialised Croats, Roma and other 'Yugoslavs' compared with the even larger Turkish and Kurdish guest-worker communities (Sieg 2002; Chin 2007; Clarkson 2008; Molnar 2014).

Yugoslav construction-workers and engineers, meanwhile, travelled to Yugoslavia's Afro-Asian trading partners to build factories, infrastructure and hotels. Historians of state socialism have recently begun investigating this form of internationalism, with Łukasz Stanek (on architects from state socialist countries in West Africa) and Vladimir Kulić (on Yugoslav architects' designing hotels and expo pavilions) both challenging the idea that architectural modernity only travelled West-to-East and North-to-South. Instead, Kulić (2014: 29) writes, these connections reveal 'alternative, more convoluted paths, which circumvented the hierarchical structures of colonialism or superpower hegemonies'. Black African, white anglophone and white state socialist European experts all competed over whose historical experiences created the best understanding of 'modernization' – with the Hungarian architect Charles Polónyi (designer of several important projects in Accra), Nkrumah and Tito himself all paralleling east European and West African experiences of colonisation (Stanek 2015: 435).[15] With 'highly-skilled', 'white-collar' Yugoslav workers in developing countries in a better structural position than lower-skilled guest-workers in western Europe (Kilibarda 2010: 39), there was not one unified Yugoslav migrant-worker subjectivity: experiences of labour migration were structured by geography and class, as well as gender (Morokvasic 1991) and intra-Yugoslav dynamics of ethnicity and development.

Non-Aligned ideology even informed the racial politics of Yugoslav popular music (Chapter 1). Early 1950s Yugoslav Communists, like authorities in many European countries, expressed reservations about jazz, and some People's Youth reports about music considered 'vulgar ... black dances' and jazz music inappropriate for the youth supposedly being remade as new socialist men and women – but they were not as concerned, Dean Vuletić (2015: 29) argues, as similar moral guardians in the West (or the USSR), because Yugoslavia lacked any 'significant black minority, colonialist tradition, and stationed African-American soldiers', and because of Yugoslav foreign policy's anti-colonial stance. Instead, race was an unstable signifier, with embodied and sonic markers of racialised identity in original contexts liable to be detached and reassembled in translation.[16] The 'sonic blackness' (Weheliye 2005: 5; see Brooks 2011) of Aretha Franklin's or Nina Simone's voices, like the qualities of French or Italian divas, became markers of virtuosity for female singers at the more urban(e), cosmopolitan pole of Yugoslav taste hierarchies.

Racialisation of Yugoslav Roma and black musicians from abroad meanwhile intertwined in unstable patterns of belonging and exoticism. One Belgrade showbusiness magazine, *RTV revija*, reported in 1981on the Boney M frontman Bobby Farrell's wedding to Jasmina Šaban, an eighteen-year-old Skopje-born Romani woman whose family were 'Yugo-gastarbeiters' in Vienna.[17] Up to 20,000 people in Skopje watched the couple arrive for a ceremony where Farrell, the magazine wrote, 'became our son-in-law', on a level with 'the sensational ceremonial of Lady Diana and Prince Charles'. This adoption of Farrell into the national collective, simultaneously reiterating Yugoslavia's international standing, accompanied a sexualised, racialised gaze towards black female entertainers: '[e]verybody anticipated the arrival of the dark-skinned black women [tamnoputih crnkinja] from the group "Boney M". The attractive trio did not appear' (Aćimović 1981). Even if the Yugoslav national 'we' accommodated Roma (somewhat) better than either 1980s Bulgarian identity narratives or the ethnicised identity narratives that overthrew Yugoslav ones (see Sardelić 2016), and even if Non-Alignment facilitated closer identifications with Africanity than in the Soviet bloc, whiteness had not been displaced from identity construction in Yugoslavia. The 1980s breakdown of state socialist ideology would make it more prominent yet, especially but not only in the north-western republics.

Race, whiteness and the breakdown of state socialist ideology after Tito

After Tito died in 1980 and Yugoslavia's debt crisis intensified in 1982, programmes to reform Yugoslav socialism and constitutionalism which sought extensive internal and external geopolitical realignments emerged from Slovenia, then also Croatia. Their invocations of 'Europe' and modernity intensified intra-Yugoslav 'nesting orientalisms' (Bakić-Hayden 1995) and also – more rarely acknowledged – rearticulated the whiteness of the north-western, especially Slovenian, ethnonational identities (Longinović 2011). The Slovenian platform, acquiring the slogan 'Europe Now!' (Paternost 1992: 52),[18] aimed to strengthen the Yugoslav republics against the federal centre and to align Slovenia with 'Europe' in general and the late-Cold-War imaginary of 'central Europe' in particular, within a reformed Yugoslavia or, as this programme clashed in 1989–90 with Milošević's authoritarian re-centralisation, outside. Within south-east European symbolic geographies, situating an ethnonational identity and its associated polity within central Europe detached it from 'the Balkans', the 'Orient', the Ottoman legacy, Islam and the civilisational hierarchies projected on to these by European racisms for centuries. The 'nesting orientalisms' that south-east European studies equipped itself through postcolonial thought to recognise in the early 1990s were also products of a deeper global raciality – even if the theory itself bracketed off race (Bjelić 2009, 2017; Kilibarda 2010).

Attachments to 'central Europe' (Boatcă 2006: 99) or discourses of 'return to Europe' (Imre 2005: 82) across late state socialist and postsocialist Europe were indeed, Manuela Boatcă and Anikó Imre argue, simultaneously attachments to whiteness. Tanja Petrović develops this further, arguing that anti-Communist narratives of national history in eastern Europe even racialised state socialism itself – by characterising Russia/the USSR as 'Asiatic', then socialism as a Russian–Soviet imposition (obscuring how far members of the nation had welcomed and, even in Soviet-dominated structures, adapted socialism). Consequently, eastern Europeans 'often treat[ed] socialism as something essentially non-European that originated in Asia and was enforced upon them', making EU accession seem like '*returning home*' (Petrović 2009: 62; emphasis original). In Yugoslav contexts the 'Asiatic' frame could also be employed against Serbia – and, in some anti-Milošević discourses by the Serbian youth movement Otpor before his fall in 2000, even within it (Kilibarda 2010: 45).[19]

'Returns to Europe' imagined by dissident intellectuals and the winners of Slovenia's and Croatia's multi-party elections might even have drawn on a transnational revival of 'Europe' in late 1980s state socialisms, from Hungarian aspirations to a bridging role in European security policy to Gorbachev's imagination of a 'common European home', at a time when elites might have been losing faith in the alternative global project of connecting the state socialist world and Global South (Mark 2015). Pragmatic–technocratic reformers, and strategists expressing fears of terrorism and Islamic fundamentalism, were both 'appropriating' this position in Yugoslavia by 1989 (Kilibarda 2010: 40). Late Yugoslav and post-Yugoslav 'nesting orientalisms' thus rejected more than just the Balkans: they also rejected the alternatives implied within the Non-Aligned ideal. Seen in postcolonial, 'worldist' terms that recognise 'the *entwinement* of … contending structures, histories, memories, and political economies' in world politics (Agathangelou and Ling 2009: 1; emphasis original), the turn away from Yugoslavia's Non-Aligned identifications – as race-blind as they were – was a further narrowing of worlds.

The silencing of Non-Alignment in post-Yugoslav accounts of the past – whether a consequence of the ethnic-antagonisms frame crowding out other topics, or willed exclusion – is just as problematic as the forgetting of coexistence across ethnonational boundaries and the marginalisation of how reformable Yugoslav socialism, even in the early 1980s, still seemed to be (topics that the 'social inequalities' turn in late Yugoslav history recovers). The literary theorist Vedrana Veličković, working on postcommunism and postcolonialism, amplifies Rada Iveković's sadness at disappearing Yugoslav translations of key anti-colonial works and adds her own memory, fifty years since Lumumba's death: 'I remember I have dined many times in the Lumumba student hall named after him in the 1990s without knowing anything about this piece of black history in Belgrade' (Veličković 2012: 172–3; see Iveković 2006).[20] A 1,400-word obituary of Guberina, published by the Croatian Academy of Sciences and Arts in 2005, positions him as a linguist conversant with Charles Bally, Noam Chomsky and Ferdinand de Saussure, and founder of the respected Phonetics Institute, but has no space for his postcolonial internationalism beyond an observation about respect for 'other peoples', appropriating it for Croatian linguistic nationalism:

> All forms of national narrow-mindedness were foreign to Petar Guberina, especially the denigration of other peoples and the contestation of their rights, but at the same time, as a humanist, he demanded respect for the national rights of his own Croatian people, Croats' right to call their own language 'Croatian' and to nurture and develop it in the spirit of their own tradition and for their own needs. (Kovačec 2005)

Both the deliberate rejection of social alternatives in post-Yugoslav ethnonationalisms, and the consequent dominance of nationalism and ethnopolitical conflict as frames for research, have created a politics of knowledge production – inside, outside and across the permeable inside–outside of, the region – that pushes state socialism's geopolitical complexity towards or beyond the margins of public consciousness. Socialist Yugoslavia's geopolitical identity, so often called 'between East and West', could involve even more than balancing Europe's privileged West and Othered East; sometimes it pulled Yugoslavia southwards out of Europe altogether, into the post-Bandung configuration that for scholars like Mignolo (2011: 273) ignited the decolonial moment. But this was not the first ambiguous racial formation in the Yugoslav region: even before unification, multiple such formations already circulated through the region, creating contradictory points of identification. Their legacies of racialised thinking and representation were translated into identity-making politics that even predated state socialism, let alone the postsocialism in which they would be expressed through transnational politics of race and whiteness that persist into the present.

Notes

1 Todorova's essay on temporalities and the history of European nationalism does not return to this point – yet it has more transformative implications than she suggested.
2 With thanks to Dario Brentin.
3 Slovenian folklore contains another coastal abduction narrative where a black stranger kidnaps a woman, 'Lepa Vida' ('Pretty Vida'). The song, adapted in 1832 by the national poet France Prešeren, terms the abductor 'črn zamorec' ('the black "zamorec"', meaning both 'man from overseas' and 'Negro', and a racial slur in modern Slovenian). Marjetka Golež Kaučić (2002: 165), referring obliquely to past criticisms of racism in 'Lepa Vida', argues that the song dates from when Arab/Moor slave-traders were capturing coastal dwellers and so 'negative attitudes towards the "zamorec" ... have nothing to do with racism' – yet a nineteenth- or twentieth-century listener would still hear contemporary as well as historic undertones in 'zamorec'. With thanks to Julija Sardelić.
4 Greek sailors had called Korčula 'Black Korčula' for its thick forests.
5 Though Woolf (2002: 177) argues that Fortis could not find 'a racial or physiognomic formula to sum up the national distinctiveness of the Morlacchi', few tropes were more common than 'the Hottentots' in producing European imaginations of race and sexuality (Gilman 1985).
6 Did this title symbolically cast satellites like East Germany as 'sons' of Soviet Russia?
7 Afghanistan, Burma, Cambodia, Ceylon, the People's Republic of China, Cyprus, Egypt, Ethiopia, the Gold Coast (soon to become Ghana), India, Indonesia, Iran, Iraq, Japan, Jordan, Laos, Lebanon, Liberia, Libya, Nepal, Pakistan, the Philippines, Saudi Arabia, Sudan, Syria, Thailand, Turkey, North Vietnam, South Vietnam and Yemen.
8 Attendees were Afghanistan, the Algerian National Liberation Front, Burma, Cambodia, Ceylon, Congo, Cuba, Cyprus, Ethiopia, Ghana, Guinea, India, Indonesia, Iraq, Lebanon, Mali, Morocco, Nepal, Saudi Arabia, Somalia, Sudan,

Tunisia, the United Arab Republic, Yemen and Yugoslavia (Alden, Morphet and Vieira 2010: 50).

9 This uses 'white but not quite' differently from Anna Agathangelou (2004b: 88), who describes stigmatisation of sex-workers from postsocialist European countries, but both point to shifting racial identifications projected on to postsocialist Europe.

10 The Croatian philosopher Rada Iveković writes: 'in the early seventies, as a well known German feminist scholar had asked us [for] contributions for a collective book and proposed to bundle us up in the Eastern block section, we asked to be put into the part concerned with the Third World. This is where we saw ourselves then' (Iveković 2006).

11 Kiiru had made *Lerman Dragutin* in 1988, about the Karlovac explorer, and was first president of the Croatian–African Friendship Society, founded in 2004.

12 Contrast Basil Davidson's anti-primitivist explanation of African postcolonial social structures, informed by his knowledge of early socialist Yugoslavia (Davidson 1992). With thanks to Sunnie Rucker-Chang.

13 A 1982 report from the Federal Institution for International Co-Operation in Science, Cultural Development and Technology, Belgrade, stated that Yugoslavia 'did not approach this co-operation as "extension of assistance", nor from the position of superiority or level of development or expert–scientific supremacy, but on the contrary from the position of common interests' (Zimić 1982: 13) – suggesting that the author of the report might have been aware it could be perceived as less solidaristic. The positioning of Yugoslavia as 'one of the most developed among Non-Aligned [countries]' (Tito to Algerian television, 1973) indeed established a hierarchy of modernity that could easily be racialised (Kilibarda 2010: 39).

14 The Yugoslav feminist Mirjana Morokvasic, writing in 1991 on 'Fortress Europe and migrant women', argued both '[t]he colonial past in some countries and economic supremacy in others' stigmatised 'migrant and minority women', including the Yugoslav and Vietnamese women workers of both Germanies who were sent home if they gave birth (Morokvasic 1991: 73–4).

15 These professions of internationalism 'contrasted uncomfortably' with evidence of everyday racism and anti-blackness in state socialist societies: while a Ghanaian journalist was writing that Bulgarians, with 'five hundred years … under the Turkish rule … understand the African and are very sympathetic with her struggle', African students in Sofia, Prague, Moscow and Beijing were mobilising against unequal conditions (Stanek 2015: 435; see Hessler 2006: 50).

16 The People's Youth of Yugoslavia (Narodna omladina Jugoslavije) was the KPJ/SKJ youth organisation, and reported on young people's internalisation of state socialist ideology as part of its work.

17 Boney M were an Afro-European band formed by a white German producer.

18 Emerging in 1989, this became the Slovenian opposition slogan in the 1990 elections.

19 One Otpor document, which for Kilibarda illustrates 'cultural racism' in Europeanness and reform discourses, argued that Serbia and the Balkans contained two political tendencies. The first was European and individualistic. The other, in the document's words, was 'Asiatic, not after the continent from which it originally comes, but because of the mentality of the Ottoman sultanates and džamahirijau (sic.), which has its origins in the nearly five-centuries of Turkish occupation strongly reinforced with the ruling ideology of pseudo-socialism in Serbia ... The attempt to preserve this model can only succeed temporarily in small societies forgotten by the world like Cuba – but is impossible at a crossroads in Europe's centre like Serbia' (Kilibarda 2010: 45).

20 The USSR, meanwhile, renamed its 'Peoples' Friendship University' in Moscow (which educated Asian, African and Latin American students, opened in 1960) after Lumumba (Matusevich 2012: 335).

4

Postsocialism, borders, security and race after Yugoslavia

The historical legacies shown in the last chapter do much to explain the contradictory racialised imaginaries of the Yugoslav region's 'cultural archive' (Chapter 1) and the shifting nature of translations of race into discourses of ethnic and national belonging (Chapter 2). Though many past applications of postcolonial thought to south-east Europe have bracketed race away, identifications with racialised narratives of Europeanness predated state socialism, yet alone the collapse of Yugoslavia which, it is sometimes thought, opened space for new postsocialist racisms. Translations of broader racialised discourses in the 1990s indeed took distinctive forms, embedded in a transnational European 'cultural racism' (Balibar and Wallerstein 1991: 26) consolidating nationalisms around a common defensive project of securing Europe against supposedly culturally alien, unassimilable migrant Others from Africa and Asia (Lentin 2004; Fekete 2009). Culturalist narratives of Europeanness-as-modernity and Europeanness-at-risk entered traditionalist–conservative and liberal national identity discourses most evidently in Slovenia (Mihelj 2005; Petrović 2009; Longinović 2011), but also elsewhere. Identity narratives at the north-west end of 'nesting orientalisms' (Bakić-Hayden 1995) trained racialising lenses south-east across the Balkans towards Muslim and dark-skinned refugees and migrants entering Europe. Slovenian and Croatian nationalism's performative rejection of Yugoslav state socialism and Yugoslav multi-ethnicity appeared to have also swept Yugoslav anti-colonial solidarities away.

While post-Yugoslav identifications with cultural racism went back too far simply to be 'consequences' of postsocialism, the region's violently inverted geopolitical position after 1990 still shaped what form they took. The ethnopolitical violence that political entrepreneurs, paramilitaries and organised criminals stimulated as the Yugoslav regime collapsed left a country that had imagined itself a hub of East–West–South cooperation, and a society that had believed Yugoslavs enjoyed greater global mobility than citizens of either East or West (Jansen 2009), subject to peacekeeping and humanitarian intervention by the very global institutions Tito's Yugoslavia had hoped to lead. Other European governments no longer saw the region as exporting skilled professionals and managed numbers of guest-workers but as a source of international instability (Hansen 2006) and disordered refugee flows, as millions escaped violent ethnicised displacement from Croatia, Bosnia-Herzegovina and later Kosovo or systemic structural inequality (exacerbated in Serbia by economic sanctions against Milošević) elsewhere. Security-minded gazes from northern and western Europe categorised Bosnia alongside Rwanda and Somalia, imagining all three complex conflicts as primarily driven by ethnic hatred (Pieterse 1997) – though conditionally white, conditionally European Bosnian refugees could still come closer to western European collective selves than black African refugees in hierarchies of foreignness based on 'cultural distance' (Eastmond 1998: 176).[1] This heavily racialised identification of the Yugoslav region and Africa from outside inverted the discourses of modernisation, anti-colonialism and solidarity through which Tito and some Non-Aligned travellers had imagined Yugoslav–African brotherhood – while participation in European/transatlantic security and border projects would create new opportunities for identification with whiteness and the West. Perceiving the postcoloniality of postsocialism requires appreciating this contradiction.

'New' postsocialist racisms and the Yugoslav wars

Societies across central and eastern Europe, not just the Yugoslav region, witnessed an 'increasingly visible ethno-nationalism' – in revivals of narratives of national victimhood, prominent public roles for religious organisations, constriction of women's public participation, demographic panics about ethnic majorities, and weakened reproductive rights – after state socialism collapsed (Verdery 1994: 250). Racism and xenophobia against Roma, Jews, other minorities and historic ethnic Others, plus undocumented migrants crossing into the EU, were another dimension of postsocialist 'nation-building' (Bošković 2006: 560), creating what the Slovenian sociologist Tonči Kuzmanić (2002: 21) termed a 'new … post-socialist race matrix' at an international workshop on xenophobia and postsocialism that he and colleagues at the Peace Institute, Ljubljana, convened in 2001. Even in comparative context, post-Yugoslav cases stood out: partly because of the distinct role that anti-colonial friendship had had in Titoist identity, and, most visibly, because postsocialism in this region entailed not just economic and political shock but war itself.

The 'newness' of post-Yugoslav racisms, Kuzmanić (2002: 22) thought, was that they targeted the 'free floating signifiers' of cultural racism rather than following older European and US racisms' biological essentialism. 'Cultural racism' also helps Julija Sardelić explain rising post-Yugoslav antiziganism, which regarded Roma as not even capable of forming their own territorial nation. Sardelić (2014: 208–9) links this form of racism into wider contexts of 1990s European racisms via perspectives from Britain (Gilroy), France (Pierre-André Taguieff) and Italy (Michael Hardt and Antonio Negri) which argue there are multiple racisms that mobilise 'constructed cultural difference' to legitimise majorities' hierarchical advantage. Gilroy's argument that '[r]acism … assumes new forms and articulates new antagonisms through time and history' (Gilroy 1987: 11), which Sardelić (2014: 208) quotes, enables him to read attacks on multi-ethnic cultural heritage in Sarajevo ordered by Republika Srpska (RS) authorities as part of the same conflict between 'neo-fascism' and pluralist democracy that motivated Front Nationale-controlled municipalities in 1990s France to seek to ban films with queer content or rap music resisting police (Gilroy 2000: 280). Still, biological racism had not disappeared: the RS leadership grounded its belief in the Otherness and inhumanity of Bosniaks not just on culture but also on vehement biological racism based on psychiatry and genetics. Radovan Karadžić's pre-war career as a psychiatrist and Biljana Plavšić's as a biologist were not surreal wartime curiosities;[2] they were articulations of science and racism that became tools for the RS leadership to graft scientific authority on to a campaign for ethnically pure territory, with Plavšić in 1993 calling Bosniaks 'genetically deformed material [South Slav stock] that embraced Islam' (Sells 1996: xiv–xv). Their pseudoscience connected the genocidal project with European rationality and modernity.[3]

More 'new antagonisms' in post-Yugoslav racisms evolved away from the frontlines and after wars' end. The most linkages between xenophobia based on post-Yugoslav ethnicised identity boundaries and xenophobia against racialised immigrants from outside the region have been found for Slovenia. Slovenian campaigners for multi-party democracy in late state socialism had framed their programme as demanding 'Europe', and Slovenia's pathway towards EU accession was indeed the Yugoslav region's quickest.[4] Amid a widening wealth gap between Slovenia and the south-eastern republics in the 1980s, Slovenian resentment towards economic migrants from these areas (especially Albanians and Roma, but also Macedonians and Serbs) – which Longinović (2011: 98) called a 'soft version of cultural racism' itself – was already perceptible. Slovenia's citizenship law passed after independence in June 1991 wrote this hierarchy into legislation by requiring non-Slovene permanent residents to apply for naturalisation, rather than granting them citizenship as it did ethnically Slovene residents; 18,000, the so-called 'erased', were left without legal status after removal from the residency register in 1992 (Zorn 2009: 289–92; Kogovšek Šalamon 2016).

Slovenian responses to the 1992–5 Bosnian refugee crisis and 2000–1's sharp increase in undocumented migrants have been seen as strikingly similar, both mobilising myths of the Slovenian border as the symbolic boundary between, first, Europe and the Balkans, and, secondly, Europe and an even less well-defined space of racialised Otherness (Žagar 2002). This was despite the same supranational Yugoslav identity having addressed Slovenes and Bosnians for decades, and indeed the solidarities with the Third World that Non-Aligned internationalism aimed to develop among Yugoslavs. Slovenian authorities gave Bosnians 'temporary protection' (not refugee) status, restricted them to refugee centres, excluded them from paid employment and educated refugee children separately, rather than foreseeing their integration into Slovenian society (Vrecer 2010). In 2000, a year when 13,000 rather than the past year's 776 people (mostly from the Middle East and south-east Asia) claimed asylum, Slovenian media revived the frame of migrants and refugees as likely criminals and public-health risks such that Slovenes might reasonably object to having refugee centres near their homes (Mihelj 2005: 120).[5] Articulations of Slovenian nationalism in both crises involved notions of autochthony linking Slovenian ethnicity to homeland, defining the nation against immediate regional Others and newer external Others at once (Mihelj 2004: 12) – to the extent that remaining Bosnian refugees in 2000–1 started being viewed as less threatening, and in this shifting racial order 'refugee' started signifying migrants with more rights than the less-deserving new 'asylum-seekers' or 'illegals' (Žagar 2002: 38). The 'xeno-racism' (Fekete 2009: 19) characterising the politics of asylum in turn-of-the-millennium Europe certainly extended into Slovenia.

Among all post-Yugoslav national identities, Slovenia's had the most resources for performing membership of a culturalist 'European' space, able to tolerate refugees in well-regulated amounts but not so much as to threaten the national socio-cultural fabric. Even other post-Yugoslav nationalisms, however, contained racialised exclusions. Croat and Serb nationalists both racialised Bosnian Muslims as Turks during the Bosnian conflict, though Croat nationalism gave them a much more ambiguous role: though Croats' identification with Catholic and Christian Europe placed Bosniaks across a major symbolic boundary, narratives of Croats and Bosniaks as joint victims of Serbian aggression, and even the NDH myth of Bosniaks as 'Islamicised Croats', could bring Bosniaks potentially closer in the eyes of Croats than in the eyes of Serbs. In practice, dominant Croatian discourses about Bosniaks followed Bosniak–Croat political/military relations in Bosnia-Herzegovina itself. When the Bosnian branch of Croatia's ruling party (HDZ BiH[6]) and the Croat Defence Council (HVO, the Bosnian Croat armed forces) were allied with the Sarajevo government and the Bosniak-nationalist Party of Democratic Action (SDA), Croatian state media depicted Bosniak refugees more sympathetically, as common victims of Serb aggression; while during the 1993–4 Bosniak–Croat conflict and after the Dayton Peace Agreement (when HDZ BiH, still antagonistic towards the settlement, looked towards future union with Croatia and demanded a 'third entity'), they highlighted Bosniaks' Islamic characteristics, plus Croat accounts of victimisation by Muslims. Yet, beyond the hardening of ethnicised boundaries into racialised categories in wartime nationalisms, post-Yugoslav racisms also surpassed the intra-regional and construct civilisational hierarchies between their white, European nation and stereotypes of black, brown and Asian (or 'Chinese') peoples, supposedly unprepared for modernity. The politics of racism and peacekeeping in the Yugoslav wars exemplified how post-Yugoslav racisms mediated the geopolitical reversal that many ex-Yugoslavs felt they had undergone.

Racism, peacekeeping and international intervention

One 'global' racism in 1990s Croatia and Bosnia-Herzegovina channelled resentment that the humanitarian and securitising Western gaze had suddenly ascribed ex-Yugoslavs the same status as Africans (i.e. objects of pity and mistrusted visa nationals) on to the figure of the African peacekeeper. In April 1995, negotiating a post-war UN peacekeeping mandate, the Croatian government was forced to deny reports it had insisted on no African or Asian states participating (O'Shea 2005: 145). Bangladesh, Pakistan, India and Malaysia had been among the larger United Nations Protection Force (UNPROFOR) contributors in Croatia and Bosnia-Herzegovina, and UNPROFOR's first commander (a public figure) was an Indian general, Satish Nambiar. Kenya and Nigeria both contributed UNPROFOR infantry battalions in 1992 and other African countries sent smaller numbers of peacekeepers or military observers (Tatalović 1993: 58).[7] Racialising UNPROFOR let harder-line Croatian nationalists express how unwanted they considered the UN presence.

The semi-anonymous, satirically named 'UNPROFOR Big Band', one of many fringe acts expressing vituperative patriotism in wartime Croatian music (Pettan 1998a), illustrated their 1993 cassette with a cartoon monkey in a blue UN helmet, 'an obvious commentary on the number of black soldiers' (Longinović 2000: 638) in UNPROFOR. Their abusive lyrics, set to Slavonian tamburica music and subjecting male and female Serb nationalist leaders to imagined sexual and scatological assault, treated UNPROFOR and Nambiar as the same kind of racialised invader[8] – conflating an occupying military/paramilitary force with a UN peacekeeping force deployed with Croatian governmental consent. Distance from internal ethnic Others (Serbs) and external racial Others (Africans, Indians, the UN) here ran together.

The internationalisation of the Bosnian conflict as humanitarian crisis and media spectacle, coinciding with failed UN interventions in Somalia (where the Somali National Alliance attacked the US-led peacekeeping force in 1993) and Rwanda (where post-civil-war peacekeepers failed to prevent the 1994 genocide), gave Western media ambiguous frames of reference for situating Bosnians and the Yugoslav region within a global geography of conflict. Western journalists' and travellers' representations of Bosnia, extending into other cultural forms, typically fell into two types, each implying a certain stance towards intervention. The 'Balkan discourse' attributed the violence to insoluble ancient 'ethnic' or even (with direct colonial overtones) 'tribal' hatreds, blamed all sides equally, and implied Western intervention would be futile. The 'genocide discourse' recognised Bosniaks (and sometimes Croats) as victims of Serb genocide and, implicitly or explicitly evoking the Holocaust, counselled military intervention to prevent another such extermination in Europe (Hansen 2006: 96). While the 'Balkan discourse' applied an orientalising lens of endemic, unknowable disorder, 'genocide discourse' brought the Balkans closer to 'Europe'. Yet both discourses – the extensive critical commentary on Western media and Bosnia notes this much more rarely – also racialised Bosnians differently: as somehow-Other (just as Europeanness and whiteness had long been constructed against African and Indigenous 'tribal' savagery) or as fellow whites.

Making 'the Balkans' a symbolic boundary-marker of distance from 'Europeanness' and modernity is, ultimately, a racialising move – dependent on imagining certain places as inherently incapable of rationality and development without the North's/West's civilising mission. This is, in critical race theory and especially for Charles Mills (1997), the underlying racialised principle behind every spatialised hierarchy of savagery versus modernity. Moreover, the rhetorical device of provoking Western audiences' shock at concentration camps being reintroduced *in Europe* (see Campbell 2002) arguably obscured genocides outside Europe and disavowed exterminations perpetrated by 'Europeans' against colonised peoples (Dauphinée 2013: 352). The implication that the unconscious biases of whiteness might have made images of suffering Bosnians easier for white Europeans and global Northerners to identify with, relative to images of black Africans experiencing conflict, hunger and genocide at the same moment, is both unsettling and necessary to confront.

Bosnia's comparability with Rwanda and Somalia had racialised undertones even in Bosnia. When the British photojournalist Paul Lowe exhibited photographs from Sarajevo side by side with others from Somalia, Susan Sontag observed objections among Sarajevans which for Himadeep Muppidi (2013: 304) could reflect a deep 'European exceptionalism':

> Undoubtedly there was a racist tinge to their indignation – Bosnians are Europeans, people in Sarajevo never tired of pointing out to their foreign friends – but they would have objected too if, instead, pictures of atrocities committed against civilians in Chechnya or in Kosovo, indeed in any other country, had been included[.] (Sontag 2003: 112–13)

Muppidi argues, against Sontag, that comparing Bosnia with other intra-European genocides (from which late-twentieth-century European understandings of genocide came) would have been different. Indeed, comparisons with Jewish suffering were an important moral instrument throughout the Yugoslav wars – even, in constructing narratives of national victimhood, among speakers implicated in ethnopolitical violence themselves (Macdonald 2003). If the attachment to urban identity that sustained besieged Sarajevans' morale and gave other cities' anti-nationalists moral faith helped 'relate one's personal narrative to the larger story of European modernity' (Jansen 2005: 162), it still contained an – almost certainly subconscious – whiteness within the racialised history of imagining 'Europe', writing Sarajevo and Somalia – however diffusely – into different parts of history.

These are sensitive, but important, identifications to contextualise when many people in the region, and those forced to emigrate by ethnopolitical violence and economic depredation, have expressed resentment at being treated like 'a third world country' (Jansen 2005: 160) or 'like Africans'. Whether to Bosnians fleeing besieged towns in the early 1990s or Serbians queuing for visas outside Western embassies in the late 2000s, this might have felt even more like a 'fall from grace' (Jansen 2009: 826) because of the state socialist myth that Non-Aligned Yugoslavia made its citizens *more* mobile than the superpower blocs'. Tanja Petrović (2009: 55) calls these discourses 'nesting colonialisms': post-Yugoslavs distancing themselves from the 'Third World' just as the EU and other Western institutions seemed to be pushing the region into it. The separation of Yugoslavs and the Third World into different geopolitical categories undid the international solidarities of Non-Alignment – though might connote either that the Yugoslav region did belong on a higher rung of the global ladder, or that the 'Third World' did not deserve such treatment either.

Race and whiteness remained perceptible in post-war Bosnian identity discourses as new, open-ended forms of post-conflict international intervention developed – yet ethnographies of post-conflict–postsocialist Bosnia rarely discuss them. NATO's multinational military force (Implementation Force (IFOR) and Stabilization Force (SFOR)), which replaced UNPROFOR after Dayton, and the UN's International Police

Task Force (IPTF) that monitored and assisted local police, occasioned numerous encounters between Bosnians and people of colour within an intervention that many Bosnians experienced as disempowering, unaccountable and indeed neo-colonial.[9] If these were neo-colonial authorities, their embodiment was visibly multiracial – the IPTF's top contributors by July 1997 were the USA, Germany, India, Jordan, France, Pakistan and Ghana[10] – and some Bosnians resented taking instructions from officers from countries they perceived were less well administered than Bosnia should have been. IFOR/SFOR involved notably fewer African forces than UNPROFOR, and none from sub-Saharan Africa. Even then, however, the colonial histories of forces from the Global North still brought a multiracial presence to Bosnia.

British forces' recruitment of Commonwealth soldiers and Gurkha regiments, a practice with colonial roots (Ware 2012), often for instance meant Bosnians encountering Nepalese and Pacific Islanders having expected predominantly white Britons, with formed Gurkha units causing most surprise. British forces leading IFOR/SFOR's Multi-National Division (North-West) stationed several Gurkha companies on bases around northern Republika Srpska in the late 1990s, and after 2003, with Britain fighting in Iraq as well as Afghanistan, depended heavily on Gurkha battalions to fulfil commitments to Bosnia-Herzegovina and Kosovo; local residents often racialised Gurkhas, at least initially, as 'Chinese'. Tuzla, meanwhile, was the centre of US military presence, which peaked at 20,000 in 1996 before scaling down to 5,000 then 1,000 in 1998–2004 (Phillips 2004). US force-protection policies, after the humiliation of Somalia, made social encounters between local residents and US personnel much more transitory in late-1990s Bosnia than during the post-Second World War Allied occupation of Germany, and African-American troops did not have similar cultural impact[11] – though Bosnians recruited through US military contractors for service occupations or translation/interpreting had more sustained contact with US troops.

One ex-interpreter, 'Tarik', whom I interviewed for a project on translation/interpreting and peacekeeping, remembered that among the US Army units posted to his Tuzla base had been an 'all-black' unit from Arkansas. He adapted to their African-American Vernacular English while building what he recalled as his best working relationship, where after a few months he already felt 'not [like] a Bosnian guy who's here to help them, but one of the team'. Their replacements, a New York unit, were not racialised the same way (speaking 'different English, without so much slang') and 'look[ed] at me like I'm from a different planet [...] if you see a Bosnian white person who speaks Ebonics, then it feels like something's wrong with this guy. But it just happened' (Kelly and Baker 2013: 183).

The co-author of our project's joint monograph read this encounter across racialised boundaries as having produced 'an identity which is not sustainable', leaving 'the cultural identity he has assumed ... in conflict with his social identity as a white Bosnian' (Kelly and Baker 2013: 184). Lenses of global raciality that I did not apply when editing our manuscript in 2012 would locate Tarik's discomfort, and perhaps even his racialisation as white, in the New Yorkers' remembered reactions to the disjuncture they perceived between appearance, ethnicity/nationality and accent/dialect, more than stemming straight from his identity as Bosnian. The resultant social identity in the new interpersonal environment might well have been unsustainable. On one level, the account (narrated at least six to seven years later) revealed a disconnect between symbolic linguistic and embodied markers of race. In a broader view, however, it reiterates many other shifting identity-performances by Yugoslavs from various social and ethnicised subject positions, and perhaps even shows obliquely how US soldiers interacted with Bosnia and Bosnians through lenses inflected by their own racialised experiences at home. How might African-American soldiers from Arkansas, compared with white soldiers from either Arkansas or New York, have interpreted postsocialist Tuzla's war-damaged, privatised landscape, Tuzla's distinctive wartime history of resisting ethnonationalism in local government or enduring a targeted VRS mortar massacre of civilian teenagers, or indeed the stakes of the wider Bosnian war? Race, as well as ethnicity, is an essential category for understanding the micropolitics of postsocialism, and for situating the Yugoslav wars more widely in late-twentieth-century European history.

The Yugoslav wars, European racisms and the 'migration–security nexus'

Popular Western reductions of the Yugoslav wars to a decontextualised 'ethnic conflict' (Banks and Wolfe Murray 1999) contributed to scholarship itself focusing predominantly on ethnicity at the expense of economic dislocations when explaining the post-Yugoslav region. While sociologists and anthropologists were extensively researching the inequalities of postsocialist 'transition' in central Europe and the eastern Balkans, the Yugoslav region stood predominantly as a 'post-conflict' area, even though the socio-economic impacts of the collapse of socialism wove through the wars' origins and course (see Woodward 1995; Bougarel, Helms and Duijzings (eds) 2007; Archer, Duda and Stubbs (eds) 2016). Although the wars and their aftermath required a 'double lens' seeing the region as postsocialist *and* post-conflict, to most Western non-specialists they were plain and simply an example of violent ethnic conflict. In this capacity, they informed post-Cold-War Western dynamics of race and an emerging 'migration–security nexus' (Faist 2006) where policymakers evaluated migrations as security threats.

To writers like Daniel Patrick Moynihan (1993), whose 'Moynihan Report' three decades earlier had stigmatised African-American family structures as the underlying cause of African-American poverty (Crenshaw 1991: 1254), or Samuel Huntington (1996), ethnic disorder characterised post-Cold-War international security. Some readings made it endemic to certain zones of the world that would threaten Western peace and prosperity unless strong borders sealed them off (Kaplan 1993);[12] others made it the inevitable result of historically and geographically defined civilisational faultlines (Huntington 1996), or a phenomenon that alongside neo-Nazi attacks on refugees in Germany and sectarian violence in Northern Ireland revealed a resurgent, ethnic 'new nationalism' of 'blood and belonging' (Ignatieff 1994). These foreign-policy discourses were the background to how people from the Yugoslav region fleeing across, settling within, transiting over or temporarily crossing Western societies' borders were categorised – with implications for their legal and social status, the conditions on which they might belong or not belong within 'host nations', and, if one accepts that racialised ideologies still structure contemporary Western migration policies (Fekete 2009), the systems of racialisation they might encounter.

The EU 'temporary protection' system developed once 500,000 Bosnian refugees fled into the EU in 1992–3, codified into a 2001 directive (Sardelić 2017), represented an evolution of the organised asylum schemes that had covered east-central European 'Displaced Persons' after the Second World War (many unable or unwilling to return to homes now under state socialist control), refugees from the 1956 Hungarian Revolution and 1970s Vietnamese refugees. Western European governments had been making asylum increasingly restrictive since the 1980s, reducing state support for refugees and under-review 'asylum-seekers' to dissuade economic migrants from seeking settlement that way (Koser and Black 1999). These tightening asylum policies firmly distinguished 'refugees', to whom states owed protection under international law, and 'economic migrants', with no inherent right to settlement and (in most western European migration policy since the 1980s recessions) liable to be turned back; yet in many conflicts 'refugees' and 'economic' migrants were as hard to disentangle as 'post-socialism' and 'post-conflictness' in Bosnia.

While the 1945–56 refugees 'were mainly of European origin, and their cultural assimilation was perceived as relatively straightforward' (or even welcome bulwarks against Communism), the 1980s 'spontaneous' arrivals were 'generally … from outside Europe' – that is, from the Global South – and appeared to be 'harbingers of mass South–North migration in the face of uneven economic development' (Koser and Black 1999: 524–5) – or, less obliquely, of ever-greater numbers of racialised migrants seeking to settle in western Europe. Indeed, Lucy Mayblin (2017) links 1980s asylum policy changes even more emphatically to most asylum-seekers from then on coming from former colonies and being racialised as non-white. This evolving history of migration and border control was the background for late-twentieth-century cultural racisms arguing that more mass migration would undermine autochthonous culture (sometimes including the liberal democratic tendencies ascribed to a certain national mentality), threaten public safety and health, and import migrants' own ethnic and religious antagonisms (Solomos 2003; Lentin 2004; Fekete 2009).

Post-Yugoslav refugees experienced EU 'protection' differently in different member states, or even German *Länder*. Most EU members gave many Bosnian refugees more permanent statuses over time, Sweden routed them into its asylum system immediately, and Germany stood out both in requiring Bosnians to return after Dayton and in devolving repatriation to individual federal units (Koser and Black 1999: 528–9). By the Kosovo War, meanwhile, western European political and media discourses had invented the category of 'bogus asylum-seeker' as a suspicious, racially different figure. Both eastern European Roma and migrants/refugees from Kosovo (some of whom were Roma) were inscribed into this category on entering or attempting to enter the EU.[13] In Britain, the construction in some towns of a colloquial 'Kosovar' category, informed by antiziganist stereotypes, for both groups prefigured the more widespread racialisation of east European migrants after 2004, when Britain did not impose transitional freedom-of-movement controls on the east European 'accession eight' states.[14] East Europeans were caught between the 'institutional racism' of migration policy favouring EU citizens over Global South citizens as labour migrants, and tabloids still directing late-1990s racialised tropes of flooding, criminality and antiziganism against them (Fox, Moroşanu and Szilassy 2012: 680).[15]

Associations between the Yugoslav region and disorder would also draw together migration and security in the case of sex work. The Yugoslav region was both an origin-point and (with so many foreign troops and officials present) a destination for sex-work migration, some facilitated by security contractors, IPTF officers and peacekeepers (Haynes 2008: 1794–8). Spatialised hierarchies of modernity (eastern Europe less modern, eastern Europeans lacking agency) have informed prevailing representations of sex-workers, and women subjected to the coercive labour of 'trafficking', since the 1990s (Andrijasevic 2007; Mai 2013; Suchland 2015). The stereotype of the east European 'prostitute' who might either migrate from the Yugoslav region or to it, 'white' by appearance yet on the margins of whiteness in global capital (Agathangelou 2004b), is one configuration of east European women's 'flexible "racing"', racialising them as white when they are being desired and 'something more ethnic' when they are being exploited or having their agency cast into doubt in others' eyes depending on their position in the global political economy (Cerwonka 2008: 823). With anti-trafficking campaigns already targeting this node in the 'migration–security nexus' in the late 1990s, the convergence of migration policy and understandings of security had already begun before 9/11, when the meanings of Islam in the Yugoslav region would intersect with transnational racialised Islamophobia.

Racialised Islamophobia and the Yugoslav region before and after 9/11

The expansion of the 'migration–security nexus' through governments and international institutions, after 9/11, made 'Muslims' and people ascribed a Muslim appearance the primary targets of surveillance and suspicion to a degree that seemed to place Muslims beyond the boundary of Western political communities, treating them as racialised Others (Razack 2008). Post-9/11 Islamophobia compounded late-twentieth-century Western cultural racisms that already stigmatised Islam as incompatible with liberal democracy, along lines inflected by specific national histories and experiences but with common assumptions that Islam was incompatible with a secular Europe or West. These myths themselves stemmed from the sixteenth- to eighteenth-century symbolic geographies that had defined first Christendom and then 'Europe' against the Ottoman Empire – the context for hierarchical Europe/Balkan oppositions in identity discourses inside and outside the Yugoslav region.

Local identity discourses in the region, as elsewhere, actively translated post-9/11 securitised and racialised Islamophobia by adapting it to existing narratives about national history and enemies, while emphasising transnational Europeanness, Westernness and whiteness in those national narratives. More than half the Croatian journalists interviewed in 2006 by two Slovenian media scholars about how they had reported Croat war crimes against Bosniaks replied through discourses of the 'We had to fight against Islamic terrorism' type, with one commenting, 'I think that Croatia had to fight against Islamic terrorists like America or the West … it is well-known that most of the Bosniaks are Islamic fundamentalists' (Erjavec and Volčič 2007: 14). Another recontextualised Croatian war aims in Bosnia as a campaign to prevent al-Qaida, specifically its then deputy leader Ayman al-Zawahiri, from establishing Bosnian cells to plot 'the plans for attacking the Western countries' (Erjavec and Volčič 2007: 15). A third respondent compared the Croat offensive with another conflict that the more powerful party had also framed as one where a democracy was defending its citizens against Islamic terrorism (Israeli operations against Hezbollah in Lebanon), and a fourth even combined ethnicised Islamophobia with neoliberal capitalism in arguing Croats had had to 'defend our property and market' against Bosniaks who had been appropriating Croat property and resisting supposedly necessary neoliberal reforms (Erjavec and Volčič 2007: 15, 17).

While the HVO was fighting the Army of the Republic of Bosnia-Herzegovina (ARBiH) in 1993–4, wartime Croatian media constructing stereotypes of that enemy had often called them 'mujahidin'. This both exaggerated the ARBiH's number of Muslim foreign fighters and capitalised on the SDA's growing religious nationalism to contend that Sarajevo ruling over Bosnian Croats would be an existential threat to their Catholic identity. The theme of anti-terrorism had, indeed, already characterised Croatian police responses to SDS militias placing roadblocks and taking over 'Serb-majority' municipalities in August 1990–May 1991. The Croatian government characterised these militias both as terrorists and illegitimate 'hajduks' (bandits) whom it was legitimate to suppress: indeed, Croatia's first paramilitary police unit, nucleus (alongside the volunteer National Guard) of the future Croatian Army, was the Anti-Terrorist Unit Lučko (a police headquarters outside Zagreb). Yet this was domestic, not global, terrorism: al-Qaida, al-Zawahiri and the notion of Islamists using Bosnia like Pakistan/Afghanistan to plan attacks on the West were not reference points in wartime Croatian media, nor did widespread wartime verbal and visual identifications between Croatian and US military strength identify Croatia with an active US/Western military struggle *against terrorism*. The journalists' post-9/11 narratives, conversely, immediately combined these. Existing xenophobias likewise became openly securitised Islamophobia in Slovenia after 9/11 in struggles over the building of a Ljubljana mosque (Vidmar Horvat 2010: 763).

Bosnian Muslims, meanwhile, performed different identity work after 9/11 by articulating Bosnian Islamic heritage as a model for a moderate, pluralist 'European Islam' comfortable with a multicultural, multifaith society. This argued that the history of Muslim–Christian coexistence in south-east Europe during and after Ottoman rule showed potential to prove Islam was not alien to European heritage (as long as the Balkans were integrally recognised as part of 'Europe'). Yet these discourses themselves arguably required a spatialising distinction between tolerant, pluralist Bosnian Islam, tempered by Europeanness, and a Middle Eastern Islam seen as fundamentalist and doctrinaire (Bougarel 2007). These arguments in turn reflected the politics and political economy of religion in postsocialist/post-conflict Bosnia, where Saudi and Emirati religious foundations were funding opulent new mosques while propagating Wahhabism – and threatening to pull Bosnia into the racialised zone of Islamist terrorism in twenty-first-century geographies of security.

'Foreign fighters', jihadism and the war in Bosnia

International Islamic voluntarism, hardly noticed by mainstream 1990s Western media when thousands of foreign Muslim men travelled to aid Bosniak refugees or fight alongside the ARBiH, appeared far more significant two decades later in Europe's contemporary history of migration, security and race. At least 300, potentially 3,000, foreign fighters volunteered as 'mujahidin' in 1992–5 to defend Bosnian Muslims and answer Islamist calls for militarised jihad. The Sarajevo government formed a 'Mujahids' Detachment' of ARBiH in August 1993 (Li 2016: 384–5), and at war's end, though Dayton required all foreign volunteers to leave, offered Bosnian citizenship to foreign fighters who had married Bosnian women or (like Libyans and Algerians) claimed they had no safe country to return to (Mustapha 2013: 746). Around this formalised, militarised production of transnational Islamist identity were much more diverse fundraising and consciousness-raising networks among Western Muslims.

Western Muslims organised aid convoys to Bosnia in similar grassroots humanitarian initiatives to those led by trades unions and left-wing movements, Christian churches, and the hundreds of private individuals who described themselves as moved by media images from Croatia and Bosnia to take action to stop the suffering.[16] They also campaigned at home, like the British Pakistani women's group Al Masoom (active in Manchester 1990–6), who adopted 'Women in Black'-style silent protest (an anti-militarist feminist tactic from Israel/Palestine taken up in countries including Serbia) to campaign against human-rights abuses in Bosnia and Kashmir, employing an egalitarian understanding of their faith that made 'Islam the rallying cry for women's rights' (Werbner 2000: 320). Al-Qaida, however, had interests in deliberately blurring the lines between humanitarianism and paramilitary fundraising or even participation, and made Bosnia a node for recruiting young European Muslim men as militants (Kohlmann 2004) – indeed, some argue Bosnia 'played the central role' in catalysing British jihadism (Birt and Hamid 2014: 171).

Racialised suspicion by the British state blurred these lines further. Before as well as after 9/11, UK authorities often suspected mosque trustees of financing terrorism if they had supported humanitarian missions to Bosnia or other sites of Muslim suffering like Chechnya or Palestine (Fekete 2004: 9). Moazzam Begg (2007: 59–60), a British

Pakistani arrested as an enemy combatant in Pakistan in 2002 and detained at Bagram and Guantánamo for three years, wrote in his autobiography that US and UK interrogators had frequently questioned him about visits to Bosnia: motivated by atrocity scenes in an amateur documentary on *Massacres in Bosnia and Croatia* and by hearing a Bosnian Muslim refugee in Birmingham narrate her rape by Serb soldiers, Begg first joined a foreign-fighter unit in Bosnia, then volunteered in Chechnya. 'Bosnia', in fact, became a site of memory and symbol of identity for some twenty-first-century Muslims facing racialised Islamophobia in the West.

Narratives of the Bosnian conflict as a genocidal attack against Muslims, part of a myth that addressed Muslims across borders and continents as part of a transnational, under-siege ummah (Roy 2004), are in retrospect as important an impact of the Yugoslav wars as the discourses of 'ethnic hatreds' or liberal internationalism that divided 1990s politicians, yet are marginal in the wars' transnational history as written to date (Li 2016: 381). Young Muslims in Europe and settler-colonial countries accessed them through Islamic bookshops, travelling preachers, student Islamic societies and mosques, where some Islamist organisers (including Abu Hamza, extradited to the USA in 2012, who preached from Finsbury Park Mosque in 1997–2003) spoke from personal experience as volunteers in Bosnia (Thomas 2014). Atrocity images from Bosnia circulated on underground videotapes around the incipient ummah just like equivalents in ethnonational diasporas, while resentment at Western failure to prevent genocide against Muslims not only helped to fuel the emergence of a separate Muslim political identity in Britain (distinct from 1970s–80s Black–Asian solidarity) but also 'led some British-born Muslims to reinvent the concept of the *Ummah* as global victims' (Modood 2006: 42) – meaning that, as Croat, Serb, Bosniak and Albanian ethnonationalists inside and outside the region pursued a politics of victimhood, similar dynamics and the same technologies were helping a globalised jihadi identity emerge.

Both technologically and thematically – in for instance the glorification of volunteers' militarised masculinities – this transnational construction of community strikingly resembled how the region's ethnonational diasporas formed networks for aiding refugees and equipping (para-)military formations in the homeland (see Hockenos 2003). Sometimes, as when a Bosnian-born preacher in Vienna recruited Austro-Bosniaks such as Sabina Selimović and Samra Kesinović for Islamic State in Iraq and Syria (ISIS), ethno-diaspora and ummah even overlapped (Franz 2015: 10).[17] Compared with ethnonationalisms with decades of associational culture behind them, the collective identity of late-twentieth/early-twenty-first-century transnational jihadism was more incipient as a political identification yet similarly dependent on victimhood narratives as explanatory myths. Addressing its audience through a shared religious identity as Muslim, cutting across boundaries of ethnicity and race, jihadism played off Muslims' lived experiences of Islamophobia at intersections of race, class and religion with a script that placed the marginalisation of young Muslims attracted to jihadism in a continuum with imperialist oppression of Muslims in Palestine and with the genocide of Muslims in Bosnia. The racialisation of Western Islamophobia, profiling all people of Arab or South Asian appearance as Muslims and potential terrorists whatever their religious heritage or practice, pervaded state surveillance and citizenship regimes after 9/11 (Razack 2008) and played into the jihadist narrative of global Muslim victimhood.

The formation of ISIS in 2014 transformed this historical narrative, previously propagated to support a transnational Islamist identity by al-Qaida as the basis for a transnational Islamist identity, into what was intended to become the foundational myth of an actual state. The techniques of building this state, on territories in Iraq and Syria taken over by militants during the Syrian civil war, were recognisable from wars and revolutions in the Yugoslav region and elsewhere – both the establishment of state structures, bureaucracy and taxation as quickly as a Communist Party in a twentieth-century civil war, and the concurrent campaigns to eliminate religious, ethnic and sexual minorities and minority/multi-ethnic cultural heritage (in this case, particularly pre-Islamic archaeological sites in Syria). While Bosnia like Palestine and Chechnya was part of jihadist collective memory, the implications of the deepening Middle East conflict for identification with/against Islam were social facts for Muslims in the Yugoslav region and (filtered through even more layers of national identification) diasporas. As hundreds of South Slav and Albanian foreign fighters travelled to Iraq/Syria, and Bosnian and Kosovar security services tried to prevent them,[18] public debates in Bosnia-Herzegovina and Kosovo about Saudi-funded mosques or religious young women choosing to wear veils (when state socialism had unveiled women) incorporated positions towards transnational Islam into local social identities (Mesarić 2013). Yet this was only the latest example of a fusion between transnational, racialised migration–security practices and post-Yugoslav collective identities that already underpinned European integration processes themselves.

The Yugoslav region inside and outside 'Fortress Europe'

Ever since the term 'Fortress Europe' emerged in the 1980s, the notion of European cooperation in securing EU borders and agreeing more restrictive immigration policies towards citizens of the Global South has been criticised as structurally racist – by giving Europeans, most of whom are white, privileged mobility over non-Europeans, most of whom are not (Balibar 2004), and reducing its racialised deportees and detainees to a state of 'bare life' outside the socio-political community (Walters 2002: 269; Vaughan-Williams 2015). The European border project has changed since the late Cold War, with material and virtual fortification of EU external borders accompanying the Schengen Area's relaxation of most internal border controls (projected in 1985 and included in the 1997 Treaty of Amsterdam). Perceived needs to keep out undocumented 'economic' migrants from eastern Europe and the Global South had already interconnected migration and security before 9/11 (Huysmans 2000; Faist 2006). After 9/11, however, the EU migration–security nexus accelerated into defending Europe from terrorism and unregulated immigration at once.

Publicly and politically, this shift was framed as necessary, first because of 9/11, then the Afghanistan/Iraq wars, then the armed conflicts and political repression following the 2011 Arab Revolutions. These developments and the concurrent contingencies of EU enlargement altered the Yugoslav region's geopolitical position(s) relative to EU border security – from wholly on the outside at the millennium, towards a situation where some of it is standing on the margins of the inside and responsible for guarding against incursions from outside, while the rest of it is on the outside and is still responsible for guarding against incursions from even further out. Rearticulating post-Yugoslav national identities in this framework, as already seen with the Slovenian frontier myth, adapted existing historical narratives to twenty-first-century European and Euro-Atlantic racialised discourses of security.

The EU border project had the twin securitised purposes of counter-terrorism (excluding people who could not be verified as non-terrorists) and restricting undocumented 'economic' migration (a security threat because of the danger they supposedly posed to nations' social peace and cultural cohesion). Its key sites included external EU land and maritime borders as well as airports in EU-adjacent states (like Bosnia-Herzegovina and Serbia) from which undocumented migrants could easily cross EU borders overground. Incorporating this 'immediate outside' into EU border controls, which the EU required its candidates and wider-partnership members to join, simultaneously widened the fortification and surveillance zone beyond the actual EU border, displaced some border management costs on to non-member states, formed part of the EU 'conditionality' regime for candidates, gave states a standard to meet in return for visa liberalisation, and offered an instrument of tutelage for disciplining neighbouring states' security services into EU border control ideologies and practices, including their racialised frameworks of governance and profiling. The Yugoslav region, covering much of the 'Balkan route' along which undocumented migrants travelling overland via Greece entered the EU (the alternative to the maritime 'Mediterranean route' between North Africa and Italy/Spain), thus took up yet another of its liminal geopolitical positions.[19]

The Schengen immediate exterior made first Slovenia, then Croatia, and eventually every ex-Yugoslav state including Kosovo a last line of 'defence' against overland migrants travelling towards Germany, Austria and Italy. The EU's own expanding external border placed Slovenia's detention and reception centres in 2004, and Croatia's in 2013, directly into the European network of camps.[20] Even states unlikely to accede soon still had to improve airport and land border security, plus other 'conditionality' requirements, to qualify for EU economic aid for the Western Balkans.[21] EU training of Croatian, Bosnian and Kosovar border police during the 2000s has been critically called both a contemporary 'semi-protectorate' and an 'off-shoring and outsourcing' of border governance paralleling UK suggestions (from 2003) that 'third countries' on major migration routes should host 'transit processing centres' for asylum-seekers and Italy's 'push-back' policy (from 2009) of returning migrants who arrived by sea to Libya (Bialasiewicz 2012).[22]

Even as they were incorporated into EU border management, most post-Yugoslav states until 2009–10 were subject to Schengen visa requirements themselves, which travellers found frustrating, expensive and humiliating.[23] Visa 'liberalisation' was thus a key EU incentive not only for achieving 'pillar' border security objectives (preventing organised crime, corruption, terrorism and undocumented migration, and introduction of biometric passports) and obtaining co-operation with the EU's external border fortification, but also, in this region, for pursuing the EU's wider vision for political integration (Flessenkemper and Bütow 2011). EU defence and security policy called for political integration of the 'Western Balkans' to prevent future ethnopolitical conflicts and, thereby, future humanitarian and security crises for the EU. The EU held out visa liberalisation to encourage Serbia, in particular, to co-operate on sensitive transitional justice matters (particularly extraditing Karadžić and Ratko Mladić) as well as border security reform; Macedonian authorities, meanwhile, prevented hundreds of Roma leaving Macedonia for fear they would seek asylum in the EU and jeopardise visa-free travel arrangements (McGarry 2017: 223). While part of the region eventually came within the racialised logic of EU–Schengen border control, other parts were still subject to them and sought, at least at governmental level, to move inside. Post-Yugoslav states were not the only part of Europe (so was Ukraine) asked to secure the EU external border while its citizens remained excluded by it – leaving border guards structurally compartable to Indian sepoys or Maghrebi spahis under a postcolonial reading of EU–eastern European relations. The Yugoslav region nevertheless stood out, not only because the EU gave border/ visa conditionality wider political aims there but also for being on a global, not just regional, route into the EU and, most distinctively, for what its inhabitants perceived as the rupture in their mobilities over time, compared with the Yugoslav era when most Yugoslavs believed they had much more freedom of travel than citizens of the Soviet bloc.

Following the visa restrictions imposed during the Yugoslav wars when EU states profiled post-Yugoslav and Albanian travellers as potential asylum-seekers and overstayers – with racialised suspicion of 'bogus' asylum-seeker falling hardest on Roma (Guild (ed.) 2014 2014) – symbolic geographies of European mobility in the 2000s shrank further. Slovenia's EU accession in 2004 placed an EU external border across a Slovenia–Croatia boundary which until 1991 had required no passport to cross. This became even less permeable, except for some residents near the border with localised provisions, in December 2007 when Slovenia and other 2004 joiners (except Cyprus) joined Schengen. This inversion of the hierarchy of international mobility made post-Yugoslavs' sense of humiliation and marginalisation particularly raw. It would be harsh to dub every such reaction 'exceptionalism'; yet it was perfectly possible to agree both that EU border policy was necessary for securing Europe against migration and terrorism, and that 'we' should not be subject to it.

Participation in and simultaneous subjection to EU border control left the Yugoslav region in yet another ambiguous global structural position, especially after 9/11. Twenty-first-century post-Yugoslav meanings of 'Europe' fused contemporaneous continent-wide racialisations of 'European' belonging in migration/security discourse with longer-term national historical narratives, just as late state socialist/

postsocialist 'return to Europe' discourses had been historically infused. Bosnian Muslims could narrate their history as a contemporary and historical 'bridge' between Islam and Europe (Bougarel 2007). Equivalent Slovenian, Croatian and Serbian narratives of national identity and bordering gained credibility and moral authority from resonance with the 'antemurale'/'bulwark' myth of the nation guarding Christendom–Europe against Islam (Chapter 2), just as in central European societies like Hungary and Poland where identification with national antemurale myths was re-produced in 2015–16 in the Visegrád Group's joint opposition to EU-wide quotas for Syrian refugees.[24]

Both bulwark and bridge myths, like any historical trope, are continually reinterpreted, constructing national identities in a changing present (Žanić 2005). Slovenia's incorporation into EU border regimes, with media coverage of Slovenian police in border exercise providing public performances of security, for instance reaffirmed the bulwark myth by dramatising its relevance to a very different present from sixteenth- to-eighteenth-century Austro-Turkish warfare (Mihelj 2005). Croatia's myth shifted too: in the 1990s it related primarily to Serbs and (during the HVO–ARBiH conflict) Bosniaks, ascribing them an essential easternness and Balkanness (while ascribing the opposites, equally essentialistically, to Croatia) based on their supposedly inescapable Ottoman heritage (Razsa and Lindstrom 2004). The NDH, in 1941–5, had also used it as historical precedent for standing with Germany against 'barbarism, Byzantinism, Bolshevism, and Orthodoxy', yet accommodated Bosnian Muslims *within* the Croatian people (Kljaić 2015: 160). In post-9/11 Croatian foreign policy, the Islamic threat against which Croatia performatively stood by joining the War on Terror was global, not Balkan, and the coalition against it was Euro-Atlantic and liberal. So long-lived and flexible was the sixteenth- to eighteenth-century antemurale myth that later forms of identification with transnational whiteness were perhaps grafted on to that very root.

While alternative visions of Europeanness and bordering existed in cultural and intellectual production, post-Yugoslav leaders did not express them in the way that Tito had championed an alternative diplomatic position. Post-Yugoslav state-of-the-nation cinema, with plots that juxtaposed members of various marginalised social groups to symbolise different aspects of post-Yugoslav crisis and dislocation, not uncommonly contained undocumented migrant characters from the Global South, particularly Chinese – though most lacked agency and primarily seemed to be there so that their visible, racialised difference could represent encounters with new and stranger forms of Otherness and symbolise postsocialist alienation (Rucker-Chang 2013).[25] The new Yugoslav left, organising across post-Yugoslav borders and positioning itself within wider European struggles, linked migrant solidarity with socio-economic justice, environmentalism, anti-nationalism, LGBT equality and alter-globalisation (Razsa 2015) but found little mainstream political representation that would challenge post-Yugoslav governments' and nations' identification with Euro-Atlantic institutions and security practices. This identification, moreover, would even extend into participation in coalition warfare in Iraq and Afghanistan: as the EU induced states to harden their bulwarks within Europe, co-operation with NATO simultaneously projected that bulwark beyond national borders and even the region itself, in a conflict that many critics have described as driven by racialised constructions of security and Islam.

Post-Yugoslav armed forces in the War on Terror

Post-Yugoslav governments explaining participation in the War on Terror as a national interest adopted the same narratives as Western leaders in arguing that pre-emptive intervention against terrorist organisations that threatened European and Western values abroad was necessary to prevent them launching further attacks against the West. This placed them firmly within what European security studies calls 'Euro-Atlantic' institutions, an idea emphasising that Western diplomatic strategy for politically integrating the Yugoslav region and thus preventing future ethnopolitical conflict relied on the successor states' integration into NATO as well as the EU (Ó Tuathail 2005: 52). All post-Yugoslav states except Serbia, the target of NATO air strikes in 1999, aspired to join NATO, with Croatia and Slovenia seeking candidacy as soon as they won international recognition.

The symbolic politics of NATO as well as EU membership, for Slovenia and Croatia, performed a distancing from state socialist, Yugoslav and 'eastern' conceptions of security that in defence and foreign policy as in other political and social domains characterised the construction of Slovenian and Croatian narratives of national spatial/cultural identity. Both countries' military visual cultures – anticipated in Croatia by volunteers who, before the Croatian Army was regularised in January 1992, equipped themselves through surplus stores including Zagreb's (still-trading) 'American Shop' – drew on impressions of the contemporaneous US military freshly reimagined, post-Vietnam, by late-Cold-War film-makers as well as the US military itself (Senjković 2002). By 1994, with the Clinton administration (relatively) more involved in Bosnia, Slovenia had joined NATO's 'Partnership for Peace' (NATO's programme for potential future candidates), and Croatia was receiving US military assistance through a private contractor, eventually a decisive advantage in Croatian offensives against the Republic of Serb Krajina in 1995.[26]

NATO itself, its members and candidates, and states and politicians rejecting affiliation with it, all attached membership symbolically to broader questions of how national identity related to prevailing scripts of 'Europe' and the 'West' in Cold War and post-Cold-War Europe (Fierke and Wiener 1999). NATO's first eastward enlargement, to the Czech Republic, Hungary and Poland (invited in 1997, admitted in March 1999), simultaneously symbolised these states'/governments'/nations' search for 'identification with, and recognition by, the West' (Schimmelfennig 1998: 199); NATO's belief that military co-operation would promote liberal values and thus stabilise peace in a region where, a decade earlier, it had still expected to fight the USSR in large-scale ground warfare; a guarantee these states would not fall into Russia's sphere of influence; and a hierarchical calculation that these states had internalised NATO values most quickly (Kuus 2007). This was the central

Europe to which 1990s Slovenian and Croatian leaders aspired. With Milošević's rump Federal Republic of Yugoslavia targeted by NATO ultimatums in 1998 then air strikes in 1999 over Kosovo, and NATO-led military forces in both Bosnia-Herzegovina (having replaced UNPROFOR after Dayton) and Kosovo (after June 1999), the temporalities of which states were, might be, or might never be 'ready' for NATO drew yet another symbolic boundary through the Yugoslav region.

Slovenia's NATO accession alongside Bulgaria, Estonia, Latvia, Lithuania, Romania and Slovakia in March 2004 preceded, and almost mirrored,[27] the EU enlargement into eastern Europe in May, hardening a symbolic Slovenian 'acceleration' out of the Yugoslav region and into central Europe that gratified Slovenes who believed they had always been more naturally liberal and democratic than their 'Balkan' Others (see Longinović 2011). Croatia, a Partnership for Peace member since 2000, joined NATO with Albania in 2009. Macedonia, meanwhile, had been in Partnership for Peace since 1995 and a NATO candidate since 1999, but the Greece–Macedonia name dispute plus NATO evaluation of defence reforms held it back from accession. Bosnia-Herzegovina and Serbia both joined Partnership for Peace in 2006. The most decisive phase of NATO enlargement into the region therefore coincided with NATO's post-2001 transformation, following 9/11 and US air strikes against Taliban positions in Afghanistan, from a collective security organisation focused on defence of territory in Europe to a military coalition with combat as well as stabilisation missions overseas.

Many critics of the War on Terror, and its global structures of surveillance, intelligence, detention and interrogation in symbiosis with less covert 'kinetic' (ground combat, air strikes, anti-IED operations[28]) and 'non-kinetic' (military liaison, civil–military co-operation, training local security forces and state-building) operations in Iraq and Afghanistan, argue it employed and normalised a racialised narrative of Islamic menace to Western civilisation (Puar 2007; Razack 2008). This narrative essentialised Muslims and Islam into a global, civilisational threat, building on 1990s 'clash of civilisations' rhetoric (to which evidence from the Yugoslav wars had contributed) about religious and cultural difference as root causes of intercommunal conflict. Moreover, through US torture and interrogation methods in Iraq, Afghanistan, Guantánamo and CIA so-called 'black sites' globally, it aligned the coalition's most powerful member and thus its partners with a logic that has been argued to follow 'the racial–sexual grammar of chattel slavery' (Richter-Montpetit 2014: 58). Post-9/11 securitisation and racialisation of Islam (and of people with brown and Muslim bodies crossing borders) depended on pre-9/11 Western cultural racism. Even more deeply, the history of the Second World War's North Atlantic alliance that gave NATO its founding myth itself carries a vestigial whiteness if seen in continuity with the 'racialized peace' already forged, Srđan Vučetić (2011) argues, by Britain and the USA (later including France) at the fin-de-siècle.

Post-Yugoslav politicians and Atlanticist commentators primarily described their militaries' roles in Iraq and Afghanistan as contributing to state-building and democratisation. They might also suggest – as some post-Yugoslav troops deployed as peacekeepers in countries such as Liberia did – that their own countries' and militaries' recent experience of post-conflict reconstruction and defence/security reform gave them insights into the challenges of stabilisation after authoritarianism and war.[29] Joining these coalitions helped post-Yugoslav militaries acclimatise to NATO standards as their accession pathways required, helped officers and diplomats to gain experience and status to progress to more powerful roles inside and outside NATO, and helped post-Yugoslav societies symbolically to perform an overcoming of and redemption from legacies of the 1990s wars. Critical race scholarship on the War on Terror would view this as simultaneously performing an attachment to whiteness.

Participation in NATO after 9/11 was a 'considerably changed strategic environment' (Šimunović 2015: 179) compared with post-Yugoslav governments' late-1990s expectations. The militarised identity narratives of 1990s Slovenian and Croatian nationalism were specifically about defending the ethnonation's homeland, simultaneously thereby – as a strong bulwark against Eastern threats – defending Europe, Westernness and Christianity. The War on Terror might therefore have also seemed like a considerably changed *symbolic* environment, with the nation's soldiers acting as junior but professional partners overseas to NATO allies rather than re-enacting the nexus between national heroism, strength and territory. Continuities between pre-9/11 post-Yugoslav militarised identity discourses and post-9/11 European/international security discourses nevertheless emerge through the notion of 'postnational' defence (Kronsell 2012).[30]

The idea of 'postnational' defence in twenty-first-century European security viewed national interests and defence as 'multinational', 'achieved in solidarity with others well beyond the borders' (Kronsell 2012: 3): for instance, co-operative pursuit of terrorists in Iraq/Afghanistan protected European cities by preventing terrorists from organising attacks there. Compared with NATO's late-1990s liberal interventionism, postnational defence related more specifically to the security of *national* territory and the *nation's* population, re-identifying them as part of the threatened Europe and West. By serving overseas, Croatian or another nation's soldiers were still, discursively speaking, defending the homeland. Especially for Slovenia and Croatia, such contributions could simultaneously represent a fulfilment of the promise of independence (when one pro-independence argument had been that Yugoslavia was preventing these republics from fulfilling aspirations for greater co-operation with Europe and the West); for Bosnia-Herzegovina and Macedonia as well as Croatia, meanwhile, coalition participation overseas cast the nation as providing, rather than receiving, stabilisation.

In ostensibly an utterly different context – European television – Serbia in the symbolic eastern-enlargement year 2004 had celebrated returning to the Eurovision Song Contest by performing a pastoral, gentle, distinctly national masculinity widely read as an alternative to the violently militarised masculinities of demagogues, war criminals and paramilitaries then associated with Serbia abroad (Mitrović 2010). Post-Yugoslav militaries' international public images – even Serbia's, which did not aspire to join NATO – underwent a similar transformation around ideas of gender, violence and peace. Their re-equipment for desert operations, anti-IED protection and compliance with NATO interoperability standards gave them new uniforms that differed from, yet in

Slovenia/Croatia bore the same insignia as, those that denoted heroic defenders of the nation in the 1990s.[31] The evolution of post-Yugoslav militaries' public image was symbolic as well as practical: by participating in NATO interventions overseas, whatever else those meant, post-Yugoslav militaries could access the same reframing of militaries and their masculinities as 'forces for good' (Duncanson 2013) that characterised NATO states' public narratives about militaries in general during the wars in Iraq and Afghanistan.

This reframing also reframed, at least in part, the gender of military participation, with counter-insurgency seeming to require new culturally aware and compassionate military masculinities and NATO adding gender analysts to missions (plus encouraging members to open more military posts to women) after adopting the Women, Peace and Security (WPS) agenda in 2007. Croatia's Kolinda Grabar-Kitarović, assistant NATO secretary-general for public diplomacy in 2011–14, first embodied NATO's WPS commitment as its first female assistant secretary-general, then as Croatian president and commander-in-chief (2015–), and symbolised the evolution of Croatian military prowess since the beginning of the Homeland War (Croatia having now fulfilled Tuđman's goal of joining NATO). Yet WPS itself arguably reinforced 'racial–sexual boundaries' in international security (by perpetuating the frame of 'dangerous brown men' and failing to challenge peacekeeper sexual violence) even as it increased (white) women's equality (Pratt 2013: 772). In this postcolonial feminist perspective, even post-Yugoslav militaries' steps towards gender equality while involved with NATO were also, within deep structures of race, moves in a racialised war.

While post-Yugoslav states' contributions in Iraq/Afghanistan were subjects of public diplomacy, their involvement with the War on Terror within their borders was more covert. Though all post-Yugoslav national identity narratives interpreted the posited existential threat from Islamic terrorism through existing national myths about Islam and the (il)legitimacy of political violence,[32] the covert War on Terror had strongest impact in Bosnia-Herzegovina and Kosovo, which had both the largest proportions of Muslim inhabitants and (through peacekeeping) the largest material US military presence. In Kosovo, the US's Camp Bondsteel, built as headquarters for NATO's multinational force in 1999, was long rumoured to be part of the CIA's global 'extraordinary rendition' network of secret interrogation sites, the covert infrastructure behind the spectacle of US detention at Guantánamo. The Council of Europe's human rights commissioner, Álvaro Gil Robles, alleged this after visiting Bondsteel in 2002, as did the Kosovo ombudsman, Marek Antoni Nowicki, to a European Parliament inquiry into secret US detention sites in 2007 (Carey 2013: 456). The International Committee of the Red Cross sought to hold the Polish, Lithuanian and Romanian states accountable after finding interrogators at several CIA sites in those countries had used torture (Carey 2013: 431). Kosovo's different configuration of sovereignty and accountability, with civil administration performed by the United Nations Interim Administration Mission in Kosovo in 1999–2007, created an 'accountability gap' (Visoka 2012: 190) in international governance and an even more ambiguous space into which detainees might disappear.

Other post-Yugoslav states were implicated in secret detention. The first European Court of Human Rights hearing on secret detention was the mistaken-identity case of Khalid El-Masri, a Lebanese-German man detained by Macedonian police who handed him to the CIA knowing he faced extraordinary rendition to Afghanistan (Carey 2013: 454–5). The Bosnian state's covert co-operation in the War on Terror became international public knowledge in 2004 during the so-called 'Algerian Six' habeas corpus case in the USA, involving six Algerian ex-mujahidin who had become Bosnian citizens and who were detained at Guantánamo in January 2002 after their extradition from Bosnia-Herzegovina.The men's location had been unknown for several weeks after their arrest by Bosnian federal police, though they had been transported to Guantánamo the next day (Maljević 2010: 266–7). Bosnia's existing political problem about mujahidin given citizenship in 1995 gained extra parameters in the War on Terror's international context, anticipating how domestic polemics about Islamic militancy would combine with the wider European/international security context when ISIS escalated the jihadist campaign against European cities. Konstantin Kilibarda (2010: 44–5) reads post-Yugoslav co-operation with US interrogation and participation in 'imperialist' military intervention in conjunction with these states' adaptation to EU migration–security standards and their repatriarchalisation of social relations as expressions of the 'racialized subject positions' their collective national selves took up during accession to Euro-Atlantic institutions. These did not simply import the racialised logic of the War on Terror but, like any other transnational policy transfer (see Lendvai and Stubbs 2009), adapted international norms, discourses and practices to local conditions, exemplifying 'race in translation' (Stam and Shohat 2012) yet again.

Individuals from the Yugoslav region nevertheless took up more complexly racialised subject positions within the War on Terror, not just as troops in national militaries but also as civilian employees of the private military contractors supplying security personnel, drivers, firefighters, caterers, construction workers, logistics/IT specialists and other staff to coalition bases across Iraq, Afghanistan and rearguard locations. Such 'Third Country Nationals' (TCNs) are, even in the emerging literature on how gender and race intersect in the everyday security practices of private military security companies that recruit many Western military veterans and Gurkhas (see Chisholm 2015), often invisible, in roles further removed from person-to-person violence that still, in most twentieth-century warfare, would have been performed by state militaries (Li 2015a: 129).

Bosnia-Herzegovina is among ten countries named by Darryl Li (2015a: 129), alongside 'dozens' more all from the Global South, to have furnished significant numbers of TCNs to Iraq/Afghanistan. Its own recent history of military intervention with English as a lingua franca, plus the postsocialist, post-conflict economy's ongoing stagnation, created a stratum of Bosnians with experience of working in militarised, English-speaking settings, and few job prospects at home, who readily found TCN work (Baker 2012: 867). US forces relied on TCNs because their labour was cheaper than US citizens'; because, unlike locally recruited workers, they were not inherently suspected of belonging to local militant groups that were attempting to infiltrate coalition bases (though they could not obtain US citizens' clearance or trust levels either); and because their deaths would go unnoticed in the US, though they often became scandals in their home countries (Moore 2017).[33]

Workers from the Yugoslav region, as so often, occupied an ambiguous place in private contractors' racialised hierarchy. Keith Brown's study of Macedonian labour migration and empire suggests Macedonian and other post-Yugoslav TCNs ranked 'alongside Nepalis, Filipinos, and others whose labor, and lives, carry lower costs than those of "Westerners"' within coalition bases' ethnically and racially stratified configuration of labour and space (Brown 2010: 833). Nationality further inflected workers' exploitation: south and south-east Asian TCNs, for instance, experienced the overcrowding and wage theft to which subcontractors already exposed their co-nationals in other sectors in the Middle East, like construction in Dubai and Qatar (Moore 2017). As in so many past labour migrations from the Yugoslav region, the workers' access to whiteness was contingent and conditional, yet more available than for workers unambiguously racialised as non-white. Brown, inspired by Ann Laura Stoler's tracing of 'imperial ligaments' (Stoler 2006: xii) between Ohio tyre factories and Sumatran rubber plantations, argues through the early-twenty-first-century history of Macedonian TCNs in Iraq and early-twentieth-century labour migration to the USA from today's Republic of Macedonia that Macedonia's history, anthropology and sociology – by implication the whole Yugoslav region's – should contend with (global) empire as much as the more popular and familiar question of nation. This both facilitates and – a step beyond Brown – *requires* scholars of postsocialism explicitly considering the region's position(s) in global formations of race. In 2015–16, another 'refugee crisis' in Europe brought this home.

Race and the Yugoslav region during the refugee crisis

The spectacles of militarised border security, and of grassroots migrant solidarity, produced from the Yugoslav region as Europe's 'refugee crisis' began manifesting in 2015 were not, however newsworthy, as striking a departure in post-Yugoslav relationships with European politics of belonging as they seemed; instead, they intensified and followed the practices and discourses that had already incorporated the region into the EU's (racialised) migration–security nexus after the break-up of Yugoslavia. Across the continent, dominant early-twenty-first-century narratives of 'Europeanness' implicitly and explicitly involved a hierarchical opposition of 'European'/'democratic'/'liberal' values against 'Islam' which was both spatialised (projecting 'European' and 'Muslim' values to different zones of the world or different areas of cities) and racialised (projecting suspicion of Islam on to any brown-skinned body and anyone whose dress and behaviour suggested they practised Islam). These forms of everyday anti-Muslim racism combined the xenophobic opposition to extra-European migration of late-twentieth/early-twenty-first-century European cultural racism with the War on Terror's racialised Islamophobia. Even before hundreds of thousands of refugees fleeing acute and structural violence in Syria, Iraq, Afghanistan, Libya and elsewhere became the centre of a policing and humanitarian spectacle after travelling through south-east Europe in large numbers in 2015, European institutions' geopolitics of migration and security had already drawn in and cut across the Yugoslav region.

The so-called 'refugee crisis' of 2015–16 was also an intensification of existing patterns and policies, not the unexpected equivalent of a natural disaster to which many Europeans likened it. It manifested when an increasing number of refugees arriving in Europe from Syria in particular – 487,000 in January–September 2015, double the whole 2014 figure (Holmes and Castañeda 2016: 12) – combined with maritime migration routes from North Africa that increasingly landed migrants in Greece not Italy, to join others from the Middle East and Afghanistan who came to Greece overland via Turkey. Although the EU's Dublin Convention obliged refugees' first member state of entry to process their asylum claims, Greece (impoverished by the conditions of its EU debt bailout) struggled to provide for them, while many refugees preferred moving onwards towards greater economic prospects and existing diaspora communities in Germany, Austria and Sweden. The EU

Temporary Protection Directive of 2001 – passed after the Yugoslav wars to regularise the relocation of refugees from a catastrophic crisis around EU member states until they could safely return – remained unactivated. News media and 'migration cinema' had already made the overland 'Balkan route' through Macedonia and Serbia towards the EU (its external border now Croatia–Serbia) and Schengen (with key nodes at the Croatian–Slovenian, Croatian–Hungarian and Hungarian–Serbian borders) familiar to post-Yugoslav publics as a route along which smugglers would lead small groups of clandestine migrants into the EU. In summer 2015 the Balkan route's image became publicly visible, internationally mediated and daylit, as columns of refugees walking through post-Yugoslav rural landscapes recalled the 1990s displacements but contained differently racialised bodies.

Post-Yugoslav authorities' responses activated militarised narratives of policing, migration and security already established through participation in EU border fortification. All insisted they should be transit not host countries, indeed created 'hyper-temporary' legal statuses to facilitate refugees' movement north even before Angela Merkel overrode Dublin by appearing to invite refugees directly to Germany (Sardelić 2017: 3). In June 2015, Macedonia introduced a new temporary asylum status giving refugees seventy-two hours to transit the country (from Greece to Serbia) rather than having to make clandestine entry and exit. Those travelling by rail, on railways depleted by state cutbacks during the European financial crisis, gathered at Gevgelija near the Macedonian–Greek border, with by late August up to 1,000 people arriving daily, anxious to get ahead of Hungary's planned new border fence. Images of Macedonian police in camouflage uniforms firing stun-grenades and tear-gas at refugees who had taken direct action to board trains before Hungary closed its border briefly made Gevgelija a site of spectacularised crisis alongside Lampedusa, Kos and Calais. Belgrade, like Budapest's Keleti Station, soon became a major waypoint on the 'Balkan route', where refugees waiting to travel to Budapest first camped in a park by the main bus and railway station, then also at Miksalište, an alternative cultural centre in the Savamala district earmarked by city authorities for gentrification. Volunteers at both sites, near Croatian and Macedonian border-crossings, and in smaller towns through which refugees passed, mobilised to offer refugees food, clothing and information, well beyond what post-Yugoslav states with their few asylum centres had been equipped to provide.

The discourses with which politicians across eastern Europe rejected large numbers of Muslim refugees settling in their countries – even under EU-wide quotas finally agreed in May 2016 – made it indisputable that race and whiteness, not just ethnicity, were integral to national identity construction in early-twenty-first-century postsocialist Europe. Leaders of the Visegrád states, rejecting German proposals for EU-wide refugee relocation, openly argued (citing the Paris, Brussels and Nice shootings and the Cologne sex attack) that Muslim refugees were unacceptable national security risks who could not be integrated into national life. Post-Yugoslav leaders also constructed the scale of migration as a threat to national and European security, but with the important difference that their region was already receiving many refugees: their priority was to establish their countries as transit states not long-term resettlement/relocation destinations. Kolinda Grabar-Kitarović, speaking in September 2015 as Hungary was fencing off its border, drew on transnational discourses about terrorist infiltration in distinguishing 'real refugees' from 'people with forged Syrian passports, who … have other aims in entering the EU' and 'present[ed] a potential security threat'. Even for 'real' refugees, however, Croatia could 'only be part of the transit route' because, amid high rates of unemployment and economic emigration, 'Croatia must take account of its own people and its developmental conditions … We can show a human face, but we must, above all, take care of our own citizens' (Benčić 2015a).

The region's grassroots relief and solidarity movements, meanwhile, recreated alternative geopolitics that both evoked everyday public memories of being refugees and hosts during the Yugoslav wars and had at least potential to revive memories of everyday connections with the Middle East and North Africa that in socialist Yugoslavia had been part of many people's lifeworlds. The largest initiatives, in Belgrade, saw volunteers organise semi-permanent refugee relief centres at 'Info Park', near the stations, and 'Mikser House', in Savamala (Stojić Mitrović 2016). Groups such as Help the Refugees in Macedonia, founded in April 2015 after fourteen Somalis and Afghans were killed while walking on the railway near Veles, and Are You Syrious?, founded in Zagreb that August before expanding into 'an international citizens' initiative … from Serbia to Slovenia', used Facebook and collaborative apps to co-ordinate volunteers and donations, fundraise internationally and inform followers about conditions on the Balkan route – an important service for refugees themselves given states' frequent policy changes. Their voluntarism resembled public responses to the severe 2014 floods in the region, when grassroots solidarities across post-Yugoslav borders had likewise compensated for post-Yugoslav governments' incapacity.

The presence of so many people from Africa and the Middle East in post-Yugoslav cities, especially Belgrade, meanwhile began to evoke memories of everyday Non-Aligned connectivities, which, combined with widespread public memory of 1990s displacement, might have accounted for relatively more welcoming social attitudes towards refugees compared with the Visegrád states'. Fluent speakers of post-Yugoslav languages with heritage knowledge of Arabic, their family histories often a product of Non-Aligned mobilities, were in particular demand as volunteer interpreters and activist-translators. Some were themselves former refugees, such as Saf Alobaidi, a Syrian horticulturist and civil engineer who fled to Serbia in 2007, interpreting in 2015 for the United Nations High Commission for Refugees at the Banja Koviljača refugee centre where he had originally been sent – a centre opened in 1965 for 'exiles from South America and Eastern Europe' seeking asylum in socialist Yugoslavia (Kremer 2015). Others were former Non-Aligned students or their children, such as Tomas Valter, an Assyrian Christian from Basra who came to Yugoslavia to study medicine in 1968, or Rima Aboughazale, whose Lebanese father had moved her family from Belgrade to Beirut before Lebanon's civil war forced them to return. Here, as so often, language contacts (so often overlooked) revealed everyday yet neglected connections between regions that scholarship often keeps separate: the histories behind which languages people communicate in, who performs written/spoken mediation between languages, or how anyone involved came to know the languages they use are windows into the micropolitics of humanitarianism, migration and war (Footitt and Kelly (eds) 2012).

Official reactions to migrant solidarity movements in 2016, however, showed a politics of demobilisation as well as mobilisation around the refugee crisis. Savamala's contentious redevelopment into the 'Belgrade Waterfront', with Emirati finance and the Serbian prime minister Aleksandar Vučić's support, saw masked men clear an area including Miksalište in April 2016. Miksalište, which had helped up to 600 refugees daily, reopened elsewhere two months later but closed due to lack of capacity in July, with Info Park itself having to close in October and more than a thousand refugees camping in unheated buildings over winter (Bjelica and van Bijlert 2016). The very confluence of capital, dispossession, protest and racialised precarity surrounding Savamala was already in play before the refugee crisis: the resettlement of 178 Roma households to peripheries of Belgrade when city authorities cleared their camp under the Gazela bridge for development, and the civil society mobilisations in protest, exemplified the convergence of 'translocal discourses and institutional structures' (Kilibarda 2011: 593) later mediated through the refugee crisis. The lens of global raciality reveals that the Gazela bridge and Savamala were both part of the same 'racialized urban restructuring' (Kilibarda 2011: 593) in Belgrade.

Simultaneously, the region's border management projects and security discourses interacted with racisms elsewhere: the crisis's very course, with states opening or closing borders in response to refugees' changing routes and reported public attitudes to nations acquiring large Muslim communities, depended on complex interactions between many states' authorities, EU institutions and European legal instruments. During the June 2016 Brexit campaign, a controversial UK Independence Party poster, unveiled hours before a white man with neo-Nazi connections killed the Labour MP Jo Cox (a Remain supporter who had lobbied for the UK to accept more refugees), showed a column of mostly male, brown-skinned refugees, as if marching to Britain as invading terrorists, and read 'Breaking Point: the EU has failed us all; we must break free of the EU and take control of our borders'. Its nexus of sovereignty, securitised migration, Islamophobia, race, masculinism and take-back-control discourse epitomised the transnational populist right of 2016. The photograph came from a grassy road near the Slovenian–Croatian border, mobilising a nest of imaginaries of violence and crisis into a fantasy that Maja Lovrenović (2016) summarises as '[r]efugees from the "balkanized" Middle East marching through "the Balkans" to "balkanize" Europe'. In one sense it was entirely removed from the Balkans; in another, it showed the racisms of post-imperial Britain and the Yugoslav region were interdependent, not just parallel.

In 2015–16, the need to situate the Yugoslav region within the politics and mobilities of a refugee crisis at the convergence between the War on Terror's consequences, the suppression of the Arab Revolutions and the effects of colonial and neo-colonial structural violence on people, economies and environments in Africa made explicit what should have been apparent before: a lens limited to 'Europe' could not explain the region's history and the construction of collective identities related to (not 'contained within') it. If, as Peter Gatrell (2016: 2–3) writes, 'future historians [who] write about forced migration in and around the Mediterranean during 2015–16' will need modes of 'thinking through oceans ... beyond the boundedness of the modern nation state', a longue-durée post-Ottoman history, linking the Yugoslav region and Syria–Iraq–Libya throughout the twentieth and twenty-first centuries not just up to the nineteenth, might never have been more timely but is largely still to be told.[34] For the Yugoslav region, and other peripheralised areas where nations were not heavily involved in colonialism as political entities, centring such past and present connections does more than offer the area a global context: it also signals what routes show that race, distinct from yet related to ethnicity and religion, undeniably forms part of identity-making projects in the region.

This holds true both for the 1990s and after 9/11. Indeed, the 1990s convergence of postsocialist ethnonational homogenisation and identification with 'Europe' with transnational discourses of cultural racism in reaction against postcolonial demographic change gave race and whiteness valences that would feed directly into the convergences of the early twenty-first century, between the existing EU migration–security nexus, the War on Terror's further polarisation and securitisation of 'Europe' against 'Islam', and the campaigns of political violence in European cities that militants planned as a result. These were historically specific expressions of racialisation and whiteness, shaped in interaction with other contestations of belonging outside or projected on to the Yugoslav region. The presence of race within post-Yugoslav identity-making, however, was not a novel product of postsocialism; as previous chapters have shown, it had existed as long as, and had deeply informed, notions of nationhood itself.

Notes

1 Even though Pieterse had previously studied Western representations of Africans (1992), he did not explore race in comparing Bosnia, Rwanda and Somalia (1997).
2 Karadžić, so-called 'architect of the Bosnian Genocide' (Donia 2015), was the wartime RS president; Plavšić was one of his vice-presidents. Another psychiatrist, Jovan Rašković, founded the Serb Democratic Party (SDS) in Croatia shortly before Karadžić founded one in Bosnia-Herzegovina (Bjelić 2013: 1).
3 The Sarajevo-born writer Igor Štiks expresses this in his 2006 novel *Elijahova stolica* (*Elijah's Chair*), when a Sarajevan actress tells a Viennese journalist during the siege: 'Today's Europe may, in fact, have its true representatives in Karadžić's army, not us. Karadžić's men are the heralds of the continent's future, of ethnicization, religious hatred, division, of racial purity and resistance to the demographic threats of the racial, national, and religious others. Champions of the new European xenophobia, they are the truly European players on the Balkan playing fields, not us' (Štiks and Elias-Bursać 2016).
4 Though more difficult than for the central European 'Visegrád Group' which many Slovenians considered natural comparators: Slovenia joined the EU with them (2004), but only signed its preliminary 'Europe Agreement' in 1996, whereas Czechoslovakia, Hungary and Poland signed theirs in December 1991 (with new Czech/Slovak agreements in December 1994).
5 Slovenia's 'Chinese migrant' films (see Rucker-Chang 2013) were therefore made against this background. The 2000 rise is particularly striking since 1999 included the Kosovo War.

6 The original Croat Democratic Union (HDZ), founded by Franjo Tuđman (Croatian president 1990–9), held parliamentary power in Croatia throughout the 1990s.
7 Thomas Balmès's 1996 documentary *Bosnia Hotel* follows three Samburu men reflecting on their service as Kenyan peacekeepers in Bosnia-Herzegovina as an intercultural encounter (Ernst-Luseno 1998).
8 Their song 'Unproforci, pazite na ceste' ('UNPROFOR, caution on the roads') threatened UNPROFOR soldiers with anal rape, insulting Nambiar as 'a moustachioed faggot [brkati pederu]' who had 'let the Serbs shit on' him – implying his failure to defend Croatian sovereignty was also a failure of masculinity, possibly even projecting a 'repressed homoerotic fascination with the racial "Other"' (Longinović 2000: 638) on to the abuse.
9 Two Western European analysts called the post-Dayton order a 'European Raj' (Knaus and Martin 2003), causing some controversy in the Bosnia/peacebuilding literature.
10 Germany, India, Jordan and France all contributed 120–165 officers to that cohort, Pakistan 98 and Ghana 86; the USA contributed 228. The IPTF's 31 other contributing states in 1997 mostly sent 30–60 (UNMIBH 1998).
11 Or so it seems – however, late-1990s Tuzla also became the centre of Bosnian hip-hop, a connection deserving further research. The Tuzla-based rapper Edo Maajka's song 'Legenda o Elvisu' ('The Legend of Elvis', 2004) is about the child of a married Bosnian cleaner and an African-American soldier.
12 Kaplan's follow-up *The Coming Anarchy* reported on West Africa with even more essentialised assumptions about the causes of conflict there and even more alarm about their implications for the West (Kaplan 2000).
13 See McGarry (2017: 234) on the precarious status of Kosovar Roma once EU member states expected them to return to Kosovo.
14 In fact there were ten – but Cyprus and Malta both had the smallest populations and were former British colonies, thus were largely excluded from constructions of 'EU enlargement' as a social problem for Britain.
15 One UK study with white Hungarian/Romanian migrants in 2009–11 found they distanced themselves from xenophobia by emphasising their whiteness and Europeanness in interviews so much as to deny discrimination they were actually facing (Fox, Moroşanu and Szilassy 2015).
16 *All* grassroots foreign voluntarism during the Yugoslav wars is under-researched, but see Janković (2012).
17 Sixteen-year-old Kesinović and fifteen-year-old Selimović, whose refugee parents settled in Austria in 1992–5, travelled to Syria in 2014, becoming what Western media frequently called 'poster girls' for the ISIS propaganda strategy of promising very young Muslim women empowerment and fulfilment by separating from their families, settling in ISIS territory, marrying jihadis and raising children who would grow up in the Islamic State. Awaiting them instead was a system of sexualised coercion where they were reportedly forced into sex with arriving male jihadis – treatment to which VRS guards in eastern Bosnia had subjected captured Bosniak women in 1992–5 – while ISIS manipulated their images on social media to inspire other Muslim teenagers

to follow them (Perešin and Cervone 2015: 502). Selimović was missing by the end of 2014, and Kesinović is thought to have been beaten to death in 2015 while escaping from a house in Raqqa.
18 Gornja Maoča near Brčko in north-west Bosnia, home to a Salafist community including former mujahidin, was already a reputed 'Wahhabi village' before it provocatively flew an ISIS flag in 2015.
19 While today's 'Balkan route' primarily connotes movement of people, in the 1990s it implied drugs.
20 Croatia's first immigration detention facility opened at Ježevo in 1996. The 2000 asylum 'crisis' saw Slovenia open a new detention centre at Postojna.
21 This assistance scheme was first called PHARE (Poland and Hungary: Assistance for Restructuring their Economies) and covered eastern European states seeking EU accession, though not Serbia or Montenegro. A dedicated scheme for the Western Balkans – Community Assistance for Reconstruction, Development and Stabilisation – was founded in 2001 covering all Yugoslav successor states except Slovenia, plus Albania. This became the Instrument for Pre-Accession Assistance in 2007. The phrase 'the Western Balkans', as an EU euphemism for ex-Yugoslavia, extended to Albania, generally excluded Slovenia, related increasingly ambiguously to Croatia as Croatia's status changed, and diplomatically avoided evoking 'Yugoslavia' at all.
22 EU assistance was also linked to border security reforms in Libya, where 50 per cent of state border security and surveillance equipment purchases were EU-funded in 2009–11; authorities during the 2011 revolution used this against protestors and rebels in Libyan cities (Bialasiewicz 2012: 859).
23 Schengen permitted citizens (with biometric passports) of Macedonia, Montenegro and Serbia visa-free travel in December 2009, adding Bosnia-Herzegovina and Albania in December 2010.
24 On narratives of present/past Polish encounters with Islam, see Narkowicz and Pędziwiatr (2017). The Visegrád Group comprises the Czech Republic, Slovakia, Poland and Hungary.
25 Yugoslavs *had* of course encountered global racial Otherness in Non-Aligned students (though more were African than east Asian): here, too, the forgetting of Non-Alignment makes Yugoslav history less globally connected than it deserves.
26 Tuđman had signed the Washington Agreements in January 1994, ending the HVO–ARBiH conflict in Bosnia-Herzegovina with this incentive.
27 Romania and Bulgaria joined the EU in 2007.
28 Improvised Explosive Devices (IEDs) were heavily used in both Iraq and Afghanistan against coalition troops.
29 Much further in the background was the history of Yugoslav–Iraqi engineering/construction co-operation under Tito and Saddam (see Kulić 2014).
30 YouTube users uploading montages of Croatian soldiers in Afghanistan alongside montages celebrating Croatian soldiers in the 1990s war also drew such a continuity.
31 Bosnian defence reform had created one integrated military from the three wartime formations; the Serbian military had changed its insignia in 2006 after the separation of Serbia and Montenegro.

32 Some Croatian nationalists would both have denounced Islamic terrorism and celebrated Zvonko Bušić, the Croat émigré hijacker of a 1976 New York–Paris flight, as a patriot fighting for independence from Yugoslavia.
33 These included Iraqi militants' killing of two Macedonian contractors on video in October 2004 (Brown 2010: 816). Killers of a Croatian oil-worker in Egypt in 2015 released an image stating he had been killed 'for his country's participation in the war against the Islamic State' (Withnall 2015).
34 Thanks to Ljubica Spaskovska for prompting this observation.

Conclusion

Even though the Yugoslav region was not an imperial metropole, even though many symbolic geographies of 'Europe' allocate it to Europe's spatial and material periphery, race is part of its social and historical reality. Categorisations of race, processes of racialisation and constructions of collective identity in relation to whiteness have not even simply been a postsocialist phenomenon: accordingly, cultural racism and anti-blackness in the region cannot just be called a product of identification with the symbolic pole of 'Europe' in the late twentieth century as an aspirational alternative to the authoritarianism and financial stagnation of late state socialism. The region's imaginations and fantasies of race, sonically and visually undeniable in the everyday 'cultural archive', nevertheless reveal shifting rather than stable identifications with race, depending on which aspects of the region's historical experience are mediated through which national and collective identities. Disentangling the relationship between ethnicity, nation and race, and recognising the multiple racial formations 'translated' into the region before and during state socialism, explain the region's ambiguous position towards race in postsocialism and the confusion that trying to position the region in global racial politics can often cause. The Yugoslav region is not an anomaly or an exception when it comes to race; it reflects the same 'translations' of race that structure the rest of the world.

And yet, despite important research on 'race' and whiteness in the region (e.g. Bjelić 2009; Kilibarda 2010; Longinović 2011; see also Imre 2005; Todorova 2006), these ideas have played much smaller roles than ethnicity or religion, or even postcolonialism, in mainstream social and cultural theory about the region. Such theory is itself a transnational production, circulating between the region's academic and cultural institutions and foreign universities which are products of colonial legacies and sites of racial struggle; those producing it may be diasporic scholars, exiles, cultural outsiders or still consider themselves living in the same home country. During the Anglophone academy's postcolonial and subaltern turn, which overlapped with the end of state socialism and the Yugoslav wars, this asymmetric relationship led to a decisive theoretical conjunction when scholars brought up in the region but working in the USA applied postcolonial theory to explaining postsocialism (Bakić-Hayden and Hayden 1992; Todorova 1994, 1997; Bakić-Hayden 1995). Postcolonial thought is still closer to the centre of south-east European studies than many other fields.

An image from another discipline which (after the Yugoslav wars) shares many topics with south-east European studies, International Relations, illustrates the comparison. Anna Agathangelou and L. H. M. Ling visualise the power dynamics between IR subfields as if they were the kind of colonial family compound Ann Laura Stoler (2002) describes, with their own spatial politics and intimate inclusions/exclusions. Postcolonial International Relations is among the '"illicit" progeny' outside this 'House of IR', theoretical formations challenging the discipline's foundations from outside rather than bargaining for acceptance inside (Agathangelou and Ling 2004: 32). Postcolonial thought in a 'House of south-east European studies' would not quite be in the father's master bedroom (we might find realist studies of ethnicity and nationalism there), but with studies of identity in the region so deeply informed by theorising the 'Europe'/'Balkans' relationship, 'balkanism' is securely indoors, quite likely settling in upstairs. However, when the history of structural and material violence that globalised 'race' is also the origin of the dominations contested by postcolonial theory, it is even more curious that south-east European studies is full of postcoloniality yet, as a conversation, separate from race.

One route for (re)incorporating race has been mapping the constitutive hierarchical binary of whiteness and blackness on to what the field, informed by postcolonial thought, holds to be the foundational binary of south-east European identity construction: 'Europe' and 'the Balkans'. Some accounts equate the Balkans' marginalisation within Europe – accentuated for more than a century by how migrants from the region have been racialised in destination countries as only conditionally white or within new semi-racialised categories like 'east European' – with blackness itself (Jović Humphrey 2014) – an identification some Non-Aligned Yugoslavs readily made in solidarity with decolonised Africa (Radonjić 2015), and which re-emerged after Yugoslavia, especially in Serbia and Montenegro, for communicating resentment about the region's or country's altered international status. Another route, which goes further in accommodating the region's 'nesting orientalisms' (Bakić-Hayden 1995) where ethnicity and geopolitics intersect, views especially Slovenia, and sometimes Croatia, as sites where late socialist/postsocialist identification with 'Europe' necessarily involved identification with whiteness, giving the orientalised Othering of Roma, Albanians and Serbs racialised as well as ethnicised overtones (Longinović 2011).

Yet even beyond the north-western republics or their Habsburg and Venetian legacies, the Yugoslav region and its associated ethnonational identities have been implicated in racialising Others through civilisational hierarchies linking whiteness to 'European' belonging and modernity and blackness to their imagined opposite. They have also been subjected to racialising judgements themselves. Often, they have been involved in processes of racialisation running 'up' and 'down' simultaneously, even as the region's peripherality in European colonial history and its peripheralisation in the contemporary European economy have been adduced as reasons to disidentify Yugoslavia and its national identities from race. There are thus at least three modes for relating race to the Yugoslav region: a mode of indifference, colour-blindness or – to use the vocabulary of critical race scholars already exposing race in other parts of Europe outside the largest ex-metropoles – 'white innocence' (Wekker 2016); a mode of analogy, likening the marginalisation of part or all of the region through spatialised 'Europe'–'Balkan' hierarchies to racialised marginalisations elsewhere; and a mode of connection, seeing identity-making projects within and projected on to the region as embedded within, not just parallel to, the global circulation and translation of 'race'.

To illustrate these modes, consider how each might develop the phrase with which the anti-essentialist geographer David Campbell (1999) summarises his critique of the linkage between ethnic exclusivism and territory in the ethnopolitical logic of the Bosnian conflict and in the internationally mediated peace agreements that enshrined it: 'apartheid cartography'. The mode of indifference might not even comment on its association between the spatial politics of violence and ethnicity in post-Yugoslav Bosnia-Herzegovina and those of violence and racialisation in apartheid South Africa. The mode of analogy might invite readers to agree, through their moral stance on apartheid, that the effects of territorialised ethnopolitics in Bosnia were similarly illegitimate and deleterious, might more sceptically question whether the separate histories of South African colonialism/apartheid and Balkan nationalism make this an inappropriate comparison, or might view ethnicised Othering in Bosnia as directly equivalent to Western prejudice against racialised minorities.[1] The mode of connection might do even more.

The mode of connection might position apartheid in South Africa *and* ethnonationalism in Bosnia within global formations of thought about ethnicity, race, territory, difference, biological essentialism and the capacity for civilisation; trace links between transnational public mobilisation of civil society against apartheid and foreign journalists' and activists' campaigns for solidarity with embattled Bosnians; ask how structures of thought and feeling produced during the colonisation of South Africa *and* the anti-apartheid movement shaped responses to the Bosnian conflict and its aftermath outside and inside the region; critically interrogate discourses about Bosnians being treated 'like Africans' or 'a Third World country'; or position exclusivist ethnonationalisms in the Yugoslav region, Republika Srpska's genocidal strategy of homogenisation and apartheid's bureaucratic racism within one connected account of race, identity, territory, violence and diplomacy in the twentieth century.[2]

Of all the modes for approaching race and the Yugoslav region, the mode of connection is the most challenging and the most necessary.

Connecting race and the Yugoslav region

Just as anti-racist movements often struggle to discuss 'racism' as structural oppression rather than individual prejudice (Lentin 2004), studies of the Yugoslav region (and eastern European studies in general) struggle to thread together discussions of race. Often, texts and histories where race should come into view are scattered throughout the literature, rather than being connected into the kind of conversation that already exists about modernity, orientalism and postcoloniality in the Balkans. And yet, this well-established conversation can and should be viewed within global raciality – using conceptual tools the field already knows.

'Race', as an ideology and structure of power, is deeply tied to 'civilisation' and 'modernity', to defining self against Other, to essentialised representations of people and places stretched into global hierarchies of space and time (Mills 1997; Mignolo 2000). 'Racialization', as a process, simultaneously makes a temporal judgement, basing 'cultural dimensions of modernity on the foundation of racial hierarchy', and a spatial judgement, ascribing humans wherever they live to essentialised modern or unmodern cultural zones depending on which part of the globe their perceived race attaches them to (Winant 2001: 16). Like postcolonial theorists, critical race theorists are concerned with 'the characterization of oneself by reference to what one is not' (Mills 1997: 43), *'the reliance on difference to produce identity'* (Winant 2001: 16; emphasis original). South-east European studies, having adapted postcolonial theory, knows these dynamics well. Yet critical race scholarship adds a further meaning of 'Europe' to balkanism's 'Europe'/'Balkan' binary. If 'Europeanness' also, at some deep-rooted level, entails a notion of the collective 'self' being ready to rule over racialised Others, aspirations towards 'Europe', however unconsciously, might involve identification with such readiness. This both reframes the balkanism paradigm and destabilises the Yugoslav region's typical position in categories of coloniser/colonised.

Theories of global raciality, moreover, emphasise that racialised domination and whiteness constituted in the past, and still constitute today, a worldwide project, not limited to former imperial metropoles and lands they colonised. To accept, with Charles Mills (2015: 223), that 'white supremacy was global' implies unambiguously that south-east Europe, like any other corner of the planet, has been affected by it and incorporated within it, *even though* a weight of economic and cultural evidence testifies to the region's peripheral and uncertain position within 'Europe' throughout the twentieth and twenty-first centuries' geopolitical reconfigurations. Critical race theory's 'Europe' is a fantasy of civilisation defined against savagery, of self-determination defined against spaces requiring external intervention, of politics and civics (therefore of the city) against the wilderness, all defined according to racialised boundaries projected on to people and territory (Mills 1997: 42). Yet where does a marginalised periphery of Europe fit into the global raciality of Mignolo, Winant or Mills?

The answer is that global raciality accommodates many local racisms. The very structure of white supremacy that Mills calls the 'racial contract', a tacit agreement among whites not to know of racialised Others' suffering, involves not just creating and legitimising systemic inequality between differently racialised groups but also the boundaries of whiteness and non-whiteness altering to tend towards (without predetermining) the 'limited expansion' of whiteness over time: this, for what Mills (1997: 78–9) calls '"borderline" Europeans, white people with a question mark', including 'the Irish, Slavs, Mediterraneans, and above all … Jews', is the ambiguity of racialisation in northern European and settler-colonial societies. '*Intra*-European' forms of racism (Mills 1997: 79; emphasis original) also subdivide European meanings of race. One such is the construction of Nordic and Teutonic races versus more indolent southern European 'races' (typologies juggled by South Slav scientists throughout the early twentieth century so their nations would seem the most ideal blend). Antiziganism, though Mills does not name it, is another, which also depends on its structures not being seen (McGarry 2017: 108). Yet the fact that Mills does not theorise antiziganism specifically, although from east European perspectives it is distinctive enough to need naming and irreducible to discourses about other groups (Imre 2005; Sardelić 2014), suggests south-east (or central) Europe does not raise any further issues for him than the general 'borderline Europeans' question. Indeed, even Said, who inspired the postsocialist translation of postcoloniality, arguably struggled to account for the Western Othering of Eastern Europe (Dix 2015) or even the condition of the late Ottoman Empire (Deringil 2003: 313) at all.[3]

Walter Mignolo and Madina Tlostanova (2006: 210–11), conversely, do recognise 'the colonial and ex-colonial locales of the subaltern empires' and 'the people who were multi-marginalized and denied their voice by Western modernity', including 'the Yugoslavian bundle of contradictions in the Balkans', as experiences that would produce Mignolo's border thinking in the former Second World; the reason it is not more politically powerful, they suggest, is because 'desire to assimilate to the West' won out instead. Unpacking that bundle places state socialism, post-Ottoman heritage and Non-Aligned legacies, as well as after-effects of Austrian, Hungarian and Italian rule, on to the cloth of decolonial thought: but doing so requires integrating theories of global racial formations, 'race in translation' and the 'global colour line' (Vučetić 2013) into the study of state socialism and postsocialism. This requires reckonings south-east European studies rarely make. Where Frantz Fanon (1963: 96 in Bhambra 2014: 31) argues 'the opulence of Europe "has been founded on slavery"', does this include the opulence of Habsburg Zagreb, Venetian Split or independent Ragusa? The opulence of Ottoman Sarajevo? Would Yugoslavia's diplomatic and military assistance to the Algerian Front de Libération Nationale fighting French colonial forces retrospectively exempt the region from complicity in such a legacy? Or did the structures of knowledge, power and not-needing-to-know that have constituted 'global white ignorance' (Mills 2015) since the beginning of Atlantic slavery and the colonisation of the Americas permeate the Yugoslav region – and the rest of state socialist Europe – as they did the rest of the globe?

The answers are complex. For some scholars, balkanism is itself a form of racialisation, driven by identifications with whiteness whether open or unavowed (Longinović 2011). Within the region, especially during Non-Alignment, identifications between Yugoslav/Balkan experiences and African or African-American experiences have often been made in solidarity with victims of racial oppression; and yet for eastern Europeans racialised as white to claim *equivalent* experiences to African-Americans, Afro-Europeans or black African migrants in Europe would ring hollow for historians of global white supremacy: for them, balkanisms, even those projected and enforced by the West, would not have the same history as the racisms that European colonists first articulated to justify the subjugation of indigenous Americans and enslavement of Africans. The history of 'race' and racialisation is nevertheless inseparable from the modern and contemporary meanings of Europeanness on which balkanisms as well as orientalisms rest.

And yet neither socialist and postsocialist Europe in general, post-Ottoman Europe or the Yugoslav region with its extra geopolitics of Non-Alignment are commonly part of the globe, or even the Europe, theorised by critical race scholarship. Stam and Shohat (2012: 80), indeed, sum up US spatialised hierarchies of knowledge production about the world by noting the bounding of 'Latin American/Caribbean', 'Asian/Pacific', 'African' and 'Middle East' studies on one hand, versus western Europe and the US as the 'quietly normative headquarters' that 'strategically mapped' all other areas – yet east European or Soviet studies, equally products of the Cold War, are not even part of their map (Hajdarpašić 2009).[4] Gilroy (2004: 157), writing on European cultural racism, describes common themes in 'European racial nationalisms all the way from Sweden to Rome' – but what of those further east and south? Monica Popescu's suggestion (inspired by a story by the South African writer Ivan Vladislavić, whose paternal grandparents emigrated from Croatia (Warnes 2000: 273)) that 'the figure of translation' could mediate 'post-apartheid and post-communist' critical apparatus (Popescu

2003: 408) did not lead to critical race literature speaking directly about the Yugoslav region unless scholars of the region constructed their own hinge.[5]

One hinge – analogy – provided a title for another significant contribution to south-east European studies at the turn of the millennium: Maple Razsa and Nicole Lindstrom's article on nationalist, liberal and cosmopolitan balkanisms in 1990s Croatia. Razsa and Lindstrom (2004) applied Bakić-Hayden's and Maria Todorova's insights to examples from commentators with different relationships towards Croatian ethnonationalism, collected years after Yugoslavia collapsed, to show balkanism still structured post-Yugoslav national identities in the established successor states. The title, 'Balkan is Beautiful', playing on 'Black is Beautiful', evokes Croatian reclamations, as well as rejections, of 'Balkan' identity. Their parallel rests on how David Theo Goldberg 'writes of race, but [in ways] which could be true of the Balkans' (Razsa and Lindstrom 2004: 650).[6] Goldberg himself writes five years later of '[t]he Balkans, [which] resonate at the margins of Europe with thickly, if complex, ethnoracial undertones' (Goldberg 2009: 26) – but his own typology of twenty-first-century racisms (racial 'Americanization', 'Palestinianization', 'Europeanization', 'Latinamericanization', 'Southafricanization' and 'neoliberalism') offers no place for the Yugoslav region or other postsocialist countries except a Europe defined by the direct colonial activities of its West.

Establishing the globality and plurality of racial formations nevertheless lays ground for balancing the planetary reach of 'race' with the localised racial formations of Habsburg, Venetian and Ottoman rule, of state socialism and Yugoslavia's even more specific state socialist Non-Alignment. These, in Mills's terms, are the region's versions of 'specific subsidiary contracts' (Mills 1997: 24) that constitute any area's position in the global 'racial contract' of white supremacy. That contract is, moreover, '*continually being rewritten*' (Mills 1997: 72; emphasis original) as the racial polity adjusts to systemic crises such as – though Mills even having written on Stalinism (Mills 1994) does not make this explicit – the beginning or end of the Cold War. State socialism's racial exceptionalism, locating race and racism in American capitalism's historic wrongs while detaching race from myths of European civilisation and modernity, was one subsidiary contract (Todorova 2006); the further disidentifications from whiteness contingently available through Yugoslav Non-Aligned anti-colonialism were another.

Whiteness, still, is woven into identity narratives throughout the Yugoslav region – whether unavowed, underneath symbolic geographies contrasting 'Europe' with an Other space, or openly, in antiziganisms or anti-blackness combining ethnicised entitlement to regulate minorities' settlement on national territory with culturally and/or biologically essentialised rationales for why these racialised Others could never assimilate into the nation. Mills's figure of the contract (partially) distinguishing 'signatories' and 'beneficiaries' (Mills 1997: 37) again offers a resolution. While signatories, aware moral and material hierarchies of race and whiteness exist, choose to align themselves with these systems, beneficiaries do not align themselves with the racial contract in the same way – they may even seek to detach themselves from it through 'post-racial' or 'colour-blind' imaginations – but are still its beneficiaries, through structures and legacies dating back before they were born. People from the Yugoslav region racialised as white, and the collective selves they have imagined, may or may not have been signatories of the racial contract; to the extent that they identify with whiteness or it is ascribed to them, they are, nevertheless, among its beneficiaries. Many Yugoslav Communists might have been beneficiaries but not signatories; in postsocialist nationalisms the signatories increased.

And yet – a further complication – the region's inhabitants and ethnic-majority diasporas have not universally been granted full access to whiteness on the same terms as Anglophones and north-western Europeans. Whether through association with primitivised easts and tropicalised souths, through antiziganist ascription, through Islamophobic suspicions of bearded 'Mediterranean-appearance' men, or through markers of language and accent complicating apparently white bodies, the region's ethnic majorities as well as minorities enter the 'white but not quite' category (Agathangelou 2004b: 88) in many Western formations of race. This ambiguity often leads to forms of internalised colonialism that resist one's own Othering by a hegemonic foreign discourse by using those same techniques 'to alienate and demonize [one's] own constructed "others"' (Agathangelou and Ling 1997: 9). This might well be how a lens of global raciality would describe 'nesting orientalisms'.

This ambiguity of whiteness in relation to east European national identities – at certain times, in certain places – simultaneously suggests solidarities across difference. Commenting after the 2016 Brexit referendum on so-called 'post-referendum racism' (rising street harassment and violence against white EU citizens, often Polish, and people of colour), for instance, Akwujo Emejulu argued 'whiteness, even in discussions about racism and anti-racism, can … seemingly de-prioritis[e] the interests and experiences of people of colour' who were already protesting against 'institutionalised Islamophobia', state violence and deportation. Yet Emejulu also distinguished between 'previously "invisible" and privileged white EU migrants', primary addressees of her critique, and '"white" migrants from Eastern Europe who have been and continue to be subject to instutitionalised xenophobia as their labour value is exploited' (Emejulu 2016). Their structural position did not erase or make irrelevant their race, but was not purely determined by skin colour. Such contingencies emerge through studies of and theory from the Yugoslav region and wider state socialist/post-Ottoman Europe, yet are rarely heard in wider Anglophone theoretical production.

Postcoloniality, postsocialism and the politics of knowledge production

The Yugoslav region's most widely read theorist, outside south-east European studies, is the Slovenian philosopher Slavoj Žižek, a Lacanian and critical theorist known both for his postcolonial readings of the 'Europe'/'Balkan' division and for his suspicion of multiculturalism. While Žižek came later to balkanism than Bakić-Hayden or Maria Todorova, he transfers this critique into the field of 'theory' for readers who have not encountered the theoretical production of these Serbian- and Bulgarian-born, US-based women. His 1999 essay 'The spectre of Balkan', for instance, describes the Slovenian antemurale myth, recognises how the European–Balkan boundary shifts in differently nested nationalisms, and (like the literature scholar Vesna Goldsworthy (1998)) views cultural production as the key site where such imaginations and fantasies spread (Žižek 1999).

Žižek connects balkanism to racism in four different ways: its 'rejection of ... Balkan Otherness' in defence of civilisation; its perception of the Balkans as 'the terrain of ethnic savagery' that can only be reconciled by ascribing racism to the Other, not oneself; an 'inverted racism that celebrates the exotic authenticity of the Balkan Other', a fetishisation which for Žižek (as for the film scholar Dina Iordanova (1998)) explains why hedonistic visions of the Balkans in the cinema of directors like Emir Kusturica are so popular; and a 'logic of displaced racism' whereby '[b]ecause Balkan remains a part of Europe and is inhabited by white people, racist clichés that one wouldn't dare use in reference to some African or Asian nation can be freely applied to Balkan'. While some of this is compatible with the Longinović–Bjelić reading of balkanism as racialisation, Žižek's apparently unperceived contradiction between his fourth and second orders of racism lead him to argue that, within the region, Slovenia has been

> most exposed to this displaced racism since it is closest to Western Europe. When, in an interview regarding his [film] 'Underground', Kusturica dismissed Slovenes as a nation of servants, as 'the grooms of the Austrians', no one was bothered by the outright racism of this statement. (Žižek 1999)

There are indeed several relevant critiques of Kusturica: his self-orientalism evoking balkanist stereotypes in response to the Western gaze; the fetishising antiziganist tropes in his portrayals of Balkanness in general, Roma especially; the sympathies with Serb ethnocentricism that saw him leave Sarajevo for Belgrade when the Bosnian conflict began and to support the building up of a pseudo-independent Republika

Srpska, including co-operating with the RS government to build a neotraditional open-air museum, 'Andrićgrad', near Višegrad, where RS forces had worked to eliminate Bosniaks and their post-Ottoman cultural heritage (Halilovich and Phipps 2015: 35–6).[7] Within Bakić-Hayden's, Longinović's or Bjelić's structural terms, however, a Serbian-towards-Slovenian direction of racism would run against south-east Europe's usual north-over-south, west-over-east hierarchies – another instance where racism and ethnicity are not reducible to one another.

Critical race scholars, meanwhile, are highly critical of Žižek's position that liberal multiculturalism is a hegemony that a European anti-capitalist left should resist (see Žižek 2017). Žižek, Stam and Shohat (2012: 120–1) suggest, places multiculturalism itself, not colonial exploitation, at the apex of the global capitalist structures he opposes: by erasing bottom-up coalitions of anti-racist struggle and transversal solidarity that had to emerge before multiculturalism could acquire what little hegemony it has, Žižek can present multiculturalism as a universalising project of the powerful (Stam and Shohat 2012: 120–1). Sara Ahmed (2008) reads Žižek as taking an idea that was developed to challenge against hegemony as if it were hegemony, so he can celebrate freedom to offend as counter-hegemonic – when such deliberate offence actually reinforces the most hegemonic structures.[8] Here, as with his use of balkanism and race, Žižek has inverted the histories and power-structures behind what he critiques in order to produce an outcome akin to 'reverse racism' accusations (Lentin 2004: 31), which equalise, one might even say relativise, forms of discrimination by dehistoricising their origins and structural effects (Bjelić 2002: 21).

Žižek's emphatic, provocative identifications with 'Europe' (which one might expect a Lacanian to reflect on better) themselves encourage theorists to critique him as representing *European* theory. Stam and Shohat (2012: 93–131), for instance, frame both Žižek and the French sociologists Pierre Bourdieu and Loïc Wacquant as examples of European theorists opposing multiculturalism and 'identity politics'. While reading Žižek as a European philosopher, they do not – unlike Bjelić (2009) – additionally situate him as one whose intellectual trajectory passes through the late socialist/postsocialist Slovenian academy. Yet that discursive community is, this book shows, the product of pre-Yugoslav and state socialist racial formations, inflected by the continent-wide peripheralisation of south/eastern Europe and the 'nesting orientalisms' (Bakić-Hayden 1995) of the region's identity constructions. These formations are connected to, though not the same as, the histories of 'race' in the French academy or any other.

When other theorists, mostly women, have already expressed Žižek's main points about the Yugoslav region and spatialised hierarchies of modernity, a book about postcoloniality and south-east Europe need not even spend much time on him. Yet his work is a rare example of theoretical production from and about the region being engaged outside south-east European studies. The multi-layered reading of Žižek above, using both south-east European perspectives on postcoloniality and critical race perspectives on 'Europe' and whiteness, shows the critique of balkanism and the work of global critical race and decolonial studies can be compatible: they are not inherently ranged against each other, even though critical race perspectives unsettle many of south-east European studies' assumptions about 'Europe' by casting Europe as the metropole of colonial violence and the source of racialisation. Situating the Yugoslav region, the Balkans or eastern Europe within global formations of race does not require a flat rejection of the idea that their societies and people have been marginalised or structurally oppressed; not even of the idea they have often been targets rather than beneficiaries of racialisation. Historicising the structural power relationships and legacies of 'race', as Gilroy (2000) does, can globalise the study of identities in the Yugoslav region without inviting the essentialism that much of this field avoids.

More scholars, inspired by struggles for racial equality and black liberation in the West, New Left activism around migrant solidarity and growing feminist engagement with intersectionality, were drawing such connections even as I was writing this book. Yet the groundwork is older. Anikó Imre (2005: 80) already argued in a 2005 chapter for the volume *Postcolonial Whiteness* that 'white supremacy's function in the constitution of East European national identities is rooted much deeper than either these nations' official self-representations or the Western media portrayal of recent ethnic confrontations would suggest'; yet this unambiguous statement had little wider impact.[9] Today's scholarship – including research marginalised scholars would have done earlier if not for institutional obstacles – has existing theoretical argument about race, whiteness and postsocialist identities on which to build, even though so far it has not reframed the discipline's conversations in the way that the 1990s adaptations of Said still make 'Europe'/'Balkan' and 'western'/'eastern' Europe constructions live themes.

This is not to say that postsocialist translations of postcolonialism are static. Queer studies, in particular, have injected new energy into the postsocialism–postcolonialism conjunction, in the footsteps of eastern European feminists using postcolonial theory to explain how post-Cold-War western European feminists had marginalised eastern European women's perspectives (Slavova 2006; Cerwonka 2008; Tlostanova 2010). Robert Kulpa and Joanna Mizielińska's volume *De-Centring Western Sexualities* (Kulpa and Mizielińska (eds) 2011) fitted into a wider queer postcolonial studies framework in critiquing assumptions about 'eastern Europe lagging behind the West' (i.e. assumptions that Western trajectories of LGBTQ politics were the most advanced or only models for sexual and gender minorities' recognition elsewhere). Indeed, Mizielińska and Kulpa (2011: 19) called the volume 'an effect of merging post-communist and post-colonial studies', mirroring how postcolonial queer scholarship critiques spatial–temporal hierarchies of modernity constructed around global homophobia/biphobia/transphobia (see Rao 2014). But would studies of LGBTQ rights claims in eastern Europe, as Melanie Richter-Montpetit (2016) suggests for such claims in general, also ultimately have to account for the history of chattel slavery to connect them into a full global history of rights claims and modernities? If chattel slavery's frameworks of anti-blackness were, as Mills (1997) argues, foundational to modernity and liberalism globally, even these apparently disconnected topics exist not just as analogy/disanalogy but connection, joined through the complex history of appealing to and imagining 'Europe' in which queer politics and so many other domains of life in postsocialist Europe are embedded.[10]

Such connections nevertheless remain exceptions. How many theorists of postsocialism who were not already starting to connect their work to global formations of race, or to listen across difference as intersectional feminism mediated through the (often unremunerated) digital scholarship and activism of women of colour has had to challenge white scholars like myself to do, would have read a volume called *Postcolonial Whiteness* and thus Imre's chapter in 2005, or indeed 2015? The connections for which this book calls have not gone wholly unmade; rather, the wider field has failed to take them up. The reasons why may be a complex set of factors, though in decolonial perspective they would all appear symptoms of an underlying coloniality within academic knowledge production. Postcolonial, decolonial and some feminist critics of postsocialism have argued, like counterparts in the Global South, that white Western European and Anglophone scholarship keeps most of them in roles of 'native informants and silent subalterns' even when its arguments supposedly decentre Europe and the West (Tlostanova, Koobak and Thapar-Björkert 2016: 4). The very 'epistemic ignorance' (Alcoff 2007: 40) of whiteness, the privilege of not-needing-to-know shared by beneficiaries of Mills's 'racial contract', leads most scholars who do not already intend to read and cite theories about it to ignore it or not perceive it. Material exclusions, racialised insofar as are visa regimes and income differentials within and between nations, compound the exclusions within theory itself: precarious scholars (more likely to be minorities) with less time to publish, or prevented by visa requirements from post-doctoral work in institutions with more extensive postcolonial studies and black studies departments, would have taken their work further earlier without those barriers.[11]

The variety of engagements with race and racialisation made by scholars connected to the Yugoslav region, the breadth of diasporic experiences mediating scholars' associations with it, the fragmentations of collective identities witnessed by scholars who became refugees during the Yugoslav wars or grew up abroad within a post-Yugoslav '1.5

generation', all make it difficult to speak singly of 'theory from the Yugoslav region' about race. There is not one theory, but a range; there are multiple ways of situating the region in the post/colonial and post/socialist past and present; even 'from' is a spectrum not a binary. A certain configuration of historical experiences runs in and through the region which cannot be reduced even to 'eastern Europe', 'postsocialist Europe', 'south-east Europe' or the 'Ottoman ecumene', despite overlaps. German-speaking, Italian-speaking and Ottoman racial formations, the legacy of Non-Alignment and how the region's people have been racialised abroad across time all converge into that configuration.

This book, written by a white woman from London, England and Britain, could never be a book of theory 'from' the Yugoslav region anyway, only 'about': degrees of being 'from' the region are many, but none of them belong to me. I am among the scholars whose ethnic heritage is not linked to the region and who often benefit from initial presumptions of objectivity because they are outside the ethnopolitical and ideological (communist against nationalist) biases of which scholars in and connected to the region are more easily accused – although British nationality is no guarantee of objectivity when British scholars' capacity to pick a south-east European ethnonational claim to champion uncritically while denigrating its rivals, with overtones of colonial thinking about martial and partner races, was already evident when the First World War began. Whiteness protects me from the charge of 'identity politics' and bias when speaking about race. If I strive for objectivity in terms of avoiding the moral equivalency of relativism while being equally critical of each post-Yugoslav national position where necessary, I should be just as critical of my own national position, using tools I first learned to develop by applying them to countries that were not my own. This is not an ideologically neutral stance in today's Britain.

Encouraging other scholars of the Yugoslav region to make global raciality as central as ethnicity or social inequality in their research proceeds from, and I hope will feed back into, a drive to connect the region I study and the country where I have always lived and worked into the same cultural and historical processes. Writing at the imperial metropole, this is impossible without accounting for how 'race', racialisation and whiteness have shaped the Yugoslav region as well as Britain, since the global history of slavery and colonialism provides so many of the areas' structural differences. In many other respects – as the politics of entitlement, nationalism, borders, xenophobia and racism showed while Brexit coincided with my writing this book – the UK and Yugoslavia represent two comparable multinational states with severe regional inequalities, and unresolved histories of state and non-state political violence, with many surface parallels when fragmentation has loomed. Their different locations in the history of colonialism – though both are located there – reveal the comparison's limits most clearly (Baker 2016).

Even that limited comparison, however, makes ideas about the Yugoslav region resonate with struggles for racial justice in my own country. Scholarship on post-conflict reconciliation and transitional justice in the region suggests histories of inter-communal violence and exploitation in the past need acknowledging for a society to coexist in social peace in the present, since these divergent narratives and their politics are already social facts; but it suggests these acknowledgements must simultaneously avoid creating simplistic collective paragons and villains, and recognise the demonstrable power imbalances that did shape the war. A 'thick reconciliation' (Helms 2010: 29) in Bosnia-Herzegovina, for instance, where people not only perform everyday social tasks together but understand neighbours' divergent narratives about the conflict across ethnicised and political boundaries, would require more nuanced views of the recent past than the narratives of collective victimhood and guilt dominating Bosnian politics and mainstream media. To avoid simplistic relativisations of 'equal guilt on all sides' (with which Serb politicians in particular have evaded responsibility for the wars), however, it would also have to acknowledge the unequal distribution of resources structuring what each side could achieve (the UN arms embargo disproportionately affected the under-equipped Sarajevo government, without diplomatic and military support from any adjacent state, compared with the VRS or HVO). 'Ethnicity' is not the same as 'race', because the histories of conquest and violence that gave rise to 'race' are so grounded in a specific moment of colonial expansion; but if recognition of historic wrongs is a precondition for social peace after ethnopolitical conflict, how much more must this be the case in a society as implicated in the history of racism, slavery and colonialism as Britain.

Acknowledging the silences of race, colonialism and empire in the British national present, and having already rejected the notion that Britain and the Yugoslav region belong to separate spheres of history (whether those are 'Western'/'Eastern' European or 'postcolonial'/'postsocialist'), makes it impossible *not* to ask how race and whiteness have shaped national identities in the Yugoslav region, where I have so often researched identification with the modernity of 'Europe'. Seeking to answer the challenges to Eurocentrism and 'white ignorance' (Mills 2015) made by current struggles for racial justice inside and outside the university, I come late to questions east European women, including Anikó Imre (2005) and Miglena Todorova (2006), already posed more than ten years ago. If today's conjunction of research on postsocialist racisms, state socialist Non-Alignment and pre-socialist black histories might finally inscribe global raciality as well as ethnicity into post-Yugoslav and east European studies, it stands on these earlier shoulders, and those of scholars in critical race theory and Black European studies whose questions can now be – should always have been – applied to state socialist Europe, the post-Ottoman space and the Yugoslav region. Vedrana Veličković (2012: 173), a literary theorist educated in Belgrade and working in Brighton, asks in her own essay on postsocialism and postcolonialism: 'Let us hope that these interventions will no longer only be made by eastern European scholars'. As younger and older scholars from outside the region join the coalition, let us also hope – or make sure – that the expertise of those who first perceived those interventions could be made remains foundational. (I hope works published before this book will be cited at least as often as this one; I hope a reader who has reached this point will understand why.)

Even among the contingent and contradictory racial formations constituting 'Europe', situating race in the Yugoslav region is complex. The answer, for the imperial fin-de-siècle and the postsocialist, post-9/11 turn of the millennium, must account both for the covertly, sometimes overtly, racialised exclusions of the region and its people within other identity-making projects and for the access to whiteness its ethnic majorities, and national identities based on them, have had through skin colour and through identification with 'Europe' as a space of modernity and civilisation. Simplistically ascribing regions and peoples to history's 'good' or 'bad' box, based on which side of the colonial equation they belong, could only say the Yugoslav region or South Slav national identities have worked both ways. More granular, intersectional and anti-essentialist understandings of power, identity-making and individual and collective histories, however, reveal that – far from the region being outside 'race' – the tools necessary to contextualise it are precisely those that expose how racialisation works the spatial and socio-economic peripheries of Europe and beyond.

The politics of knowledge within global formations of race explain why this has seemed so difficult, confusing, inappropriate or even threatening – compared with the deconstruction of ethnicity in south-east European studies, where even though this represents a controversy rather than a consensus its premises are widely understood. Integrating race, and therefore the global legacies of European colonialism and Atlantic slavery, into studies of the Yugoslav region as deeply as ethnicity and nationalism might centre new questions, subjects and experiences and appear to decentre others – while requiring explicit consideration of how racialisation and whiteness work in contexts where the structural status quo sustains itself through keeping them 'invisible' (Ahmed 2007: 149).

This is so in world politics, where racism militates against empathy with victims of colonial structural violence and with victims of wars which were framed as liberal interventionist necessities but have been resisted as neo-imperialist wars fought amid racialised constructions of security and threat; in discourses that keep 'Europe' coherent as an ideal and legitimise the administrative, material and virtual fortification of European borders; and in knowledge production and the academy. The gap between the mode of analogy and the mode of connection is perhaps the same gap between lenses critiquing racism as individual prejudice – as progressive discourses of tolerance and inclusion have since the late Cold War – and lenses understanding racism as structural not individual, the product of historical and present-day violence and exploitation (Lentin 2004). Where progressive politics – including state socialist anti-imperialism – has often projected a 'racism without racists' (Bonilla-Silva 2013), conflating race and ethnicity in post-Yugoslav – and wider east European – studies has created a postcoloniality without race.

Yet accounting explicitly for race, racialisation and whiteness does not suddenly unmake existing approaches to postsocialist marginalisation and exclusion. Quite the opposite: a field which has already internalised some premises of postcolonial thought might, as Anna Carastathis (2014: 4) suggests to scholars of Greece, be better equipped than other disciplines to situate itself within the global history of race.[12] The spatial hierarchies of modernity versus primitivism which ascribe essentialised stigma through imagined links between people, bodies, cultures and territory are both, for Charles Mills, the basic division of the globe underneath racialised ascriptions of identity and, in south-east European studies, the bases of anthropological, literary and historical accounts of the symbolic construction of the region's ethnicised and socio-economic boundaries. Recognising that global formations of race travel through the region, translated into its own identity-making projects, does not erase the region's own history of imperial subjugation, and does not imply the Balkans have not been, in the past and present, economically, politically and culturally marginalised. If one is already comfortable with 'nesting orientalisms', it is not so far a stretch to conceive of race, or its many formations, as an axis of exclusion nesting even further around others. What needs to be unmade, instead, is the exceptionalism that presupposes the Yugoslav region or postsocialist eastern Europe does not need to be connected into a history of race and coloniality which for centuries has permeated, and depended on permeating, the whole globe. The work of weighing up this balance, in a world of interconnected struggle, can both signal and inspire other ways in which solidarities between and across marginalised people and places are possible, imaginable and necessary.

Notes

1 In contemporary activism south-east Europeans will likely find more scope for building solidarities with the African diaspora through comparisons of periphery, dependence and xenophobia rather than claiming equivalent histories of enslavement – as the violence of chattel slavery, and its effect for the global black diaspora, was unique (Sharpe 2016).
2 See, for instance, Jeremy Crampton's study of 'race mapping and the Balkans' at the Paris Peace Conference in 1919 (Crampton 2006).
3 Hywel Dix (2015: 981), for instance, argues, 'Said appears not to consider the differences or conflations between Western, Eastern, Central and Balkan Europe at all' (wherever their boundaries are) – which has not prevented theorists *from* the Balkans filtering *orientalism* through their own knowledge to produce new theory.
4 The Yugoslav region only appears in a passage mentioning VRS soldiers raping and impregnating Bosniak women to show (counter to a Brazilian national identity myth) that 'miscegenation is the ambiguous product of a painful power-laden process of contact and domination, not something to be praised for its own sake' (Stam and Shohat 2012: 27).
5 With thanks to a reviewer of the book proposal.
6 Razsa and Lindstrom cite Goldberg's *Racist Culture*: 'although race has tended historically to define conditions of oppression, it could, under a culturalist interpretation – and under some conditions perhaps – be the site of a counterassault, a ground or field for launching liberatory projects or from which to expand freedom(s) and open up emancipatory spaces' (Goldberg 1993: 211 in Razsa and Lindstrom 2004: 650).
7 Named after the Yugoslav novelist Ivo Andrić.
8 See Marina Gržinić (2015) recommending Ahmed to scholars of post-Yugoslav identities and gender politics.
9 A few authors on postcoloniality and postsocialism do cite it (Owczarzak 2009; Veličković 2012). Google Scholar, though more limited for non-Anglophone scholarship, lists twenty-one citations, including two on migration cinema in Europe, seven on Hungarian and/or Romanian antiziganism, three on critical whiteness studies, one on postsocialist feminisms and five on postsocialism/postcoloniality (plus duplicates). 'Balkan is Beautiful', published in a well-known area-studies journal by a large English-language publisher

(Razsa and Lindstrom 2004), has eighty-eight citations there though only one year older.
10 With thanks to Melanie Richter-Montpetit for further discussion.
11 Paralleling University College London's 'Why is My Curriculum White?' campaign was 'Why Isn't My Professor Black?' – recognising that exclusions outside the curriculum also affect production and validation of knowledge.
12 Indeed, the margins-to-centre move through which south-east European translations of postcoloniality, taught to white Anglophones and Europeans in Western universities, has equipped researchers trained since the late 1990s to understand their own investments in orientalism and thence coloniality itself deserves recognition.

Bibliography

Aćimović, Draško. 1981. 'Čoček za Mister Bobija'. *RTV revija* (August). www.yugopapir.com/2015/06/makedonska-svadba-decenije-bobby.html (accessed 19 August 2016).

Adebajo, Adekeye. 2016. 'The revolt against the West: intervention and sovereignty'. *Third World Quarterly* 37 (7): 1187–202.

Adrović, Samir. 2013. '"Bogami sam znao da smo crni, ali toliko, ne"'. *Vijesti*, 17 June. www.vijesti.me/vijesti/bogami-sam-znao-da-smo-crni-ali-toliko-ne-133926 (accessed 29 June 2016).

Agathangelou, Anna M. 2004a. 'Gender, race, militarization, and economic restructuring in the former Yugoslavia and at the U.S.–Mexico border'. In *Women and Globalization*, ed. Delia D. Aguilar and Anne E. Lacsamana: 347–86. Amherst, NY: Humanity Books.

Agathangelou, Anna M. 2004b. *The Global Political Economy of Sex: Desire, Violence and Insecurity in Mediterranean Nation States*. London and New York: Routledge.

Agathangelou, Anna M., and L. H. M. Ling. 1997. 'Postcolonial dissidence within dissident IR: transforming master narratives of sovereignty in Greco-Turkish Cyprus'. *Studies in Political Economy* 54 (1): 7–38.

Agathangelou, Anna M., and L. H. M. Ling. 2004. 'The house of IR: from family power politics to the poisies of worldism'. *International Studies Review* 6 (4): 21–49.

Agathangelou, Anna M., and L. H. M. Ling. 2009. *Transforming World Politics: From Empire to Multiple Worlds*. London and New York: Routledge.

Ahmed, Sara. 2007. 'A phenomenology of whiteness'. *Feminist Theory* 8 (2): 149–68.

Ahmed, Sara. 2008. '"Liberal multiculturalism is the hegemony – it's an empirical fact": a response to Slavoj Žižek'. *Dark Matter*, 19 February. www.darkmatter101.org/site/2008/02/19/%E2%80%98liberal-multiculturalism-is-the-hegemony-%E2%80%93-its-an-empirical-fact%E2%80%99-a-response-to-slavoj-zizek/ (accessed 4 November 2016).

Ahmed, Sara. 2015. 'Introduction: sexism – a problem with a name'. *New Formations* 86: 5–13.

Al-Ali, Nadje. 2002. 'Gender relations, transnational ties and rituals among Bosnian refugees'. *Global Networks* 2 (3): 249–62.

Alcoff, Linda Martín. 1998. 'What should white people do?'. *Hypatia* 13 (3): 6–26.

Alcoff, Linda Martín. 2007. 'Epistemologies of ignorance: three types'. In *Race and Epistemologies of Ignorance*, ed. Shannon Sullivan and Nancy Tuana: 39–58. Albany, NY: SUNY Press.

Alden, Chris, Sally Morphet and Marco Antonio Vieira. 2010. *The South in World Politics*. Basingstoke: Palgrave Macmillan.

Alim, H. Samy, Awad Ibrahim and Alastair Pennycook (eds). 2008. *Global Linguistic Flows: Hip Hop Cultures, Youth Identities, and the Politics of Language*. London and New York: Routledge.

Alleyne, Mike. 1998. '"Babylon makes the rules": the politics of reggae crossover'. *Social and Economic Studies* 47 (1): 65–77.

Andrijasevic, Rutvica. 2007. 'Beautiful dead bodies: gender, migration and representation in anti-trafficking campaigns'. *Feminist Review* 86 (1): 24–44.

Anthias, Floya, and Nira Yuval-Davis. 1993. *Racialized Boundaries: Race, Nation, Gender, Colour and Class and the Anti-Racist Struggle*. London and New York: Routledge.

Archer, Rory, Igor Duda and Paul Stubbs. 2016. 'Bringing class back in: an introduction'. In *Social Inequalities and Discontent in Yugoslav Socialism*, ed. Rory Archer, Igor Duda and Paul Stubbs: 1–20. London and New York: Routledge.

Armitage, David. 2001. 'The red Atlantic'. *Reviews in American History* 29 (4): 479–86.

Babović, Jovana. 2015. 'Belgrade's "black star": gender, race, and Josephine Baker in interwar Yugoslavia'. Paper presented at the Association for Slavonic, East European and Eurasian Studies convention, Philadelphia, 21 November.

Bach, Ulrich E. 2016. *Tropics of Vienna: Colonial Utopias of the Habsburg Empire*. Oxford: Berghahn.

Bain, Zara. 2015. 'Contract, cognition, ideology: understanding the foundations of Charles W. Mills's "white ignorance"'. Paper presented at SWAP/MAP 10th Anniversary Conference on the Work of Charles W. Mills, Florida State University, 27 March.

Baker, Catherine. 2008. 'Wild dances and dying wolves: simulation, essentialization, and national identity at the Eurovision Song Contest'. *Popular Communication* 6 (3): 173–89.

Baker, Catherine. 2010. *Sounds of the Borderland: Popular Music, War and Nationalism in Croatia since 1991*. Farnham: Ashgate.

Baker, Catherine. 2012. 'Prosperity without security: the precarity of interpreters in postsocialist, postconflict Bosnia-Herzegovina'. *Slavic Review* 71 (4): 849–72.

Baker, Catherine. 2013. 'Language, cultural space and meaning in the phenomenon of "Cro-dance"'. *Ethnologie française* 43 (2): 313–24.

Baker, Catherine. 2015. *The Yugoslav Wars of the 1990s*. London: Palgrave Macmillan.

Baker, Catherine. 2016. 'Brexit has echoes of the break-up of Yugoslavia'. *EUROPP: European Politics and Policy*, 5 July. http://blogs.lse.ac.uk/europpblog/2016/07/05/brexit-echoes-yugoslavia/ (accessed 8 November 2016).

Bakić-Hayden, Milica. 1995. 'Nesting orientalisms: the case of former Yugoslavia'. *Slavic Review* 54 (4): 917–31.

Bakić-Hayden, Milica, and Robert M. Hayden. 1992. 'Orientalist variations on the theme "Balkans": symbolic geography in recent Yugoslav cultural politics'. *Slavic Review* 51 (1): 1–15.

Baldwin, Kate A. 2002. *Beyond the Color Line and the Iron Curtain: Reading Encounters Between Black and Red, 1922–1963*. Durham, NC: Duke University Press.

Baldwin, Kate A. 2016. *The Racial Imaginary of the Cold War Kitchen: From Sokol'niki Park to Chicago's South Side*. Hanover, NH: Dartmouth College Press.

Balibar, Étienne. 2004. *We, the People of Europe?: Reflections on Transnational Citizenship*. Trans. James Swenson. Princeton, NJ: Princeton University Press.

Balibar, Etienne, and Immanuel Wallerstein. 1991. *Race, Nation, Class: Ambiguous Identities*. Trans. Chris Turner. London: Verso.

Ballantyne, Tony, and Antoinette Burton (eds). 2005. *Bodies in Contact: Rethinking Colonial Encounters in World History*. Durham, NC: Duke University Press.

Ballinger, Pamela. 2004. '"Authentic hybrids" in the Balkan borderlands'. *Current Anthropology* 45 (1): 31–60.

Bancroft, Angus. 2001. 'Closed spaces, restricted places: marginalisation of Roma in Europe'. *Space and Polity* 5 (2): 145–57.

Banić Grubišić, Ana. 2011. 'Kulturni identitet kao afirmacija manjinske grupe: romske hip-hop'. In *Kulturni identiteti kao nematerijalno kulturno nasleđe: zbornik radova sa naučnog skupa Kulturni identiteti u XXI veku*, ed. Bojan Žikić: 93–110. Belgrade: Odeljenje za etnologiju i antropologiju Filozofskog fakulteta Univerziteta u Beogradu.

Banks, Marcus, and Monica Wolfe Murray. 1999. 'Ethnicity and reports of the 1992-95 Bosnian conflict'. In *The Media of Conflict: War Reporting and Representations of Ethnic Violence*, ed. Tim Allen and Jean Seaton: 147-61. London: Zed.

Barker, Martin. 1981. *The New Racism: Conservatives and the Ideology of the Tribe*. London: Junction Books.

Bartulin, Nevenko. 2008. 'The ideology of nation and race: the Croatian Ustasha regime and its policies towards the Serbs in the Independent State of Croatia 1941-1945'. *Croatian Studies Review* 5: 75-102.

Bartulin, Nevenko. 2009. 'The ideal Nordic-Dinaric racial type: racial anthropology in the Independent State of Croatia'. *Review of Croatian History* 5 (1): 189-219.

Bartulin, Nevenko. 2013. *Honorary Aryans: National-Racial Ideology and Protected Jews in the Independent State of Croatia*. Basingstoke: Palgrave Macmillan.

Bartulin, Nevenko. 2014. *The Racial Idea in the Independent State of Croatia: Origins and Theory*. Leiden: Brill.

Begg, Moazzam. 2007. *Enemy Combatant: The Terrifying True Story of a Briton in Guantanamo*. London: Simon and Schuster.

Behnke, Andreas (ed.). 2016. *The International Politics of Fashion: Being Fab in a Dangerous World*. London and New York: Routledge.

Bellamy, Alex J. 2003. *The Formation of Croatian National Identity: A Centuries-Old Dream?* Manchester and New York: Manchester University Press.

Benčić, Luka. 2015a. 'Hrvatska će pomoći i brinuti se o izbjeglicama: ali sigurnost hrvatskih građana je na prvom mjestu'. *Jutarnji list*, 17 September.

Benčić, Luka. 2015b. 'Modni mačci s Kantride: igrači promoviraju morčić: "Rijeka je turistički grad i ovi dresovi su turistički suvenir"'. *Jutarnji list*, 30 October. www.jutarnji.hr/sport/modni-macci-s-kantride-igraci-promoviraju-morcic-%E2%80%98rijeka-je-turisticki-grad-i-ovi-dresovi-su-turisticki-suvenir%E2%80%99/181162/ (accessed 10 July 2016).

Bhabha, Homi K. 1994. *The Location of Culture*. London and New York: Routledge.

Bhambra, Gurminder K. 2014. *Connected Sociologies*. London: Bloomsbury Academic.

Bialasiewicz, Luiza. 2012. 'Off-shoring and out-sourcing the borders of EUrope: Libya and EU border work in the Mediterranean'. *Geopolitics* 17 (4): 843-66.

Bilge, Sirma. 2013. 'Intersectionality undone: saving intersectionality from feminist intersectionality studies'. *Du Bois Review* 10 (2): 405-24.

Bilić, Bojan, and Sanja Kajinić. 2016a. 'LGBT activist politics and intersectionality in Croatia and Serbia: an introduction'. In *Intersectionality and LGBT Activist Politics: Multiple Others in Croatia and Serbia*, ed. Bojan Bilić and Sanja Kajinić: 1–30. London: Palgrave Macmillan.

Bilić, Bojan, and Sanja Kajinić (eds). 2016b. *Intersectionality and LGBT Activist Politics: Multiple Others in Croatia and Serbia*. London: Palgrave Macmillan.

Biondich, Mark. 2002. 'Persecution of Roma–Sinti in Croatia, 1941–1945'. In *Roma and Sinti: Under-Studied Victims of Nazism*, ed. Paul A. Shapiro and Robert M. Ehrenreich: 33–48. Washington, DC: United States Holocaust Memorial Museum.

Birt, Yahya, and Sadek Hamid. 2014. 'Jihadi movements in the United Kingdom'. In *Islamic Movements of Europe*, ed. Frank Peter and Rafael Ortega: 171–3. London: Tauris.

Bjelić, Dušan I. 2002. 'Introduction: blowing up the "bridge"'. In *Balkan as Metaphor: Between Globalization and Fragmentation*, ed. Dušan I. Bjelić and Obrad K. Savić: 1–22. Cambridge, MA: MIT Press.

Bjelić, Dušan I. 2009. 'The Balkans: radical conservatism and desire'. *South Atlantic Quarterly* 108 (2): 53–72.

Bjelić, Dušan I. 2013. *Normalizing the Balkans: Geopolitics of Psychoanalysis and Psychiatry*. Farnham: Ashgate.

Bjelić, Dušan I. 2014. 'Toward a racial genealogy of the Great War'. *The Disorder of Things*, 3 November. http://thedisorderofthings.com/2014/11/03/toward-a-racial-genealogy-of-the-great-war/ (accessed 20 June 2016).

Bjelić, Dušan I. 2016. 'The class–nation ambiguity and the post-communist war of races'. Paper presented at the Association for Slavonic, East European and Eurasian Studies annual convention, Washington DC, 17–20 November.

Bjelić, Dušan I. 2017. 'Bulgaria's Zionism, the colonization of Palestine and the question of Balkan postcoloniality'. *Interventions* 19 (2): 218–37.

Bjelić, Dušan I., and Obrad K. Savić (eds). 2002. *Balkan as Metaphor: Between Globalization and Fragmentation*. Cambridge, MA: MIT Press.

Bjelica, Jelena, and Martine van Bijlert. 2016. 'Afghan exodus: notes from a Belgrade squat'. *Afghanistan Analysts Network*, 30 November. www.afghanistan-analysts.org/afghan-exodus-notes-from-a-belgrade-squat/ (accessed 5 January 2017).

Blagojević, Gordana. 2009. 'Savremeni stereotipi Srba o Kinezima u Beogradu: "kada kažeš Kina, mislim na Blok 70 ili …"'. *Zbornik Matice srpske za društvene nauke* 128: 47–61.

Blakely, Allison. 1986. *Russia and the Negro: Blacks in Russian History and Thought.* Washington, DC: Howard University Press.

Blanchard, Pascal, Gilles Boëtsch and Nanette Jacomijn Snoep. 2011. 'Human zoos: the invention of the savage'. In *Human Zoos: The Invention of the Savage*, ed. Pascal Blanchard, Gilles Boëtsch and Nanette Jacomijn Snoep: 20–53. Arles: Actes Sud.

Blažević, Robert, and Amina Alijagić. 2010. 'Antižidovstvo i rasno zakonodavstvo u fašističkoj Italiji, nacističkoj Njemačkoj i ustaškoj NDH'. *Zbornik Pravnog fakulteta Sveučilišta u Rijeci* 31 (2): 879–916.

Blumi, Isa. 2011a. 'Neither eastern nor welcome: the confused lives of Berlin's Balkan migrants, 1950–2000'. In *The German Wall: Fallout in Europe*, ed. Marc Silberman: 145–64. Basingstoke: Palgrave Macmillan.

Blumi, Isa. 2011b. *Reinstating the Ottomans: Alternative Balkan Modernities, 1800–1912.* Basingstoke: Palgrave Macmillan.

Boatcă, Manuela. 2006. 'No race to the swift: negotiating racial identity in past and present eastern Europe'. *Human Architecture* 5 (1): 91–104.

Bolin, Göran. 2006. 'Visions of Europe: cultural technologies of nation-states'. *International Journal of Cultural Studies* 9 (2): 189–206.

Bondarenko, Dimitri M., Elena A. Googueva, Sergey N. Serov and Ekaterina V. Shakhbazyan. 2009. '"Postsocialism meets postcolonialism": African migrants in the Russian capital'. *Anthropological Journal of European Cultures* 18 (2): 87–105.

Bonfiglioli, Chiara. 2012. 'Revolutionary networks: women's political and social activism in Cold War Italy and Yugoslavia (1945–1957)'. PhD thesis, Utrecht University.

Bonilla-Silva, Eduardo. 2013. *Racism Without Racists: Color-Blind Racism and the Persistence of Racial Inequality in America.* 4th ed. Lanham, MD: Rowman and Littlefield.

Bonnett, Alastair. In press. 'Multiple racializations in a multiply modern world'. *Ethnic and Racial Studies.* www.tandfonline.com/doi/full/10.108 0/01419870.2017.1287419 (accessed 30 April 2017).

Borstelmann, Thomas. 2001. *The Cold War and the Color Line: American Race Relations in the Global Arena.* Cambridge, MA: Cambridge University Press.

Bosanac, Jana. 2004. 'Transkulturacija u glazbi: primjer hrvatskog hip hopa'. *Narodna umjetnost* 41 (2): 105–22.

Bošković, Aleksandar. 1997. 'Vinko Paletin's discovery of the New World'. *Anthropos* 92 (1–3): 200–5.

Bošković, Aleksandar. 2006. 'Balkan ghosts revisited: racism – Serbian style'. *Anthropos* 101 (2): 559–64.

Bougarel, Xavier. 2007. 'Bosnian Islam as "European Islam": limits and shifts of a concept'. In *Islam in Europe: Diversity, Identity and Influence*, ed. Aziz al-Azmeh and Effie Fokas: 96–124. Cambridge: Cambridge University Press.

Bougarel, Xavier, Elissa Helms and Ger Duijzings (eds). 2007. *The New Bosnian Mosaic: Identities, Memories, and Moral Claims in a Post-War Society*. Farnham: Ashgate.

Bozic-Vrbancic, Senka. 2005. '"After all, I am partly Māori, partly Dalmatian, but first of all I am a New Zealander"'. *Ethnography* 6 (4): 717–42.

Bozic-Vrbancic, Senka. 2006. 'Mysterious degrees of whiteness: stereotypes about Croats in colonial New Zealand'. *Revija za sociologiju* 37 (3–4): 181–92.

Bracewell, Wendy. 2011. 'Lovrich's joke: authority, laughter and savage breasts in an 18th-c. travel polemic'. *Études balkaniques* 2–3: 224–49.

Bradley, Mark Philip. 2010. 'Decolonization, the global South, and the Cold War, 1919–62'. In *The Cambridge History of the Cold War*, vol. 1, ed. Melvyn P. Leffler and Odd Arne Westad: 464–85. Cambridge: Cambridge University Press.

Brooks, Daphne A. 2010. '"This voice which is not one": Amy Winehouse sings the ballad of sonic blue(s)face culture'. *Women and Performance* 20 (1): 37–60.

Brooks, Daphne A. 2011. 'Nina Simone's triple play'. *Callaloo* 34 (1): 176–97.

Brown, Jacqueline Nassy. 2009. *Dropping Anchor, Setting Sail: Geographies of Race in Black Liverpool*. Princeton, NJ: Princeton University Press.

Brown, Keith. 2010. 'From the Balkans to Baghdad (via Baltimore): labor migration and the routes of empire'. *Slavic Review* 69 (4): 816–34.

Brubaker, Rogers. 1996. *Nationalism Reframed: Nationhood and the National Question in the New Europe*. Cambridge: Cambridge University Press.

Brubaker, Rogers. 2004. *Ethnicity Without Groups*. Cambridge, MA: Cambridge University Press.

Buchanan, Donna A. (ed.). 2007. *Balkan Popular Culture and the Ottoman Ecumene: Music, Image, and Regional Political Discourse*. Lanham, MD: Scarecrow Press.

Burton, Antoinette. 1996. 'Contesting the zenana: the mission to make "lady doctors" for India, 1874–1885'. *Journal of British Studies* 35 (3): 368–97.

Burton, Antoinette. 2007. 'Not even remotely global? Method and scale in world history'. *History Workshop Journal* 64 (1): 323–8.

Byrne, Jeffrey James. 2015. 'Beyond continents, colours, and the Cold War: Yugoslavia, Algeria, and the struggle for non-alignment'. *International History Review* 37 (5): 912–32.

Campbell, David. 1999. 'Apartheid cartography: the political anthropology and spatial effects of international diplomacy in Bosnia'. *Political Geography* 18 (4): 395–435.

Campbell, David. 2002. 'Atrocity, memory, photography: imaging the concentration camps of Bosnia: the case of ITN versus *Living Marxism*, Part 2'. *Journal of Human Rights* 1 (2): 143–72.

Campt, Tina M. 1993. 'Afro-German cultural identity and the politics of positionality: contests and contexts in the formation of a German ethnic identity'. *New German Critique* 58: 109–26.

Campt, Tina M. 2004. *Other Germans: Black Germans and the Politics of Race, Gender, and Memory in the Third Reich*. Ann Arbor, MI: University of Michigan Press.

Canka, Mustafa. 2013. 'Only memories and emptiness remain: the history of Ulcinj's Afro-Albanian community in Montenegro'. *LeftEast*, 30 September. www.criticatac.ro/lefteast/only-memories-and-emptiness-remain-the-history-of-ulcinjs-afro-albanian-community-in-montenegro/ (accessed 21 December 2016).

Car, Maja. 2015. 'Voljela bih malo podići lice, ali još mi je strah'. *Večernji list*, 20 September. www.vecernji.hr/estrada/voljela-bih-malo-podici-lice-ali-jos-me-strah-nisam-ludakinja-koja-misli-da-mozes-zaustaviti-starenje-1025552 (accessed 11 August 2016).

Carastathis, Anna. 2014. 'Is Hellenism an Orientalism? Reflections on the boundaries of "Europe" in an age of austerity'. *Critical Race and Whiteness Studies* 10 (1). www.acrawsa.org.au/files/ejournalfiles/214Carastathis201413.pdf (accessed 7 January 2017).

Carew, Joy Gleason. 2015. 'Black in the USSR: African diasporan pilgrims, expatriates and students in Russia, from the 1920s to the first decade of the twenty-first century'. *African and Black Diaspora* 8 (2): 202–15.

Carey, Henry Frank. 2013. 'The domestic politics of protecting human rights in counter-terrorism: Poland's, Lithuania's, and Romania's secret detention centers and other east European collaboration in extraordinary rendition'. *East European Politics and Societies* 27 (3): 429–65.

Carlos, Marjon. 2015. 'Rita Ora's not black, but her hair sure thinks she is'. *Fusion*, 26 May. http://fusion.net/story/138506/rita-oras-not-black-but-her-hair-sure-thinks-she-is/ (accessed 14 October 2016).

Cederberg, Maja. 2005. 'Everyday racism in Malmö, Sweden: the experiences of Bosnians and Somalis'. PhD thesis, Nottingham Trent University.

Cervinkova, Hana. 2012. 'Postcolonialism, postsocialism and the anthropology of east-central Europe'. *Journal of Postcolonial Writing* 48 (2): 155–63.

Cerwonka, Allaine. 2008. 'Traveling feminist thought: difference and transculturation in central and eastern European feminism'. *Signs* 33 (4): 809–32.

Césaire, Aimé. 2000 [1972]. *Discourse on Colonialism*. Trans. Joan Pinkham. New York: Monthly Review Press.

Chakrabarty, Dipesh. 2000. *Provincializing Europe: Postcolonial Thought and Historical Difference*. Princeton, NJ: Princeton University Press.

Chang, Felix B. 2013a. 'The Chinese under Serbian laws'. In *Chinese Migrants in Russia, Central Asia and Eastern Europe*, ed. Felix B. Chang and Sunnie T. Rucker-Chang: 153–83. London and New York: Routledge.

Chang, Felix B. 2013b. 'Myth and migration: Zhejiangese merchants in Serbia'. In *Chinese Migrants in Russia, Central Asia and Eastern Europe*, ed. Felix B. Chang and Sunnie T. Rucker-Chang: 137–52. London and New York: Routledge.

Chang, Felix B., and Sunnie T. Rucker-Chang (eds). 2013. *Chinese Migrants in Russia, Central Asia and Eastern Europe*. London and New York: Routledge.

Chari, Sharad, and Katherine Verdery. 2009. 'Thinking between the posts: postcolonialism, postsocialism, and ethnography after the Cold War'. *Comparative Studies in Sociology and History* 51 (1): 6–34.

Chatterjee, Partha. 1993. *The Nation and its Fragments: Colonial and Postcolonial Histories*. Princeton, NJ: Princeton University Press.

Chin, Rita. 2007. *The Guest Worker Question in Postwar Germany*. Cambridge: Cambridge University Press.

Chisholm, Amanda. 2015. 'Postcoloniality and race in global private security markets'. In *The Routledge Handbook of Private Security Studies*, ed. Rita Abrahamsen and Anna Leander: 177–86. London and New York: Routledge.

Ciarlo, David. 2011. *Advertising Empire: Race and Visual Culture in Imperial Germany*. Cambridge, MA: Harvard University Press.

Clarkson, Alexander. 2008. 'Home and away: immigration and political violence in the Federal Republic of Germany, 1945–90'. *Cold War History* 8 (1): 1–21.

Colic-Peisker, Val. 2005. '"At least you're the right colour": identity and social inclusion of Bosnian refugees in Australia'. *Journal of Ethnic and Migration Studies* 31 (4): 615–38.

Colic-Peisker, Val. 2008. *Migration, Class and Transnational Identities: Croatians in Australia and America*. Urbana, IL: University of Illinois Press.

Collins, Patricia Hill. 2011. 'What is "critical" about critical racial theory?'. In *The Routledge Handbook of Contemporary Social and Political Theory*, ed. Gerard Delanty and Stephen P. Turner: 160–76. London and New York: Routledge.

Collins, Patricia Hill, and Sirma Bilge. 2016. *Intersectionality*. Cambridge: Polity.

Čolović, Ivan. 1994. *Bordel ratnika: folklor, politika i rat*. Belgrade: XX vek.

Čolović, Ivan. 2006. *Etno: priče o muzici sveta na Internetu*. Belgrade: XX vek.

Condry, Ian. 2007. 'Yellow B-Boys, black culture, and hip-hop in Japan: toward a transnational cultural politics of race'. *Positions: East Asia Cultures Critique* 15 (3): 637–71.

Crampton, Jeremy W. 2006. 'The cartographic calculation of space: race mapping and the Balkans at the Paris Peace Conference of 1919'. *Social and Cultural Geography* 7 (5): 731–52.

Crenshaw, Kimberlé. 1991. 'Mapping the margins: intersectionality, identity politics, and violence against women of color'. *Stanford Law Review* 43 (6): 1241–99.

Croegaert, Ana. 2015. '#BiHInSolidarity/Be in solidarity: Bosnian Americans, Islam, and whiteness in post-9/11 America'. *North American Dialogue* 18 (2): 63–76.

Čupković, Gordana. 2015. 'Diachronic variations of slurs and levels of derogation: on some regional, ethnic, and racial slurs in Croatian'. *Language Sciences* 52: 215–30.

Cvjetičanin, Biserka. 1979. 'Kontinuitet i dinamičnost afričkih kultura'. *Naše teme* 23 (3): 785–95.

Daniel, Ondřej. 2007. '*Gastarbajteri*: rethinking Yugoslav economic migrations towards the European north-west through transnationalism and popular culture'. In *Imagining Frontiers, Contesting Identities*, ed. Steven G. Ellis and Luďa Klusáková: 277–302. Pisa: Pisa University Press.

Dauphinée, Elizabeth. 2013. 'Writing as hope: reflections on *The Politics of Exile*'. *Security Dialogue* 44 (4): 347–61.

Davidson, Basil. 1992. *The Black Man's Burden: Africa and the Curse of the Nation-State*. New York: Times Books.

Denning, Michael. 2015. *Noise Uprising: The Audiopolitics of a World Musical Revolution*. London: Verso.

Deringil, Selim. 2003. '"They live in a state of nomadism and savagery": the late Ottoman Empire and the post-colonial debate'. *Comparative Studies in Society and History* 45 (2): 311–42.

Deroo, Éric, and Pierre Fournié. 2011. 'From postcard to cinematograph: inventing reality'. In *Human Zoos: The Invention of the Savage*, ed. Pascal Blanchard, Gilles Boëtsch and Nanette Jacomijn Snoep: 268–91. Arles: Actes Sud.

Dević, Ana. 1997. 'Anti-war initiatives and the unmaking of civic identities in the former Yugoslav republics'. *Journal of Historical Sociology* 10 (2): 127–56.

Dević, Ana. 2016. 'What nationalism has buried: Yugoslav social scientists on the crisis, grassroots powerlessness and Yugoslavism'. In *Social Inequalities and Discontent in Yugoslav Socialism*, ed. Rory Archer, Igor Duda and Paul Stubbs: 21–37. London and New York: Routledge.

DiAngelo, Robin. 2011. 'White fragility'. *International Journal of Critical Pedagogy* 3 (3). http://libjournal.uncg.edu/index.php/ijcp/article/view/249%3E (accessed 3 January 2017).

Dittmer, Jason. 2010. *Popular Culture, Geopolitics, and Identity*. Lanham, MD: Rowman and Littlefield.

Dix, Hywel. 2015. 'On Balkanism and Orientalism: undifferentiated patterns of perception in literary and critical representations of Eastern Europe'. *Textual Practice* 29 (5): 973–91.

Djokić, Dejan (ed.). 2003. *Yugoslavism: Histories of a Failed Idea, 1918–1992*. London: Hurst.

Djokić, Dejan. 2007. *Elusive Compromise: A History of Interwar Yugoslavia*. London: Hurst.

Dokić Mrša, Sanja, and Nataša Miljević Jovanović. 2015. 'Like fun: kvantitetno-kvalitativna analiza zabavnog programa u BiH'. *In Medias Res: časopis filozofije medija* 4 (7): 1112–19.

Donia, Robert. 2015. *Radovan Karadžić: Architect of the Bosnian Genocide*. Cambridge: Cambridge University Press.

Dragićević-Šešić, Milena. 1994. *Neofolk kultura: publika i njene zvezde*. Novi Sad: Izdavačka knjižarnica Zorana Stojanovića.

Dragović-Soso, Jasna. 2007. 'Why did Yugoslavia disintegrate? An overview of contending explanations'. In *State Collapse in South-Eastern Europe: New Perspectives on Yugoslavia's Disintegration*, ed. Lenard J. Cohen and Jasna Dragović-Soso: 1–39. West Lafayette, IL: Purdue University Press.

Du Bois, W. E. B. 1994 [1903]. *The Souls of Black Folk*. New York: Dover.

Dudziak, Mary L. 2000. *Cold War Civil Rights: Race and the Image of American Democracy*. Princeton, NJ: Princeton University Press.

Dulić, Tomislav. 2006. 'Mass killing in the Independent State of Croatia, 1941–1945: a case for comparative research'. *Journal of Genocide Research* 8 (3): 255–81.

Duncanson, Claire. 2013. *Forces for Good? Military Masculinities and Peacebuilding and Afghanistan and Iraq*. Basingstoke: Palgrave Macmillan.

Dyer, Richard. 1997. *White: Essays on Race and Culture*. London and New York: Routledge.

Dzenovska, Dace. 2013. 'Historical agency and the coloniality of power in postsocialist Europe'. *Anthropological Theory* 13 (4): 394–416.

Eastmond, Marita. 1998. 'Nationalist discourses and the construction of difference: Bosnian Muslim refugees in Sweden'. *Journal of Refugee Studies* 11 (2): 161–81.

El-Tayeb, Fatima. 2011. *European Others: Queering Ethnicity in Postnational Europe*. Minneapolis, MN: University of Minnesota Press.

Emejulu, Akwujo. 2016. 'On the hideous whiteness of Brexit: "let us be honest about our past and our present if we truly seek to dismantle white supremacy"'. *Verso Books Blog*, 28 June. www.versobooks.com/blogs/2733-on-the-hideous-whiteness-of-brexit-let-us-be-honest-about-our-past-and-our-present-if-we-truly-seek-to-dismantle-white-supremacy (accessed 2 November 2016).

Enstad, Nan. 2016. 'Smoking hot: cigarettes, jazz, and the production of global imaginaries in interwar Shanghai'. In *Audible Empire: Music, Global Politics, Critique*, ed. Ronald Radano and Tejumola Olaniyan: 45–65. Durham, NC: Duke University Press.

Erdeljac, Filip. 2015. 'Ordinary people, extraordinary times: everyday life in Karlovac under Ustasha rule'. In *The Utopia of Terror: Life and Death in Wartime Croatia*, ed. Rory Yeomans: 61–85. Rochester, NY: University of Rochester Press.

Erjavec, Karmen, and Zala Volčič. 2007. 'Recontextualizing traumatic pasts: Croatian justification of war crimes in Bosnia-Herzegovina'. *Global Media Journal: Mediterranean Edition* 2 (1): 10–22. http://globalmedia.emu.edu.tr/images/stories/ALL_ARTICLES/2007/spring2007/ErjavecVolcicWordComplete2.pdf (accessed 12 October 2016).

Erlmann, Veit. 1999. *Music, Modernity and the Global Imagination: South Africa and the West*. Oxford: Oxford University Press.

Ernst-Luseno, Heidi. 1998. 'Review: *Bosnia Hotel*: Kenyan warriors in Bosnia'. *American Anthropologist* 100 (4): 1021–2.

Essed, Philomena. 1991. *Understanding Everyday Racism: An Interdisciplinary Theory*. London: Sage.

Evans, Daniel. 1985. 'Slave coast of Europe'. *Slavery and Abolition* 6 (1): 45–58.

Faist, Thomas. 2006. 'The migration–security nexus: international migration and security before and after 9/11'. In *Migration, Citizenship, Ethnos*, ed. Y. Michal Bodemann and Gökçe Yurkadul: 103–19. Basingstoke: Palgrave Macmillan.

Fanon, Frantz. 1963. *The Wretched of the Earth*. Trans. Constance Farrington. New York: Grove Press.

Fanon, Frantz. 1986 [1952]. *Black Skin, White Masks*. Trans. Charles Lam Markmann. London: Pluto.

Fekete, Liz. 2004. 'Anti-Muslim racism and the European security state'. *Race and Class* 46 (1): 3–29.

Fekete, Liz. 2009. *A Suitable Enemy: Racism, Migration and Islamophobia in Europe*. London: Pluto.

Fierke, K. M., and Wiener, Antje. 1999. 'Constructing institutional interests: EU and NATO enlargement'. *Journal of European Public Policy* 6 (5): 721–42.

Fikes, Kesha, and Alaina Lemon. 2002. 'African presence in former Soviet spaces'. *Annual Review of Anthropology* 31: 497–524.

Fine, John V. A., Jr. 2006. *When Ethnicity Did Not Matter in the Balkans: A Study of Identity in Pre-Nationalist Croatia, Dalmatia, and Slavonia in the Medieval and Early-Modern Periods*. Ann Arbor, MI: University of Michigan Press.

Flessenkemper, Tobias, and Tobias Bütow. 2011. 'Building and removing visa walls: on European integration of the Western Balkans'. *Sicherheit und Frieden* 29 (3): 162–8.

Footitt, Hilary, and Michael Kelly (eds). 2012. *Languages at War: Policies and Practices of Language Contacts in Conflict*. Basingstoke: Palgrave Macmillan.

Fox, Jon E., Livia Moroşanu and Eszter Szilassy. 2012. 'The racialization of the new European migration to the UK'. *Sociology* 46 (4): 680–95.

Fox, Jon E., Livia Moroşanu and Eszter Szilassy. 2015. 'Denying discrimination: status, "race", and the whitening of Britain's new Europeans'. *Journal of Ethnic and Migration Studies* 41 (5): 729–48.

Frankenberg, Ruth. 1993. *White Women, Race Matters: The Social Construction of Whiteness*. Minneapolis, MN: University of Minnesota Press.

Franz, Barbara. 2015. 'Popjihadism: why young European Muslims are joining the Islamic State'. *Mediterranean Quarterly* 26 (2): 5–20.

Fryer, Peter. 1984. *Staying Power: The History of Black People in Britain*. London: Pluto.

Fuchs, Brigitte. 2011. 'Orientalizing disease: Austro-Hungarian policies of "race", gender, and hygiene in Bosnia and Herzegovina, 1874–1914'. In *Health, Hygiene and Eugenics in Southeastern Europe to 1945*, ed. Christian Promitzer, Sevasti Trubeta and Marius Turda: 57–85. Budapest: CEU Press.

Gagnon, V. P., Jr. 2004. *The Myth of Ethnic War: Serbia and Croatia in the 1990s*. Ithaca, NY: Cornell University Press.

Gal, Susan, and Gail Kligman. 2000. *The Politics of Gender after Socialism*. Princeton, NJ: Princeton University Press.

Garner, Steve. 2007. *Whiteness: An Introduction*. London and New York: Routledge.

Garner, Steve. 2010. *Racisms: An Introduction*. London: Sage.

Gatrell, Peter. 2016. 'Refugees – what's wrong with history?'. *Journal of Refugee Studies* 30 (2): 170–89.

Gille, Zsuzsa. 2010. 'Is there a global postsocialist condition?'. *Global Society* 24 (1): 9–30.

Gilman, Sander L. 1982. *On Blackness Without Blacks: Essays on the Image of the Black in Germany*. Boston, MA: G. K. Hall.

Gilman, Sander L. 1985. *Difference and Pathology: Stereotypes of Sexuality, Race, and Madness*. Ithaca, NY: Cornell University Press.

Gilroy, Paul. 1987. *There Ain't No Black in the Union Jack: The Cultural Politics of Race and Nation*. London and New York: Routledge.

Gilroy, Paul. 1993. *The Black Atlantic: Modernity and Double Consciousness*. London: Verso.

Gilroy, Paul. 2000. *Between Camps: Nations, Cultures and the Allure of Race*. London: Penguin.

Gilroy, Paul. 2004. *After Empire: Melancholia or Convivial Culture?* London and New York: Routledge.

Giovannetti, Jorge L. 2006. 'Grounds of race: slavery, racism and the plantation in the Caribbean'. *Latin American and Caribbean Ethnic Studies* 1 (1): 5–36.

Giraldo, Isis. 2016. 'Coloniality at work: decolonial critique and the postfeminist regime'. *Feminist Theory* 17 (2): 157–73.

Glajar, Valentina. 2001. 'From *Halb-Asien* to Europe: contrasting representations of Austrian Bukovina'. *Modern Austrian Literature* 34 (1–2): 15–35.

Goebel, Michael. 2016. '"The capital of the men without a country": migrants and anticolonialism in interwar Paris'. *American Historical Review* 121 (5): 1444–67.

Gökay, Bülent, and Lily Hamourtziadou. 2016. '"Whiter than white": race and otherness in Turkish and Greek national identities'. *Journal of Balkan and Near Eastern Studies* 18 (2): 177–89.

Goldberg, David Theo. 1993. *Racist Culture: Philosophy and the Politics of Meaning*. Cambridge, MA: Blackwell.

Goldberg, David Theo. 2009. *The Threat of Race: Reflections on Racial Neoliberalism*. Oxford: Blackwell.

Goldstein, Ivo. 2003. 'The Catholic Church in Croatia and the "Jewish problem", 1918–1941'. *East European Jewish Affairs* 33 (2): 121–34.

Goldsworthy, Vesna. 1998. *Inventing Ruritania: The Imperialism of the Imagination*. London: Hurst.

Golež Kaučić, Marjetka. 2002. 'The Slovenian ballad at the turn of the millennium'. *Lied und populäre Kultur* 47: 157–69.

Goral, Pawel. 2014. *Cold War Rivalry and the Perception of the American West*. Basingstoke: Palgrave Macmillan.

Gordy, Eric D. 1999. *The Culture of Power in Serbia: Nationalism and the Destruction of Alternatives*. University Park, PA: Pennsylvania State University Press.

Greer, Margaret R., Walter D. Mignolo and Maureen Quilligan. 2007. 'Introduction'. In *Rereading the Black Legend: The Discourses of Religious and Racial Difference in the Renaissance Empires*, ed. Margaret R. Greer, Walter D. Mignolo and Maureen Quilligan: 1–26. Chicago, IL: University of Chicago Press.

Grünenberg, Kristina. 2005. 'Constructing "sameness" and "difference": Bosnian diasporic experiences in a Danish context'. *Balkanologie* 9 (1–2): 173–93.

Gržinić, Marina. 2015. 'Sara Ahmed and the analysis of critical whiteness and racism in post-former-Yugoslavia'. In *European Theories in Former Yugoslavia: Trans-Theory Relations between Global and Local Discourses*, ed. Miško Šuvaković, Žarko Cvejić and Andrija Filipović: 46–51. Cambridge: Cambridge Scholars Publishing.

Gubar, Susan. 1997. *Racechanges: White Skin, Black Face in American Culture*. Oxford: Oxford University Press.

Guberina, Petar. 1961. 'Tragom afričke crnačke kulture'. *Naše teme* 5 (7): 985–1019.

Guild, Elspeth (ed.). 2014. 'Going nowhere? Western Balkan Roma and visa liberalisation'. Special issue of *Roma Rights* 1. www.errc.org/cms/upload/file/roma-rights-1-2014-going-nowhere-western-balkan-roma-and-eu-visa-liberalisation.pdf (accessed 27 March 2017).

Gülçür, Leyla, and Pınar İlkkaracan. 2002. 'The "Natasha" experience: migrant sex workers from the former Soviet Union and eastern Europe in Turkey'. *Women's Studies International Forum* 25 (4): 411–21.

Gupta, Akhil. 1992. 'The song of the Nonaligned world: transnational identities and the reinscription of space in late capitalism'. *Cultural Anthropology* 7 (1): 63–79.

Gye, Hugo. 2013. 'Is this the most tasteless talent show performance ever? Greek pop star "blacks up" to perform as Stevie Wonder'. *Daily Mail*, 1 August. www.dailymail.co.uk/news/article-2382432/Greek-pop-star-Mando-blacks-Stevie-Wonder-Your-Face-Sounds-Familiar.html (accessed 14 October 2016).

Habel, Ylva. 2005. 'To Stockholm, with love: the critical reception of Josephine Baker, 1927–35'. *Film History* 17 (1): 125–38.

Habel, Ylva. 2012. 'Challenging Swedish exceptionalism? Teaching while black'. In *Education in the Black Diaspora: Perspectives, Challenges, and Prospects*, ed. Kassie Freeman and Ethan Johnson: 99–122. London and New York: Routledge.

Hadžiahmetović, J. 2011. 'Video: reper Smooth Deep: Sarajevo je moja inspiracija'. *Klix.ba*, 29 December. www.klix.ba/vijesti/bih/reper-smooth-deep-sarajevo-je-moja-inspiracija/111228101 (accessed 16 December 2016).

Hajdarpašić, Edin. 2009. 'Locations of knowledge: area studies, nationalism, and "theory" in Balkan Studies since 1989'. *Kakanien Revisited*, 17 July. www.kakanien-revisited.at/beitr/balkans/EHajdarpasic1.pdf (accessed 6 January 2017).

Hale, Charles. 1999. 'Travel warning: elite appropriations of hybridity, *mestizaje*, antiracism, equality, and other progressive-sounding discourses in highland Guatemala'. *Journal of American Folklore* 112 (445): 297–315.

Halilovich, Hariz. 2013. *Places of Pain: Forced Displacement, Popular Memory and Trans-local Identities in Bosnian War-Torn Communities*. Oxford: Berghahn.

Halilovich, Hariz, and Peter Phipps. 2015. 'Atentat! Contested histories at the one hundredth anniversary of the Sarajevo assassination'. *Communication, Politics and Culture* 48 (3): 29–40.

Hall, Stuart. 1993. 'What is this "black" in black popular culture?'. *Social Justice* 20 (1–2): 104–14.

Hall, Stuart. 1996 [1987]. 'Minimal selves'. In *Black British Cultural Studies: A Reader*, ed. Houston A. Baker Jr, Manthia Diawara and Ruth H. Lindeborg: 114–19. Chicago, IL: University of Chicago Press.

Hall, Stuart. 1997. 'The spectacle of the "Other"'. In *Representation: Cultural Representations and Signifying Practices*, ed. Stuart Hall: 225–79. London: Sage.

Hanke, Lewis. 1964. 'More heat and some light on the Spanish struggle for justice in the conquest of America'. *Hispanic American Historical Review* 44 (3): 293–340.

Hansen, Lene. 2006. *Security as Practice: Discourse Analysis and the Bosnian War*. London and New York: Routledge.

Haritaworn, Jin. 2015. *Queer Lovers and Hateful Others: Regenerating Violent Times and Places*. London: Pluto.

Harrington, Carol. 2005. 'The politics of rescue: peacekeeping and anti-trafficking programmes in Bosnia-Herzegovina and Kosovo'. *International Feminist Journal of Politics* 7 (2): 175–206.

Harris, Max, and Lada Čale Feldman. 2003. 'Blackened faces and a veiled woman: the early Korcula moreska'. *Comparative Drama* 37 (3–4): 297–320.

Haynes, Dina Francesca. 2008. 'Lessons from Bosnia's Arizona Market: harm to women in a neoliberalized postconflict reconstruction process'. *University of Pennsylvania Law Review* 158: 1779–829.

Hegghammer, Thomas. 2010. 'The rise of Muslim foreign fighters: Islam and the globalization of jihad'. *International Security* 35 (3): 53–94.

Helbig, Adriana. 2014. *Hip Hop Ukraine: Music, Race, and African Migration*. Bloomington, IN: Indiana University Press.

Helms, Elissa. 2008. 'East and west kiss: gender, orientalism, and balkanism in Muslim-majority Bosnia-Herzegovina'. *Slavic Review* 67 (1): 88–119.

Helms, Elissa. 2010. 'The gender of coffee: women and reconciliation initiatives in post-war Bosnia and Herzegovina'. *Focaal* 57: 17–32.

Helms, Elissa. 2013. *Innocence and Victimhood: Gender, Nation, and Women's Activism in Postwar Bosnia-Herzegovina*. Madison, WI: University of Wisconsin Press.

Herza, Filip. 2016. 'Black Don Juan and the Ashanti from Asch: representations of "Africans" in Prague and Vienna, 1892–1899'. In *Visualizing the Orient: Central Europe and the Near East in the 19th and 20th Centuries*, ed. Adéla Jůnová Macková, Lucie Storchová and Libor Jůn: 95–106. Prague: Academy of Performing Arts in Prague.

Hessler, Julie. 2006. 'Death of an African student in Moscow: race, politics, and the Cold War'. *Cahiers du monde russe* 47 (1): 33–63.

Hirsch, Francine. 2002. 'Race without the practice of racial politics'. *Slavic Review* 61 (1): 30–43.

Hoare, Marko Attila. 2007. *The History of Bosnia: From the Middle Ages to the Present Day*. London: Saqi.

Hockenos, Paul. 2003. *Homeland Calling: Exile Patriotism and the Balkan Wars*. Ithaca, NY: Cornell University Press.

Hofman, Ana. 2015. 'Music (as) labour: professional musicianship, affective labour and gender in socialist Yugoslavia'. *Ethnomusicology Forum* 24 (1): 28–50.

Holmes, Seth M., and Heide Castañeda. 2016. 'Representing the "European refugee crisis" in Germany and beyond: deservingness and difference, life and death'. *American Ethnologist* 43 (1): 12–24.

Hong, Young-Sun. 2015. *Cold War Germany, the Third World, and the Global Humanitarian Regime*. Cambridge: Cambridge University Press.

Hooks, Bell. 1992. *Black Looks: Race and Representation*. Boston, MA: South End Press.

Hozić, Aida. 2016. 'Tito's journey(s) through Africa: race and nation in international politics'. Paper presented at Racialized Realities in World Politics, *Millennium* conference, LSE, 22–3 October.

Hromadžić, Azra. 2015. *Citizens of an Empty Nation: Youth and State-Making in Post-War Bosnia-Herzegovina*. Philadelphia, PA: University of Pennsylvania Press.

Hund, Wulf D. 2013. 'Advertising white supremacy: capitalism, colonialism and commodity racism'. In *Colonial Advertising and Commodity Racism*, ed. Wulf D. Hund, Michael Pickering and Anandi Ramamurthy: 21–68. Münster: Lit Verlag.

Huntington, Samuel P. 1996. *The Clash of Civilizations and the Remaking of World Order*. New York: Simon and Schuster.

Hutson, Scott R. 1999. 'Technoshamanism: spiritual healing in the rave subculture'. *Popular Music and Society* 23 (3): 53–77.

Huttunen, Laura. 2009. 'Historical legacies and neo-colonial forms of power? A postcolonial reading of the Bosnian diaspora'. In *Complying with Colonialism: Gender, Race and Ethnicity in the Nordic Region*, ed. Suvi Keskinen, Salla Tuori, Sari Irni and Diana Mulinari: 101–16. Aldershot: Ashgate.

Huysmans, Jef. 2000. 'The European Union and the securitization of migration'. *Journal of Common Market Studies* 38 (5): 751–77.

Ignatieff, Michael. 1994. *Blood and Belonging: Journeys into the New Nationalism*. London: Vintage.

Ignatiev, Noel. 1995. *How the Irish Became White*. London and New York: Routledge.

Imre, Anikó. 2005. 'Whiteness in post-socialist eastern Europe: the time of the Gypsies, the end of race'. In *Postcolonial Whiteness: A Critical Reader on Race and Empire*, ed. Alfred J López: 79–102. Albany, NY: SUNY Press.

Imre, Anikó. 2006. 'Play in the ghetto: global entertainment and the European "Roma problem"'. *Third Text* 20 (6): 659–70.

Imre, Anikó. 2008. 'Roma music and transnational homelessness'. *Third Text* 22 (3): 325–36.

Imre, Anikó. 2014. 'Postcolonial media studies in postsocialist Europe'. *Boundary 2* 41 (1): 113–34.

Intihar, Simon. 2013. 'Peter Bossman dobrodošel'. YouTube, 3 November. www.youtube.com/watch?v=C45PU2fAXlY (accessed 23 March 2017).

Iordanova, Dina. 1998. 'Balkan film representations since 1989: the quest for admissibility'. *Historical Journal of Film, Radio and Television* 18 (2): 263–80.

Iordanova, Dina. 2001. *Cinema of Flames: Balkan Film, Culture and the Media*. London: BFI.

Iveković, Rada. 2006. 'The general desemantisation: global language and hegemony: *traduire le silence de la plebe*'. *Transversal* 11. http://eipcp.net/transversal/1206/ivecovic/en (accessed 2 January 2017).

Jahoda, Gustav. 2009. 'Intra-European racism in nineteenth-century anthropology'. *History and Anthropology* 20 (1): 37–56.

Janković, Vesna. 2012. 'International peace activists in the former Yugoslavia: a sociological vignette on transnational agency'. In *Resisting the Evil: (Post-) Yugoslav Anti-War Contention*, ed. Bojan Bilić and Vesna Janković: 225–42. Baden-Baden: Nomos.

Jansen, Stef. 2005. 'Who's afraid of white socks? Towards a critical understanding of post-Yugoslav urban self-perceptions'. *Ethnologia Balkanica* 9: 151–67.

Jansen, Stef. 2006. 'The privatisation of home and hope: return, reforms and the foreign intervention in Bosnia-Herzegovina'. *Dialectical Anthropology* 30 (3–4): 177–99.

Jansen, Stef. 2009. 'After the red passport: towards an anthropology of the everyday geopolitics of entrapment in the EU's "immediate outside"'. *Journal of the Royal Anthropological Institute* 15 (4): 815–32.

Jansen, Stef. 2011. '*Refuchess*: locating Bosniac repatriates after the war in Bosnia-Herzegovina'. *Population, Space and Place* 17: 140–52.

Jelača, Dijana. 2014. 'The girl-child, the outlaw, and the land/woman: or how the imaginary of the Western permeated a distant war'. *Cultural Studies/Critical Methodologies* 14 (3): 250–9.

Jelača, Dijana. 2015. 'Feminine libidinal entrepreneurship: towards a reparative reading of the sponzoruša in turbo folk'. *Feminist Media Studies* 15 (1): 36–52.

Jensen, Lars. 2012. 'Danishness as whiteness in crisis: emerging post-imperial and development aid anxieties'. In *Whiteness and Postcolonialism in the Nordic Region: Exceptionalism, Migrant Others and National Identities*, ed. Kristín Loftsdóttir and Lars Jensen: 105–19. Farnham: Ashgate.

Jonjić, Tomislav. 2012. 'Bartulin's tilting at windmills: manipulation as a historiographic method (a reply to Nevenko Bartulin's "Intellectual discourse on race and culture in Croatia 1900–1945")'. *Review of Croatian History* 8 (1): 207–68.

Jović Humphrey, Anja. 2014. 'Aimé Césaire and "another face of Europe"'. *MLN* 129 (5): 1117–48.

Judson, Pieter M. 2007. *Guardians of the Nation: Activists on the Language Frontiers of Imperial Austria*. Cambridge, MA: Harvard University Press.

Kalapoš, Sanja. 2002. *Rock po istrijanski: o popularnoj kulturi, regiji i identiteta*. Zagreb: Jesenski i Turk.

Kallis, Aristotle. 2015. 'Recontextualizing the fascist precedent: the Ustasha movement and the transnational dynamics of interwar fascism'. In *The Utopia of Terror: Life and Death in Wartime Croatia*, ed. Rory Yeomans: 260–83. Rochester, NY: University of Rochester Press.

Kaplan, Paul H. D. 2011. 'Black Turks: Venetian artists and perceptions of Ottoman ethnicity'. In *The Turk and Islam in the Western Eye, 1450–1750: Visual Imagery before Orientalism*, ed. James G. Harper: 41–66. Farnham: Ashgate.

Kaplan, Robert D. 1993. *Balkan Ghosts: A Journey Through History*. New York: St Martin's.

Kaplan, Robert D. 2000. *The Coming Anarchy: Shattering the Dreams of the Post-Cold War*. New York: Vintage.

Kelley, Robin D. G. 1999. 'A poetics of anticolonialism'. *Monthly Review* 51 (6): 1–21.

Kelly, Michael, and Catherine Baker. 2013. *Interpreting the Peace: Peace Operations, Conflict and Language in Bosnia-Herzegovina*. Basingstoke: Palgrave Macmillan.

Kilibarda, Konstantin. 2010. 'Non-aligned geographies in the Balkans: space, race and image in the construction of new "European" foreign policies'. In *Security Beyond the Discipline: Emerging Dialogues on Global Politics*, ed. Abhinava Kumar and Derek Maisonville: 27–57. Toronto: York Centre for International and Security Studies.

Kilibarda, Konstantin. 2011. 'Clearing space: an anatomy of urban renewal, social cleansing and everyday life in a Belgrade *mahala*'. *Cambridge Review of International Affairs* 24 (4): 593–612.

King, Russell, and Nicola Mai. 2008. *Out of Albania: From Crisis Migration to Social Inclusion in Italy*. London: Berghahn.

Kisić-Kolanović, Nada. 2015. 'Envisioning the "Other" East: Bosnia-Herzegovina, Muslims, and modernization in the Ustasha state'. In *The Utopia of Terror: Life and Death in Wartime Croatia*, ed. Rory Yeomans: 188–216. Rochester, NY: University of Rochester Press.

Kljaić, Stipe. 2015. 'Apostles, saints' days, and mass mobilization: the sacralization of politics in the Ustasha state'. In *The Utopia of Terror: Life and Death in Wartime Croatia*, ed. Rory Yeomans: 145–64. Rochester, NY: University of Rochester Press.

Knaus, Gerhard, and Felix Martin. 2003. 'Travails of the European Raj'. *Journal of Democracy* 14 (3): 60–74.

Kočevar, Sanda. 2012. 'Svoj o svome: ondašnji karlovački tisak o karlovačkim putnicima–istraživačima Afrike i Južne Amerike druge polovine XIX. i prve polovine XX. stoljeća'. *Časopis za suvremenu povijest* 44 (1): 93–109.

Kogovšek Šalamon, Neža. 2016. *Erased: Citizenship, Residence Rights and the Constitution in Slovenia*. Frankfurt am Main: Peter Lang.

Kohlmann, Evan. 2004. *Al-Qaida's Jihad in Europe: The Afghan–Bosnian Network*. New York: Berg.

Kolstø, P. I. 2011. 'The Serbian–Croatian controversy over Jasenovac'. In *Serbia and the Serbs in World War Two*, ed. Sabrina P. Ramet and Ola Listhaug: 225–46. Basingstoke: Palgrave Macmillan.

Koobak, Redi, and Raili Marling. 2014. 'The decolonial challenge: framing post-socialist Central and Eastern Europe within transnational feminist studies'. *European Journal of Women's Studies* 21 (4): 330–43.

Korać, Maja. 2013a. 'Transnational entrepreneurs: Chinese in Serbia and their translocal strategies of betterment and incorporation'. In *Diaspora as a Resource: Comparative Studies in Strategies, Networks and Urban Space*, ed. Waltraud Kokot, Christian Giordano and Mijal Gandelsman-Trier: 223–44. Vienna: Lit Verlag.

Korać, Maja. 2013b. 'Transnational pathways to integration: Chinese traders in Serbia'. *Sociologija* 55 (2): 245–60.

Koser, Khalid, and Richard Black. 1999. 'Limits to harmonization: the "temporary protection" of refugees in the European Union'. *International Migration* 37 (3): 521–43.

Kovačec, August. 2005. 'Akademik Petar Guberina'. Zagreb: Hrvatska akademija znanosti i umjetnosti. http://info.hazu.hr/hr/clanovi_akademije/osobne_stranice/pguberina (accessed 19 August 2016).

Kremer, Dragan. 2015. 'Making sure no-one is lost in translation'. *Open Society Foundations Voices*, 30 October. www.opensocietyfoundations.org/voices/making-sure-no-one-lost-translation (accessed 26 October 2016).

Kronja, Ivana. 2001. *Smrtonosni sjaj: masovna psihologija i estetika turbo-folka*. Belgrade: Tehnokratia.

Kronsell, Annica. 2012. *Gender, Sex, and the Postnational Defense: Militarism and Peacekeeping*. Oxford: Oxford University Press.

Kulić, Vladimir. 2009. '"East? West? Or both?" Foreign perceptions of architecture in socialist Yugoslavia'. *Journal of Architecture* 14 (1): 129–47.

Kulić, Vladimir. 2014. 'Building the non-aligned Babel: Babylon Hotel in Baghdad and mobile design in the global Cold War'. *ABE: Architecture Beyond Europe* 6. https://abe.revues.org/924 (accessed 19 August 2016).

Kulpa, Robert, and Joanna Mizielińska (eds). 2011. *De-Centring Western Sexualities: Central and Eastern European Perspectives*. Farnham: Ashgate.

Kunt, Metin Ibrahim. 1974. 'Ethnic-regional (*cins*) solidarity in the seventeenth-century Ottoman establishment'. *International Journal of Middle East Studies* 5: 233–9.

Kurtić, Vera. 2013. *Džuvljarke: Roma Lesbian Existence.* Niš: European Roma Rights Centre. www.errc.org/cms/upload/file/dzuvljarke-roma-lesbian-existence.pdf (accessed 2 December 2016).

Kuus, Merje. 2007. *Geopolitics Reframed: Security and Identity in Europe's Eastern Enlargement.* Basingstoke: Palgrave Macmillan.

Kuzmanić, Tonči. 2002. 'Postsocialism, racism and the reinvention of politics'. In *Xenophobia and Post-Socialism*, ed. Mojca Pajnik: 17–36. Ljubljana: Mirovni institut.

Lalić, Dražen. 2003. *Split kontra Splita.* Zagreb: Jesenski i turk.

Laušić, Ante. 2003. 'Hrvatska katolička misija u službi južnoafričkih Hrvata'. *Migracijske i etničke teme* 19 (2–3): 239–51.

Law, Ian. 2012. *Red Racisms: Racism in Communist and Post-Communist Contexts.* Basingstoke: Palgrave Macmillan.

Lazarević, Alexandra Sanja. 1975. 'Two Croatian travellers in southern Ethiopia: a biographical note'. *Africa: rivista trimestrale di studi e documentazione dell'Istituto italiano per l'Africa e l'Oriente* 30 (4): 596–9.

Lemaire, Sandrine, Guido Abbattista, Nicola Labanca and Hilke Thode-Arora. 2011. 'Travelling villages or the democratisation of the "savage"'. In *Human Zoos: The Invention of the Savage*, ed. Pascal Blanchard, Gilles Boëtsch and Nanette Jacomijn Snoep: 292–317. Arles: Actes Sud.

Lendvai, Noémi, and Paul Stubbs. 2009. 'Assemblages, translation, and intermediaries in south east Europe: rethinking transnationalism and social policy'. *European Societies* 11 (5): 673–95.

Lentin, Alana. 2004. *Racism and Anti-Racism in Europe.* London: Pluto.

Lentin, Alana. 2008. 'Europe and the silence about race'. *European Journal of Social Theory* 11 (4): 487–503.

Li, Darryl. 2015a. 'Offshoring the army: migrant workers and the U.S. military'. *UCLA Law Review* 62: 124–74.

Li, Darryl. 2015b. 'Translator's preface: a note on settler colonialism'. *Journal of Palestine Studies* 45 (1): 69–76.

Li, Darryl. 2016. 'Jihad in a world of sovereigns: law, violence, and Islam in the Bosnia crisis'. *Law and Social Inquiry* 41 (2): 371–401.

Linke, Uli. 1999. *Blood and Nation: The European Aesthetics of Race.* Philadelphia, PA: University of Pennsylvania Press.

Lipsitz, George. 2007. *Footsteps in the Dark: The Hidden Histories of Popular Music.* Minneapolis, MN: University of Minnesota Press.

Lisinski, Hrvoje. 1964. 'Amerika između mit i odluke'. *Naše teme* 8 (12): 1998–2012.

Loftsdóttir, Kristín. 2009. '"Pure manliness": the colonial project and Africa's image in nineteenth century Iceland'. *Identities* 16 (3): 271–93.

Loftsdóttir, Kristín. 2010. 'Becoming civilized: Iceland and the colonial project during the 19th century'. *Kult* 7. www.postkolonial.dk/artikler/kult_7/becoming_civilized.pdf (accessed 5 December 2016).

Loftsdóttir, Kristín, and Helga Björnsdóttir. 2015. 'Nordic exceptionalism and gendered peacekeeping: the case of Iceland'. *European Journal of Women's Studies* 22 (2): 208–22.

Loftsdóttir, Kristín, and Lars Jensen. 2012a. 'Nordic exceptionalism and the Nordic "others"'. In *Whiteness and Postcolonialism in the Nordic Region: Exceptionalism, Migrant Others and National Identities*, ed. Kristín Loftsdóttir and Lars Jensen: 1–12. Farnham: Ashgate.

Loftsdóttir, Kristín, and Lars Jensen (eds). 2012b. *Whiteness and Postcolonialism in the Nordic Region: Exceptionalism, Migrant Others and National Identities*. Farnham: Ashgate.

Longinović, Tomislav. 2000. 'Music wars: blood and song at the end of Yugoslavia'. In *Music and the Racial Imagination*, ed. Ronald Radano and Philip V. Bohlman: 622–43. Chicago, IL: University of Chicago Press.

Longinović, Tomislav Z. 2011. *Vampire Nation: Violence as Cultural Imaginary*. Durham, NC: Duke University Press.

Lopashich, Alexander. 1958. 'A Negro community in Yugoslavia'. *Man* 58: 169–73.

Lopašić, Aleksandar. 1971. *Commissaire General Dragutin Lerman, 1863–1918: A Contribution to the History of Central Africa*. Tervuren: Musée royal de l'Afrique central.

Lordi, Emily J. 2016. 'Souls intact: the soul performances of Audre Lorde, Aretha Franklin, and Nina Simone'. *Women and Performance* 26 (1): 55–71.

Lott, Eric. 1993. *Love and Theft: Blackface Minstrelsy and the American Working Class*. Oxford: Oxford University Press.

Lovrenović, Maja. 2016. 'The Balkans specter of Brexit'. *Confessions from the Field*, 30 June. https://fieldconfessions.wordpress.com/2016/06/30/the-balkans-specter-of-brexit/ (accessed 26 October 2016).

Lubotina, Paul. 2015. 'Corporate supported ethnic conflict on the Mesabi Range, 1890–1930'. *Upper Country: A Journal of the Lake Superior Region* 3 (1): 29–52. http://commons.nmu.edu/upper_country/vol3/iss1/2?utm_source=commons.nmu.edu%2Fupper_country%2Fvol3%2Fiss1%2F2&utm_medium=PDF&utm_campaign=PDFCoverPages (accessed 7 June 2016).

Macdonald, David Bruce. 2003. *Balkan Holocausts? Serbian and Croatian Victim-Centred Propaganda and the War in Yugoslavia*. Manchester: Manchester University Press.

Mackenzie, David. 1984. 'Serbia as Piedmont and the Yugoslav idea, 1804–1914'. *East European Quarterly* 28 (2): 153–83.

Mai, Nick. 2013. 'Embodied cosmopolitanisms: the subjective mobility of migrants working in the global sex industry'. *Gender, Place and Culture* 20 (1): 107–24.

Majstorović, Danijela, and Zoran Vučkovac. 2016. 'Rethinking Bosnia and Herzegovina's post-coloniality: challenges of Europeanization discourse'. *Journal of Language and Politics* 15 (2): 147–72.

Malcolm, Noel. 1998. *Kosovo: A Short History*. London: Papermac.

Maljević, Almir. 2010. 'Extraordinary renditions: shadow proceedings, human rights, and the "Algerian six": the war on terror in Bosnia and Herzegovina'. In *A War on Terror? The European Stance on a New Threat, Changing Laws and Human Rights Implications*, ed. Marianne Wade and Almir Maljević: 261–76. New York: Springer.

Mark, James. 2015. 'Expert cultures, state socialism and global circulation in the Cold War'. Paper presented at the Eastern Europe Without Borders conference, UCL SSEES, 10 November.

Markowitz, Fran. 2010. *Sarajevo: Aa Bosnian Kaleidoscope*. Urbana, IL: University of Illinois Press.

Martin, Charles H. 1997. 'Internationalizing "the American dilemma": the Civil Rights Congress and the 1951 genocide petition to the United Nations'. *Journal of American Ethnic History* 16 (4): 35–61.

Matusevich, Maxim (ed.). 2007. *Africa in Russia, Russia in Africa: Three Centuries of Encounters*. Trenton, NJ: Africa World Press.

Matusevich, Maxim. 2012. 'Expanding the boundaries of the Black Atlantic: African students as Soviet moderns'. *Ab Imperio* 2: 325–50.

Mayblin, Lucy. 2017. *Asylum after Empire: Colonial Legacies in the Politics of Asylum Seeking*. Lanham, MD: Rowman and Littlefield International.

Mazower, Mark. 2002. *The Balkans: From the End of Byzantium to the Present Day*. London: Phoenix.

McClintock, Anne. 1994. 'Soft-soaping empire: commodity racism and imperial advertising'. In *Travellers' Tales: Narratives of Home and Displacement*, ed. George Robertson, Melinda Mash, Lisa Tickner, Jon Bird, Barry Curtis and Tim Putnam: 128–52. London and New York: Routledge.

McClintock, Anne. 1995. *Imperial Leather: Race, Gender, and Sexuality in the Colonial Contest*. London and New York: Routledge.

McGarry, Aidan. 2017. *Romaphobia: the Last Acceptable Form of Racism*. London: Zed.

McGee, Kristin. 2012. 'Orientalism and erotic multiculturalism in popular culture: from Princess Rajah to the Pussycat Dolls'. *Music, Sound, and the Moving Image* 6 (2): 209–38.

Mesarić, Andreja. 2013. 'Wearing *hijab* in Sarajevo: dress practices and the Islamic revival in post-war Bosnia-Herzegovina'. *Anthropological Journal of European Cultures* 22 (2): 12–34.

Mignolo, Walter D. 2000. *Local Histories/Global Designs: Coloniality, Subaltern Knowledges, and Border Thinking*. Princeton, NJ: Princeton University Press.

Mignolo, Walter D. 2008. 'Racism as we sense it today'. *PMLA* 123 (5): 1737–42.

Mignolo, Walter D. 2011. 'Geopolitics of sensing and knowing: on (de)coloniality, border thinking and epistemic disobedience'. *Postcolonial Studies* 14 (3): 273–83.

Mignolo, Water D., and Madina V. Tlostanova. 2006. 'Theorizing from the borders: shifting to geo- and body-politics of knowledge'. *European Journal of Social Theory* 9 (2): 205–21.

Mihelj, Sabina. 2004. 'Negotiating European identity at the periphery: "Slovenian nation", "Bosnian refugees" and "illegal migration"'. In *European Culture and the Media*, ed. Ib Bondebjerg and Peter Golding: 165–89. Bristol: Intellect.

Mihelj, Sabina. 2005. 'To be or not to be a part of Europe: appropriations of the symbolic borders of Europe in Slovenia'. *Journal of Borderlands Studies* 20 (2): 109–28.

Mihelj, Sabina. 2012. 'The dreamworld of new Yugoslav culture and the logic of Cold War binaries'. In *Divided Dreamworlds? The Cultural Cold War in East and West*, ed. Peter Romijn, Giles Scott-Smith and Joes Segal: 97–114. Amsterdam: Amsterdam University Press.

Mills, Charles W. 1994. 'The moral epistemology of Stalinism'. *Politics and Society* 22 (1): 31–57.

Mills, Charles W. 1997. *The Racial Contract*. Ithaca, NY: Cornell University Press.

Mills, Charles W. 2007. 'White ignorance'. In *Race and Epistemologies of Ignorance*, ed. Shannon Sullivan and Nancy Tuana: 11–38. Albany, NY: SUNY Press.

Mills, Charles W. 2015. 'Global white ignorance'. In *The Routledge Handbook of Ignorance Studies*, ed. Matthias Gross and Lindsey McGoey: 217–27. London and New York: Routledge.

Mišina, Dalibor. 2010. '"Spit and sing, my Yugoslavia": New Partisans, social critique and Bosnian poetics of the patriotic'. *Nationalities Papers* 38 (2): 265–89.

Mišina, Dalibor. 2013. *Shake, Rattle and Roll: Yugoslav Rock Music and the Poetics of Social Critique*. Farnham: Ashgate.

Mišković, Nataša. 2009. 'The pre-history of the Non-Aligned Movement: India's first contacts with the Communist Yugoslavia, 1948–50'. *India Quarterly* 65 (2): 185–200.

Mišković, Nataša, Harald Fischer-Tiné and Nada Boskovska (eds). 2014. *The Non-Aligned Movement and the Cold War: Delhi–Bandung–Belgrade*. London and New York: Routledge.

Mitchell, Tony (ed.). 2001. *Global Noise: Rap and Hip-Hop Outside the USA*. Middletown, CT: Wesleyan University Press.

Mitrović, Marijana. 2010. '"New face of Serbia" at the Eurovision Song Contest: international media spectacle and national identity'. *European Review of History* 17 (2): 171–85.

Mizielińska, Joanna, and Robert Kulpa. 2011. '"Contemporary peripheries": queer studies, circulation of knowledge and east/west divide'. In *De-Centring Western Sexualities: Central and Eastern European Perspectives*, ed. Robert Kulpa and Joanna Mizielińska: 11–26. Aldershot: Ashgate.

Modood, Tariq. 2006. 'British Muslims and the politics of multiculturalism'. In *Multiculturalism, Muslims and Citizenship: A European Approach*, ed. Tariq Modood, Anna Triandafyllidou and Ricard Zapata-Barrero: 37–56. London and New York: Routledge.

Mohanty, Chandra Talpade. 1988. 'Under western eyes: feminist scholarship and colonial discourses'. *Feminist Review* 30: 61–88.

Molnar, Christopher A. 2014. 'Imagining Yugoslavs: migration and the Cold War in postwar West Germany'. *Central European History* 47 (1): 138–69.

Molvaer, Reidulf. 2011. 'The Seljan brothers and the expansionist policies of Emperor Minïlik II of Ethiopia'. *International Journal of Ethiopian Studies* 5 (2): 79–90.

Moore, Adam. 2017. 'U.S. military logistics outsourcing and the everywhere of war'. *Territory, Politics, Governance* 5 (1): 5–27.

Morić, Danijela Ana. 1995. 'Ja sam tip "glavom kroz zid"'. *Večernji list*, 14 July.

Morokvasic, Mirjana. 1991. 'Fortress Europe and migrant women'. *Feminist Review* 39: 69–84.

Mostov, Julie. 2000. 'Sexing the nation/desexing the body: politics of national identity in the former Yugoslavia'. In *Gender Ironies of Nationalism: Sexing the Nation*, ed. Tamar Mayer: 89–112. London and New York: Routledge.

Moynihan, Daniel Patrick. 1993. *Pandaemonium: Ethnicity in International Politics*. Oxford: Oxford University Press.

Mujanović, Jasmin. 2017. 'Nothing left to lose: hip hop in Bosnia-Herzegovina'. In *Hip Hop at Europe's Edge: Music, Agency, and Social Change*, ed. Milos Miszczynski and Adriana Helbig: 28–44. Bloomington, IN: Indiana University Press.

Müller, Tanja R. 2014. *Legacies of Socialist Solidarity: East Germany in Mozambique*. Lanham, MD: Rowman and Littlefield.

Muppidi, Himadeep. 2013. 'On *The Politics of Exile*'. *Security Dialogue* 44 (4): 299–313.

Mustapha, Jennifer. 2013. 'The Mujahideen in Bosnia: the foreign fighter as cosmopolitan citizen and/or terrorist'. *Citizenship Studies* 17 (6-7): 742–55.

Narkowicz, Kasia, and Konrad Pędziwiatr. 2017. 'From unproblematic to contentious: mosques in Poland'. *Journal of Ethnic and Migration Studies* 43 (3): 441–57.

Newman, John Paul. 2015. *Yugoslavia in the Shadow of War: Veterans and the Limits of State Building, 1903–1945*. Cambridge: Cambridge University Press.

Novikova, Irina. 2004. 'Black music, white freedom: times and spaces of jazz countercultures in the USSR'. In *Blackening Europe: The African American Presence*, ed. Heike Raphael-Hernandez: 73–86. London and New York: Routledge.

Novikova, Irina. 2013. 'Imagining Africa and blackness in the Russian empire: from extra-textual *arapka* and distant cannibals to Dahomey amazon shows – live in Moscow and Riga'. *Social Identities* 19 (5): 571–91.

Obermeier, Karin. 1989. 'Afro-German women: recording their own history'. *New German Critique* 46: 172–80.

Oberschall, Anthony. 2000. 'The manipulation of ethnicity: from ethnic cooperation to violence and war in Yugoslavia'. *Ethnic and Racial Studies* 23 (6): 982–1001.

Okey, Robin. 2007. *Taming Balkan Nationalism: The Habsburg 'Civilizing Mission' in Bosnia, 1878–1914*. Oxford: Oxford University Press.

Omi, Michael, and Howard Winant. 1994. *Racial Formation in the United States: From the 1960s to the 1990s*. London and New York: Routledge.

Orlović, David. 2012. '"More than a cordial reception": Ethiopian emperor Haile Selassie's visit to Yugoslavia in 1954, with a special reference to the passage to and stay in Croatia'. *Carnival: Journal of the International Students of History Association* 14: 151–65.

Oroz, Tomislav. 2009. 'The Turk on Lastovo: social memory preserved in the legend of a Catalan attack on the island'. In *The Black Arab as a Figure of*

Memory, ed. Kata Kulavkova: 159-77. Skopje: Macedonian Academy of Sciences and Arts.

O'Shea, Brendan. 2005. *The Modern Yugoslav Conflict 1991-1995: Perception, Deception and Dishonesty*. London and New York: Routledge.

Osumare, Halifa. 2012. 'Global breakdancing and the intercultural body'. *Dance Research* 34 (2): 30-45.

Tuathail, Gearóid Ó. 2005. 'Embedding Bosnia-Herzegovina in Euro-Atlantic structures: from Dayton to Brussels'. *Eurasian Geography and Economics* 46 (1): 51-67.

Owczarzak, Jill. 2009. 'Introduction: postcolonial studies and postsocialism in Eastern Europe'. *Focaal* 53: 3-19.

Papović, Jovana, and Astrea Pejović. 2016. 'The potential of popular culture for the creation of left populism in Serbia: the case of the hip-hop collective "The Bombs of the Nineties"'. *Contemporary Southeastern Europe* 3(2): 107-26. www.suedosteuropa.uni-graz.at/cse/sites/default/files/papers/pejovic_papovic_the_bombs_of_the_nineties.pdf (accessed 13 December 2016).

Paternost, Joseph. 1992. 'Symbols, slogans and identity in the Slovene search for sovereignty, 1987-1991'. *Slovene Studies* 14 (1): 51-68.

Pavelić, Boris. 2012. 'Euro Black Nation: hip hop kao izraz marginaliziranih mladih Roma'. *Novi list*, 28 May. www.novilist.hr/Scena/Glazba/Euro-Black-Nation-Hip-hop-kao-izraz-marginaliziranih-mladih-Roma?meta_refresh=true (accessed 14 December 2016).

Perešin, Anita, and Alberto Cervone. 2015. 'The Western *muhajirat* of ISIS'. *Studies in Conflict and Terrorism* 38 (7): 495-509.

Perica, Vjekoslav. 2001. 'United they stood, divided they fell: nationalism and the Yugoslav school of basketball, 1968-2000'. *Nationalities Papers* 29 (2): 267-91.

Perry, Marc D. 2008. 'Global black self-fashionings: hip hop as diasporic space'. *Identities* 15 (6): 635-64.

Petrić, Antonija. 2015. 'Popularna glazba i konstrukcije europskog identiteta: hrvatski predstavnici na Euroviziji'. Master's dissertation, Muzička akademija Zagreb.

Petrović, Đurđica. 1972. 'Crnci u Ulcinju'. *Etnološki pregled* (Cetinje) 10: 31-6.

Petrović, Tanja. 2009. *A Long Way Home: Representations of the Western Balkans in Political and Media Discourses*. Ljubljana: Peace Institute.

Petrović, Vladimir (ed.). 2015. 'Yugoslavia III (Serbia)'. In *The History of East-Central European Eugenics, 1900-1945: Sources and Commentaries*, ed. Marius Turda: 473-516. London: Bloomsbury Academic.

Pettan, Svanibor. 1998a. 'Music, politics and war in Croatia in the 1990s: an introduction'. In *Music, Politics, and War: Views from Croatia*, ed. Svanibor Pettan: 9–27. Zagreb: IEF.

Pettan, Svanibor (ed.). 1998b. *Music, Politics and War: Views from Croatia*. Zagreb: IEF.

Pettan, Svanibor. 2010. *Lambada na Kosovu: etnomuzikološki ogledi*. Belgrade: XX vek.

Petzen, Jennifer. 2012. 'Queer trouble: centring race in queer and feminist politics'. *Journal of Intercultural Studies* 33 (3): 289–302.

Phillips, R. Cody. 2004. *Bosnia-Herzegovina: The U.S. Army's Role in Peace Enforcement Operations, 1995–2004*. Washington, DC: U.S. Army Center of Military History.

Pieterse, Jan Nederveen. 1992. *White on Black: Images of Africa and Blacks in Western Popular Culture*. New Haven, CT: Yale University Press.

Pieterse, Jan Nederveen. 1997. 'Sociology of humanitarian intervention: Bosnia, Rwanda and Somalia compared'. *International Political Science Review* 18 (1): 71–93.

Popescu, Monica. 2003. 'Translations: Lenin's statues, post-communism, and post-apartheid'. *Yale Journal of Criticism* 16 (2): 406–23.

Posen, Barry R. 1993. 'The security dilemma and ethnic conflict'. *Survival* 35 (1): 27–47.

Potter, Simon J., and Jonathan Saha. 2015. 'Global history, imperial history and connected histories of empire'. *Journal of Colonialism and Colonial History* 16 (1). https://muse.jhu.edu/article/577738 (accessed 29 June 2016).

Pratt, Mary Louise. 2008. *Through Imperial Eyes: Travel Writing and Transculturation*. 2nd ed. London and New York: Routledge.

Pratt, Nicola. 2013. 'Reconceptualizing gender, reinscribing racial–sexual boundaries in international security: the case of UN Security Council Resolution 1325 on "Women, Peace and Security"'. *International Studies Quarterly* 57 (4): 772–83.

Pred, Allen. 2000. *Even in Sweden: Racisms, Racialized Spaces, and the Popular Geographical Imagination*. Berkeley, CA: University of California Press.

Predić, Zoran. 1986. 'Rizo Šurla, crnac iz Crne Gore, učesnik NOB-a: ponosan sam što sam rođen ovde!'. *RTV Revija*, January. www.yugopapir.com/2014/08/rizo-surla-crnac-iz-crne-gore-ucesnik.html (accessed 29 June 2016).

Pryke, Sam. 2003. 'British Serbs and long distance nationalism'. *Ethnic and Racial Studies* 26 (1): 152–72.

Puar, Jasbir. 2007. *Terrorist Assemblages: Homonationalism in Queer Times*. Durham, NC: Duke University Press.

Purtschert, Patricia, and Harald Fischer-Tiné (eds). 2015. *Colonial Switzerland: Rethinking Colonialism from the Margins*. Basingstoke: Palgrave Macmillan.

Radano, Ronald M., and Philip V. Bohlman (eds). 2000. *Music and the Racial Imagination*. Chicago, IL: University of Chicago Press.

Radano, Ronald M., and Tejumola Olaniyan. 2016. 'Introduction: hearing empire – imperial listening'. In *Audible Empire: Music, Global Politics, Critique*, ed. Ronald M. Radano and Tejumola Olaniyan: 1–24. Durham, NC: Duke University Press.

Radinović, Vladimir. 2014. 'Kako su afrički student doneli fank u Jugoslaviju'. *Vice Serbia*, 16 December. www.vice.com/rs/read/kako-su-africki-studenti-doneli-fank-u-jugoslaviju (accessed 13 December 2016).

Radonjić, Nemanja. 2015. '"From Kragujevac to Kilimanjaro": imagining and re-imagining Africa in Yugoslav travelogues'. Paper presented at the Alternative Global Geographies conference, University of Leipzig, 13–14 November.

Railton, Diane, and Paul Watson. 2012. *Music Video and the Politics of Representation*. Edinburgh: Edinburgh University Press.

Ramet, Sabrina P., and Slađana Lazić. 2011. 'The collaborationist regime of Milan Nedić'. In *Serbia and the Serbs in World War Two*, ed. Sabrina P. Ramet and Ola Listhaug: 17–43. Basingstoke: Palgrave Macmillan.

Rao, Rahul. 2014. 'The locations of homophobia'. *London Review of International Law* 2 (2): 169–99.

Rasmussen, Ljerka V. 2002. *Newly-Composed Folk Music of Yugoslavia*. London and New York: Routledge.

Razack, Sherene H. 2008. *Casting Out: The Eviction of Muslims from Western Law and Politics*. Toronto: University of Toronto Press.

Razsa, Maple. 2015. *Bastards of Utopia: Living Radical Politics after Socialism*. Bloomington, IN: Indiana University Press.

Razsa, Maple, and Nicole Lindstrom. 2004. 'Balkan is beautiful: Balkanism in the political discourse of Tuđman's Croatia'. *East European Politics and Societies* 18 (4): 628–50.

Reinhartz, Dennis. 1999. 'Unmarked graves: the destruction of the Yugoslav Roma in the Balkan Holocaust, 1941–1945'. *Journal of Genocide Research* 1 (1): 81–9.

Rexhepi, Piro. 2016. 'EUrientation anxieties: Islamic sexualities and the construction of Europeanness'. In *EU, Europe Unfinished: Mediating Europe and the Balkans in a Time of Crisis*, ed. Zlatan Krajina and Nebojša Blanuša: 145–61. London: Rowman and Littlefield International.

Richter-Montpetit, Melanie. 2014. 'Beyond the erotics of Orientalism: lawfare, torture and the racial–sexual grammars of legitimate suffering'. *Security Dialogue* 45 (1): 43–62.

Richter-Montpetit, Melanie. 2016. 'Queer temporalities, "Atlantic genealogies"'. Paper presented at the International Studies Association annual convention, Atlanta, 16–19 March.

Robertson, James. 2015. 'Speaking Titoism: student opposition and the socialist language regime of Yugoslavia'. In *The Vernaculars of Communism: Language, Ideology and Power in the Soviet Union and Eastern Europe*, ed. Petre Petrov and Lara Ryazanova-Clarke: 112–29. London and New York: Routledge.

Robinson, Cedric. 1983. *Black Marxism: The Making of the Black Radical Tradition*. Chapel Hill, NC: University of North Carolina Press.

Rodriquez, Jason. 2006. 'Color-blind ideology and the cultural appropriation of hip-hop'. *Journal of Contemporary Ethnography* 35 (6): 645–68.

Roediger, David. 2005. *Working Towards Whiteness: How America's Immigrants Became White: The Strange Journey from Ellis Island to the Suburbs*. New York: Basic Books.

Rogin, Michael. 1998. *Blackface, White Noise: Jewish Immigrants in the Hollywood Melting Pot*. Berkeley, CA: University of California Press.

Roman, Meredith L. 2012. *Opposing Jim Crow: African Americans and the Soviet Indictment of U.S. Racism, 1928–1937*. Lincoln, NE: University of Nebraska Press.

Ross, Thomas. 1990. 'The rhetorical tapestry of race: white innocence and black abstraction'. *William and Mary Law Review* 32 (1): 1–40.

Rothman, E. Natalie. 2009. 'Interpreting dragomans: boundaries and crossings in the early modern Mediterranean'. *Comparative Studies in Society and History* 51 (4): 771–800.

Rothman, E. Natalie. 2015. *Brokering Empire: Trans-Imperial Subjects Between Venice and Istanbul*. Ithaca, NY: Cornell University Press.

Roy, Olivier. 2004. *Globalized Islam: The Search for a New Ummah*. New York: Columbia University Press.

Rucker-Chang, Sunnie T. 2013. 'Filmic representations of the Chinese presence in Serbia, Croatia, Bosnia and Slovenia'. In *Chinese Migrants in Russia, Central Asia and Eastern Europe*, ed. Felix B. Chang and Sunnie T. Rucker-Chang: 199–220. London and New York: Routledge.

Ruthner, Clemens. 2002. 'Central Europe goes postcolonial: new approaches to the Habsburg Empire around 1900'. *Cultural Studies* 16 (6): 877–83.

Rydell, Robert W. 2013. 'Buffalo Bill's "Wild West": the racialisation of the cosmopolitan imagination'. In *Colonial Advertising and Commodity Racism*, ed. Wulf D. Hund, Michael Pickering and Anandi Ramamurthy: 97–118. Münster: Lit Verlag.

Said, Edward W. 1978. *Orientalism*. London: Routledge and Kegan Paul.

Said, Edward W. 1993. *Culture and Imperialism*. London: Chatto and Windus.

Samson, Jim. 2013. *Music in the Balkans*. Leiden: Brill.

Sardelić, Julija. 2014. 'Antiziganism as cultural racism: before and after the disintegration of Yugoslavia'. In *When Stereotype Meets Prejudice: Antiziganism in European Societies*, ed. Timofey Agarin: 205–27. Stuttgart: Ibidem Verlag.

Sardelić, Julija. 2015. 'Romani minorities and uneven citizenship access in the post-Yugoslav space'. *Ethnopolitics* 14 (2): 159–79.

Sardelić, Julija. 2016. 'Roma between ethnic group and an "underclass" as portrayed through newspaper discourses in socialist Slovenia'. In *Social Inequalities and Discontent in Yugoslav Socialism*, ed. Rory Archer, Igor Duda and Paul Stubbs: 95–111. London and New York: Routledge.

Sardelić, Julija. 2017. 'Transforming transit migration along the Western Balkan route: a socio-legal analysis'. Paper presented at Transit Migration and the Politics of Search and Rescue workshop, European University Institute, Florence, 28 February.

Sastre, Alexandra. 2014. 'Hottentot in the age of reality TV: sexuality, race, and Kim Kardashian's visible body'. *Celebrity Studies* 5 (1–2): 123–37.

Sauer, Walter. 2012. 'Habsburg colonial: Austria-Hungary's role in European overseas expansion reconsidered'. *Austrian Studies* 20: 5–23.

Sawyer, Lena. 2002. 'Routings: "race", African diasporas, and Swedish belonging'. *Transforming Anthropology* 11 (1): 13–35.

Schimmelfennig, Frank. 1998. 'NATO enlargement: a constructivist explanation'. *Security Studies* 8 (2–3): 198–234.

Schneider, William H. 2011. 'The jardin d'acclimatation, zoos and naturalization'. In *Human Zoos: The Invention of the Savage*, ed. Pascal Blanchard, Gilles Boëtsch and Nanette Jacomijn Snoep: 130–51. Arles: Actes Sud.

Scott, Marilyn. 1997. 'A zoo story: Peter Altenberg's *Ashantee* (1897)'. *Modern Austrian Literature* 30 (2): 48–64.

Seferović, Nina. 2015 [1981]. 'The Herzegovinian Muslim colony in Caesarea, Palestine'. Trans. Darryl Li. *Journal of Palestine Studies* 45 (1): 76–83.

Sekelj, Laslo. 1988. 'Anti-Semitism in Yugoslavia, 1918–1945'. *East European Quarterly* 22 (2): 159–72.

Sells, Michael A. 1996. *The Bridge Betrayed: Religion and Genocide in Bosnia*. Berkeley, CA: University of California Press.

Senjković, Reana. 2002. *Lica društva, likovi države*. Zagreb: IEF.

Sharpe, Christina. 2016. *In the Wake: On Blackness and Being*. Durham, NC: Duke University Press.

Shilliam, Robbie. 2013. 'Race and research agendas'. *Cambridge Review of International Affairs* 26 (1): 152–8.

Shilliam, Robbie. 2015. *The Black Pacific: Anti-Colonial Struggles and Oceanic Connections*. London: Bloomsbury Academic.

Shonick, Kaja. 2009. 'Politics, culture, and economics: reassessing the West German guest worker agreement with Yugoslavia'. *Journal of Contemporary History* 44 (4): 719–36.

Sieg, Katrin. 2002. *Ethnic Drag: Performing Race, Nation, Sexuality in West Germany*. Ann Arbor, MI: University of Michigan Press.

Siegel, Micol. 2000. 'Cocoliche's romp: fun with nationalism at Argentina's carnival'. *The Drama Review* 44 (2): 56–83.

Silverman, Carol. 2012. *Romani Routes: Cultural Politics and Balkan Music in Diaspora*. Oxford: Oxford University Press.

Silverstein, Paul A. 2005. 'Immigrant racialization and the new savage slot: race, migration, and immigration in the new Europe'. *Annual Review of Anthropology* 34: 363–84.

Simeziane, Sarah. 2010. 'Roma rap and the *Black Train*: minority voices in Hungarian hip hop'. In *The Languages of Global Hip Hop*, ed. Marina Terkourafi: 96–119. London: Bloomsbury Academic.

Simić, Tanja, Marina Biluš and Ante Pavić. 2007. 'Afričke priče iz Hrvatske'. *Nacional*, 29 May. http://arhiva.nacional.hr/clanak/34814/africke-price-iz-hrvatske (accessed 7 January 2017).

Šimunović, Pjer. 2015. 'Making of an ally: NATO membership conditionality implemented on Croatia'. *Journal of Transatlantic Studies* 13 (2): 175–203.

Sirbegović, Amila. 2011. 'Disrupting the visual paradigm'. In *Space (Re)Solutions: Intervention and Research in Visual Culture*, ed. Peter Mörtenböck and Helge Mooshammer: 165–74. Bielefeld: Transcript.

Slavova, Kornelia. 2006. 'Looking at western feminisms through the double lens of eastern Europe and the Third World'. In *Women and Citizenship in Central and Eastern Europe*, ed. Jasmina Lukić, Joanna Regulska and Darja Zaviršek: 245–63. Aldershot: Ashgate.

Slobodian, Quinn. 2015a. 'Introduction'. In *Comrades of Color: East Germany in the Cold War World*, ed. Quinn Slobodian: 1–19. Oxford: Berghahn.

Slobodian, Quinn. 2015b. 'Socialist chromatism: race, racism, and the racial rainbow in East Germany'. In *Comrades of Color: East Germany in the Cold War World*, ed. Quinn Slobodian: 23–39. Oxford: Berghahn.

Slobodian, Quinn (ed.). 2015c. *Comrades of Color: East Germany in the Cold War World*. Oxford: Berghahn.

Sluga, Glenda. 2001. 'Bodies, souls and sovereignty: the Austro-Hungarian empire and the legitimacy of nations'. *Ethnicities* 1 (2): 207–32.

Slukan-Altić, Mirela. 2003. 'Mirko Seljan (1871–1913): Croatian explorer and cartographer of Africa'. In *The History of Cartography of Africa*, ed. Elri Liebenberg: 19–28. Cape Town: ICA Commission on the History of Cartography.

Slukan-Altić, Mirela. 2008. 'Croatian explorer Dragutin Lerman (1863–1918) and his contribution in the mapping of Central Africa'. In *Proceedings of the Symposium 'Shifting Boundaries: History of Cartography in the 19th and 20th Centuries'*, ed. Elri Liebenberg and Peter Coolier. [n. p.]: Commission on the History of Cartography of the International Cartographic Association.

Slukan-Altić, Mirela. 2012. 'Ferdinand Konšćak: cartographer of the Compañia de Jesús and his maps of Baja California'. In *History of Cartography: International Symposium of the ICA Commission, 2010*, ed. Elri Liebenberg and Imre Josef Demhardt: 3–20. Berlin: Springer.

Šmitek, Zmago, Aleksandra-Sanja Lazarević and Djurdjica Petrović. 1993. 'Notes sur les voyageurs et explorateurs slovènes, croates et serbes en Afrique avant 1918 et sur leurs collections'. *Revue française d'histoire d'outre-mer* 80 (300): 389–408.

Solomos, John. 2003. *Race and Racism in Britain*. 3rd ed. Basingstoke: Palgrave Macmillan.

Sontag, Susan. 2003. *Regarding the Pain of Others*. London: Penguin.

Spivak, Gayatri Chakravorty. 1988. 'Can the subaltern speak?' In *Marxism and the Interpretation of Culture*, ed. Cary Nelson and Lawrence Grossberg: 271–313. Urbana, IL: University of Illinois Press.

Stam, Robert, and Ella Shohat. 2012. *Race in Translation: Culture Wars around the Postcolonial Atlantic*. New York: New York University Press.

Stanek, Łukasz. 2015. 'Architects from socialist countries in Ghana (1957–67): modern architecture and mondialisation'. *Journal of the Society of Architectural Historians* 74 (4): 417–42.

Stefanović, Đorđe. 2005. 'Seeing the Albanians through Serbian eyes: the inventors of the tradition of intolerance and their critics, 1804–1939'. *European History Quarterly* 35 (3): 465–92.

Štiks, Igor, and Ellen Elias-Bursać. 2016. 'Putting on a play in wartime Sarajevo'. *TriQuarterly*, 15 July. www.triquarterly.org/issues/issue-150/putting-play-wartime-sarajevo (accessed 4 January 2017).

Stoever, Jennifer Lynn. 2016. *The Sonic Color Line: Race and the Cultural Politics of Listening*. New York: NYU Press.

Stojić Mitrović, Marta. 2016. 'Changing dynamics of the refugee crisis in Serbia'. Paper presented at the Refugee Crisis in South East Europe workshop, Aston University, 21 June.

Stokes, Martin. 2003. 'Globalization and the politics of world music'. In *The Cultural Study of Music: A Critical Introduction*, ed. Martin Clayton, Trevor Herbert and Richard Middleton: 297–309. London and New York: Routledge.

Stoler, Ann Laura. 1995. *Race and the Education of Desire: Foucault's History of Sexuality and the Colonial Order of Things*. Durham, NC: Duke University Press.

Stoler, Ann Laura. 2002. *Carnal Knowledge and Imperial Power: Race and the Intimate in Colonial Rule*. Berkeley, CA: University of California Press.

Stoler, Ann Laura. 2006. *Haunted by Empire: Geographies of Intimacy in North American History*. Durham, NC: Duke University Press.

Stoler, Ann Laura. 2009. *Along the Archival Grain: Epistemic Anxieties and Colonial Common Sense*. Princeton, NJ: Princeton University Press.

Stromberg Childers, Kristen. 2016. *Seeking Imperialism's Embrace: National Identity, Decolonization, and Assimilation in the French Caribbean*. Oxford: Oxford University Press.

Subotić, Jelena, and Srđan Vučetić. 2016. 'Anti-racist politics and the limits of non-aligned internationalism'. Paper presented at Racialized Realities in World Politics, *Millennium* Conference, LSE, 22–3 October.

Subotić, Jelena, and Srđan Vučetić. Forthcoming. 'Performing solidarity: whiteness and status-seeking in the non-aligned world'. *Journal of International Relations and Development*. https://link.springer.com/article/10.1057/s41268-017-0112-2 (accessed 18 September 2017).

Subrahmanyam, Sanjay. 1997. 'Connected histories: notes towards a reconfiguration of early modern Eurasia'. *Modern Asian Studies* 31 (3): 735–62.

Suchland, Jennifer. 2015. *Economies of Violence: Transnational Feminism, Postsocialism, and the Politics of Sex Trafficking*. Durham, NC: Duke University Press.

Sugar, Peter F. 1977. *Southeastern Europe under Ottoman Rule, 1354–1804*. Seattle, WA: University of Washington Press.

Švob-Đokić, Nada. 1979. 'Razvoj i promjena u Africi: promjena nasuprot tradiciji i mitologiji'. *Naše teme* 23 (3): 796–803.

Taguieff, Pierre-André. 1990. 'The new cultural racism in France'. *Télos* 83: 109–22.
Tatalović, Siniša. 1993. 'Military aspects of the peacekeeping operation in Croatia'. *Politička misao* 2 (2): 55–63.
Thomas, Dominique. 2014. 'Abu Hamza al-Masri and supporters of Shari'a'. In *Islamic Movements of Europe*, ed. Frank Peter and Rafael Ortega: 174–6. London: Tauris.
Timutimu, Ngareta, Judith Simon and Kay Morris Matthews. 1998. 'Historical research as a bicultural project: seeking new perspectives on the New Zealand Native Schools system'. *History of Education* 27 (2): 109–24.
Tlostanova, Madina. 2010. *Gender Epistemologies and Eurasian Borderlands*. Basingstoke: Palgrave Macmillan.
Tlostanova, Madina, Redi Koobak and Suruchi Thapar-Björkert. 2016. 'Border thinking and disidentification: postcolonial and postsocialist feminist dialogues'. *Feminist Theory* 17 (2): 211–28.
Todorova, Maria. 1994. 'The Balkans: from discovery to invention'. *Slavic Review* 53 (2): 453–82.
Todorova, Maria. 1997. *Imagining the Balkans*. Oxford: Oxford University Press.
Todorova, Maria. 2005a. 'Spacing Europe: what is a historical region?'. *East Central Europe* 32 (1–2): 59–78.
Todorova, Maria. 2005b. 'The trap of backwardness: modernity, temporality, and the study of Eastern European nationalism'. *Slavic Review* 64 (1): 140–64.
Todorova, Maria. 2009. 'Afterword to the updated edition'. In *Imagining the Balkans*, 2nd ed.: 190–202. Oxford: Oxford University Press.
Todorova, Miglena S. 2006. 'Race travels: whiteness and modernity across national borders'. PhD thesis, University of Minnesota.
Tuhkanen, Mikko. 2009. 'Queer hybridity'. In *Deleuze and Queer Theory*, ed. Chrysanthi Nigianni and Merl Storr: 92–114. Edinburgh: Edinburgh University Press.
Turda, Marius. 2014. *Eugenics and Nation in Early 20th Century Hungary*. Basingstoke: Palgrave Macmillan.
Turda, Marius, and Paul J. Weindling (eds) 2007. *Blood and Homeland: Eugenics and Racial Nationalism in Central and Southeast Europe, 1900–1940*. Budapest: CEU Press.
UNMIBH. 1998. 'United Nations Mission in Bosnia and Herzegovina: background'. New York: Department of Public Information, United Nations. www.un.org/Depts/DPKO/Missions/unmibh_b.htm#UNIPTF (accessed 7 October 2016).

Valenta, Marko, and Zan Strabac. 2011. 'Bosnians in Norway: how do they adjust compared with other refugee groups?'. In *The Bosnian Diaspora: Integration in Transnational Communities*, ed. Marko Valenta and Sabrina P. Ramet: 83–104. Farnham: Ashgate.

Vathi, Zana. 2015. *Migrating and Settling in a Mobile World: Albanian Migrants and their Children in Europe*. Cham: Springer International.

Vaughan-Williams, Nick. 2015. *Europe's Border Crisis: Biopolitical Security and Beyond*. Oxford: Oxford University Press.

Veličković, Vedrana. 2012. 'Belated alliances? Tracing the intersections between postcolonialism and postcommunism'. *Journal of Postcolonial Writing* 48 (2): 164–75.

Verdery, Katherine. 1994. 'From parent-state to family patriarchs: gender and nation in contemporary Eastern Europe'. *East European Politics and Societies* 8 (2): 225–55.

Vernallis, Carol. 2004. *Experiencing Music Video: Aesthetics and Cultural Context*. New York: Columbia University Press.

Vidmar Horvat, Ksenija. 2010. 'Multiculturalism in time of terrorism: re-imagining Europe post-9/11'. *Cultural Studies* 24 (5): 747–66.

Visoka, Gezim. 2012. 'The "Kafkaesque accountability" of international governance in Kosovo'. *Journal of Intervention and Statebuilding* 6 (2): 189–212.

Volčič, Zala. 2013. 'Connecting the disconnected: Balkan cultural studies'. *Communication and Critical/Cultural Studies* 10 (2–3): 333–9.

Von Eschen, Penny M. 2006. *Satchmo Blows Up the World: Jazz Ambassadors Play the Cold War*. Cambridge, MA: Harvard University Press.

Vrecer, Natalija. 2010. 'Living in limbo: integration of forced migrants from Bosnia and Herzegovina in Slovenia'. *Journal of Refugee Studies* 23 (4): 484–502.

Vučetić, Radina. 2012. *Koka-kola socijalizam: amerikanizacija jugoslovenske popularne kulture šezdesetih godina XX veka*. Belgrade: Službeni glasnik.

Vučetić, Radina. 2016. 'Tito's Africa: representations of power on Tito's trips to Africa'. Paper presented at the (Re)Thinking Yugoslav Internationalism: Cold War Global Entanglements and Their Legacies conference, University of Graz, 29 September–1 October.

Vučetić, Srđan. 2011. 'A racialized peace? How Britain and the US made their relationship special'. *Foreign Policy Analysis* 7 (4): 403–22.

Vučetić, Srđan. 2013. 'Black banker, white banker: philosophies of the global colour line'. *Cambridge Review of International Affairs* 26 (1): 27–48.

Vukadinović, Radovan. 1979. 'Afrika i američko-sovjetski odnosi'. *Naše teme* 23 (3): 537–55.

Vuletić, Dean. 2015. 'Swinging between east and west: Yugoslav communism and the dilemmas of popular music'. In *Youth and Rock in the Soviet Bloc: Youth Cultures, Music, and the State in Russia and Eastern Europe*, ed. William Jay Risch: 25–42. Lexington, MD: Rowman and Littlefield.

Wachtel, Andrew Baruch. 1998. *Making a Nation, Breaking a Nation: Literature and Cultural Politics in Yugoslavia*. Stanford, CA: Stanford University Press.

Wachtel, Andrew Baruch. 2008. *The Balkans in World History*. Oxford: Oxford University Press.

Wade, Peter. 2004. 'Images of Latin American *mestizaje* and the politics of comparison'. *Bulletin of Latin American Research* 23 (3): 355–66.

Walters, William. 2002. 'Deportation, expulsion, and the international police of aliens'. *Citizenship Studies* 6 (3): 265–92.

Ware, Vron. 2012. *Military Migrants: Fighting for YOUR Country*. Basingstoke: Palgrave Macmillan.

Warnes, Christopher. 2000. 'Interview with Ivan Vladislavić'. *Modern Fiction Studies* 46 (1): 273–81.

Weheliye, Alexander G. 2005. *Phonographies: Grooves in Sonic Afro-Modernity*. Durham, NC: Duke University Press.

Wekker, Gloria. 2016. *White Innocence: Paradoxes of Colonialism and Race*. Durham, NC: Duke University Press.

Werbner, Pnina. 2000. 'Divided loyalties, empowered citizenship? Muslims in Britain'. *Citizenship Studies* 4 (3): 307–24.

West, Cornel. 1990. 'The new cultural politics of difference'. In *Out There: Marginalization and Contemporary Cultures*, ed. Russell Ferguson, Martha Gever, Trinh T. Minh-ha and Cornel West: 19–38. Cambridge, MA: MIT Press.

Westad, Odd Arne. 2005. *The Global Cold War: Third World Interventions and the Making of Our Times*. Cambridge: Cambridge University Press.

White, George W. 2000. *Nationalism and Territory: Constructing Group Identity in Southeastern Europe*. Lanham, MD: Rowman and Littlefield.

Winant, Howard. 2001. *The World is a Ghetto: Race and Democracy since World War II*. New York: Basic.

Wipplinger, Jonathan. 2007. 'The aural shock of modernity: Weimar's experience of jazz'. *The Germanic Review* 82 (4): 299–320.

Wipplinger, Jonathan. 2011. 'The racial ruse: on blackness and blackface comedy in fin-de-siècle Germany'. *German Quarterly* 84 (4): 457–76.

Withnall, Adam. 2015. 'Isis "executes" Croatian hostage Tomislav Salopek in Egypt after demands deadline passes'. *The Independent*, 12 August. www.

independent.co.uk/news/world/middle-east/isis-executes-croatian-hostage-tomislav-salopek-in-egypt-after-demands-deadline-passes-10451526.html (accessed 27 March 2017).
Woodward, Susan L. 1995. *Balkan Tragedy: Chaos and Dissolution after the Cold War*. Washington, DC: Brookings Institution.
Woolf, Larry. 2002. *Venice and the Slavs: The Discovery of Dalmatia in the Age of Enlightenment*. Stanford, CA: Stanford University Press.
Wright, Peter. 2016. 'The ambivalence of socialist anti-racism: the case of black African students in 1960s Yugoslavia'. Paper presented at the (Re)Thinking Yugoslav Internationalism: Cold War Global Entanglements and Their Legacies conference, University of Graz, 29 September–1 October.
Yarbro-Bejarano, Yvonne. 1994. 'Gloria Anzaldúa's Borderlands/La frontera: cultural studies, "difference", and the non-unitary subject'. *Cultural Critique* 28: 5–28.
Yeomans, Rory. 2015. 'Introduction: utopia, terror, and everyday experience in the Ustasha state'. In *The Utopia of Terror: Life and Death in Wartime Croatia*, ed. Rory Yeomans: 1–40. Rochester, NY: University of Rochester Press.
Young, Robert J. C. 1995. *Colonial Desire: Hybridity in Theory, Culture and Race*. London and New York: Routledge.
Young, Robert J. C. 2016. *Postcolonialism: An Historical Introduction*. 2nd ed. Oxford: Wiley-Blackwell.
Yuval-Davis, Nira. 1997. *Gender and Nation*. London: Sage.
Yuval-Davis, Nira. 2011. *The Politics of Belonging: Intersectional Contestations*. London: Sage.
Žagar, Igor Ž. 2002. 'Xenophobia and Slovenian media: how the image of the other is constructed (and what it looks like)'. In *Xenophobia and Post-Socialism*, ed. Mojca Pajnik: 37–44. Ljubljana: Mirovni institut.
Zakharov, Nikolai. 2015. *Race and Racism in Russia*. London: Palgrave Macmillan.
Žanić, Ivo. 2005. 'The symbolic identity of Croatia in the triangle "crossroads"–"bulwark"–"bridge"'. In *Myths and Boundaries in South-Eastern Europe*, ed. Pål Kolstø: 35–76. London: Hurst.
Zantop, Suzanne. 1997. *Colonial Fantasies: Conquest, Family, and Nation in Precolonial Germany, 1770–1870*. Durham, NC: Duke University Press.
Žarkov, Dubravka. 2007. *The Body of War: Media, Ethnicity, and Gender in the Break-Up of Yugoslavia*. Durham, NC: Duke University Press.
Žarkov, Dubravka. 2011. 'Exposures and invisibilities: media, masculinities and the narratives of wars in an intersectional perspective'. In *Framing Intersectionality: Debates on a Multi-Faceted Concept in Gender Studies*, ed.

Helma Lutz, María Teresa Herrera Vivar and Linda Supik: 105–20. London and New York: Routledge.

Zimić, Darinka. 1982. 'Yugoslav universities and developing countries'. *Higher Education in Europe* 7 (1): 13–16.

Životić, Aleksandar, and Jovan Čavoski. 2016. 'On the road to Belgrade: Yugoslavia, Third World neutrals, and the evolution of global Non-Alignment, 1954–1961'. *Journal of Cold War Studies* 18 (4): 79–97.

Žižek, Slavoj. 1999. 'The spectre of Balkan'. *Journal of the International Institute* 6 (2). http://quod.lib.umich.edu/j/jii/4750978.0006.202/-spectre-of-balkan?rgn=main;view=fulltext (accessed 4 November 2016).

Žižek, Slavoj. 2017. *Against the Double Blackmail: Refugees, Terror and Other Troubles with Neighbours*. London: Penguin.

Zorn, Jelka. 2009. 'A case for Slovene nationalism: initial citizenship rules and the erasure'. *Nations and Nationalism* 15 (2): 280–98.

Index

activism 3, 14, 20, 22, 29, 51, 57, 86, 92, 98, 105, 159, 169, 179, 181, 187
Afghanistan 119, 131, 138, 143, 147, 149–54, 156, 164
Africa
  Cold War and 104, 112
  colonisation of 78, 99–101, 110, 112; *see also* slavery
  music and 34, 43, 45, 53, 74–8
  representations of 3, 27–8, 36–7
  soldiers from 65, 127–8
  south-east European identifications with 39, 110, 116, 173, 187
  students from 9, 18, 27, 29, 49, 92, 112–13, 120, 164
Africa, South 76, 87–8, 93, 111, 169, 173
  apartheid 76, 111, 169
Agathangelou, Anna 72, 80, 120, 167
Albanian identity 44, 63, 66–7, 73, 84, 95
Algeria 111, 119, 120, 139, 153, 172
antemurale myth 20, 21, 125–6, 137, 145–6, 150–1
anti-colonialism 2, 4, 9, 29, 35, 46–51, 77, 104, 105, 107, 109–10, 111–13, 115, 118, 122, 123, 124, 175
anti-racism x, 2, 13, 17–18, 29, 38, 46–51, 57, 96, 98, 105, 106, 113, 170, 175, 176, 178, 186
anti-Semitism 18, 67, 68–9, 124
antiziganism 10, 18, 20, 69, 73, 83, 98, 124, 125, 135, 144, 168, 172, 175
Asia, West 6, 15, 34, 65, 77, 82, 126, 138, 142, 155–9, 161, 173
Australia 83–4, 87, 100
Austria 26, 40, 100, 141, 144, 156, 163, 177

Austria-Hungary, *see* Empire, Habsburg

Baker, Catherine viii, 2–3, 182–3
Baker, Josephine 23, 49
Bakić-Hayden, Milica 6–7, 174, 176, 178
balkanism viii, 6–7, 19, 32–3, 64, 73, 88, 128–9, 176–9; *see also* Balkans
Balkans
  ambiguity of 43, 45, 107, 121, 172
  'Balkan route' 143, 157–9, 164
  blackness and 2, 77, 173, 174
  coherence as region 19, 58, 94–5
  'Europe' and 2–3, 6, 16, 19, 20–1, 32, 64, 72, 73, 107, 116, 125, 129, 136, 138, 162, 167, 168, 178–9
  globalisation and 43, 50, 52, 88, 179
  marginality of ix, 18, 62, 77, 168, 186
  nationalism and 15, 62, 71, 128–9, 133, 169
  otherness of 20, 21, 117, 125, 146, 149, 161, 174, 177
  postcolonial/decolonial theory and 6, 15, 19, 88, 170, 176, 187; *see also* balkanism
  race and 7, 16–22, 52, 80, 122, 129, 170, 173, 177, 178, 187
  representation 5–6, 128–9, 133, 161, 177
  tradition and 34, 45, 55, 66
  'Western Balkans' 144, 164
  whiteness and 19, 55, 64, 86, 177
Bangoura, Hamed 2, 3, 112–13
Belgrade 39, 48, 49, 51, 62, 80, 107, 111, 113, 115, 118, 157–60, 177, 184

Bhabha, Homi 6, 70
Bjelić, Dušan viii, 19, 63, 64–5, 88, 177, 178–9
Black European Studies 10, 22–3, 99, 184
blackface 4, 38–42, 93, 96–8
blackness
  celebrity and 42–3, 52
  hypervisibility of 23
  identifications with 39, 40, 47–8, 50–1, 77–8, 110, 132
  Montenegro and 77
  stereotypes of 3, 49, 69, 75, 95, 98
Bosnia-Herzegovina 8–9, 39–40, 92, 138
  popular music 47–8, 50, 56
  war in 1990s 124, 126–7, 138–9, 140, 169, 183–4
    Dayton Peace Agreement 81, 92, 127, 130, 135, 139, 149, 163
Brazil 71, 94, 187
Bulgaria 12, 17, 83, 88–9, 95, 105–6, 111, 120

Césaire, Aimé 4, 108–9
China 18, 80–2, 92, 147
Christianity 19–21, 30, 59, 64, 97, 126, 138, 139, 150, 159
  Catholic 21, 59–60, 67, 69, 126, 137
  Orthodox 59–61, 63, 69, 146
civilisation 1–2, 171
  Balkans and 21, 62, 64, 101, 177
  'civilising mission' 26, 62, 87, 95, 101, 106, 129
  clash of 133, 149–50
  empire and 24, 26, 58, 62, 78, 101, 175, 185
  hierarchies of 6, 16–17, 24, 58, 101, 116, 127, 129, 168, 169, 171
  race and 16–17, 21, 24, 49, 78, 116, 127, 129, 149, 168, 170, 185
  see also modernity
Cold War 18, 25, 53, 96, 103, 148
  academia and 107, 173–4
  aftermath of 5, 8, 13, 18, 99, 116–19, 133–6, 142, 148, 180, 186

cultural diplomacy and 33–4, 49, 108
East–West divisions and 11, 12, 106, 108, 148
migration and 27, 92
race and 25, 30, 49, 89, 91, 95, 103–19, 174
see also Non-Aligned Movement; state socialism
colonialism
  'Europe' and 18, 26, 63, 109, 168, 174
  gender and 36, 52, 167
  identifications against 48, 51, 77, 111, 123, 175
  identifications with 27, 37, 51, 62, 64, 112, 130, 176, 185
  imagination of 3, 18, 26, 32, 35, 38–42, 44, 51, 64, 100, 128
  legacies of x, 2, 9, 16, 28, 33, 51–2, 161, 167, 181, 182, 185
  neo-colonialism 111, 131, 161
  race and 5, 11, 15, 21, 23, 26, 38–42, 61, 63, 70, 75, 86, 111, 171, 184
  settler 10, 24, 26, 61, 62, 72, 86, 103
  South Slavs' implication in 62–3, 77–9, 90, 110, 112
  violence and 11, 16, 131, 161, 172, 179, 185
  Yugoslav region apparently beyond 10, 15, 19, 41–2, 90, 99, 115, 161
coloniality, global ix, 4, 7, 14, 28, 33, 64–5, 89–90, 101, 168–70, 183, 185, 186–7
cosmopolitanism 16, 24, 70, 89, 115, 174
critical race theory viii, 2, 3, 6, 7, 16–17, 19–20, 22, 28, 36, 52, 106, 109, 129, 150, 168, 170–1, 173–4, 178–9, 184
Croatia
  Independent State of 68–9, 92, 96, 126, 146

national identity 6, 21, 40, 68–70, 72–3, 126–7, 139, 146, 151–2, 174
  popular music 2–3, 35–8, 47
  rejection of Yugoslavia in 118, 122
'cultural archive' 31–2, 91, 99, 122, 166
Cyprus 80, 107, 119, 145, 163

Dalmatia 4, 60, 87, 96–8, 102, 109–10, 114
decolonisation 4, 7–8, 17–18, 104–5, 107, 168
diaspora 58, 82–9, 91, 140–2, 156, 175
  black 43, 53, 91, 187
  race translated through 82–9, 107–8
Đorđević, Vladan 63, 64, 95
Dubrovnik 60, 77, 97, 172
Dvorniković, Vladimir 21, 66–7

East, the
  Balkans and 2, 6, 34, 146, 180
  Cold War and 46, 108, 113–14, 117–18, 123, 148
  racialisation of 21, 69, 175
  threats imagined from 20, 116, 135–6, 142, 150, 158
  see also balkanism; Empire, Ottoman; Islam; orientalism
education 24, 67, 87, 105, 112, 121, 126; *see also* Africa, students from; United Kingdom, Yugoslav region studied in; whiteness, academia and
empire, *see* colonialism
Empire, Habsburg 4, 25, 55–6, 59–63, 66, 70, 91–2, 95, 97, 168
  colonialism and 40, 55, 61–2, 77–8, 92, 99–101
  race and 98–101, 172, 174
  wars with Ottoman Empire 21, 59–60
Empire, Ottoman 4, 15, 41, 57–63, 74, 79, 96, 172

colonialism and 19, 52, 58–62, 90, 94, 172
  legacies of 19–20, 25, 29, 32, 34, 43, 56, 68, 80, 101, 116, 121, 146, 161, 172, 178, 182, 184
  race and 97, 173, 174, 184
  rejection of 73, 121, 146, 1
  religion and 59, 90, 116, 136, 138, 178
ethnicity 1, 4, 5, 8, 25
  race and 11, 21, 81, 89–90, 184
  study of 17, 57–8, 91, 133, 166, 167, 185
Eurocentrism 3, 18, 19, 30, 106–7, 111–12, 184
Europe
  definitions of 7, 156, 168, 170–1
  identifications with 98, 148, 162, 170–1, 178
  'return to Europe' 116–17, 145–6
  see also balkanism; Europe, eastern; European Union
Europe, eastern 1, 2, 4, 6, 7, 12–14, 18, 94–5, 99, 109, 149, 164, 182
  ethnonationalism and 10, 12–13, 57, 64, 91, 123–4, 179–80
  marginality of 80, 83–5, 135–6, 145, 172, 176, 180
  postcoloniality and 8, 29, 32, 180, 186–7
  race and 11, 26, 33, 45–7, 80, 81, 83–5, 99–100, 104–5, 117, 135, 168, 170, 172, 173, 176, 179, 184
European Union (EU)
  border security 21, 123, 133–6, 142–7, 150–1
  enlargement of 20–1, 84, 145, 148, 154, 162, 163, 164
exceptionalism, racial 10–12, 19, 22–4, 26, 102, 104, 129–30, 145, 174–5, 186–7
exoticism 7, 17, 18, 23, 27–8, 33, 37, 43, 51, 54, 80, 90, 98–102, 113, 115, 177; *see also* Africa, stereotypes of; orientalism

Fanon, Frantz 17, 36, 52, 172
feminism viii, 3, 57–8, 72, 120, 139
  black 14, 31–2, 41–2, 181
  Chicana 14, 71–2
  intersectionality and 13–14, 29, 45, 179, 181
  media and viii, 10, 38, 42, 45, 181
  postcolonialism and 139, 152, 180
  postsocialist 13–14, 15, 38, 45, 180–1, 187
film 81–2, 102–3, 147, 157, 177
France 22, 23, 26, 34, 35, 41, 61, 65, 83, 94, 99, 113, 115, 124, 131, 150, 163, 172, 178–9

gender 19, 41, 42, 101, 104, 108, 114–15
  ideologies of 5, 58, 151–2
  postsocialism and 12–14, 180, 187
  race and 13–14, 24, 44–5, 55, 58, 74, 152, 154
  study of 8, 12–14, 180
  see also feminism; masculinities; sexuality
genocide 1, 39, 58, 68, 91, 128–30, 140–1, 162
Germany 29, 34, 35, 64, 101, 120, 131, 163
  migration and 52, 72, 84, 88, 92, 120, 135, 144, 156–8
  race and 10, 14, 22–3, 26, 29, 38–9, 91, 92, 95–6, 98–103, 110, 133–4, 182
    East Germany 102–3, 105
    Imperial Germany 23, 40, 99–100
    Third Reich 68–9, 146
    West Germany 114
  study of 22, 99
Ghana 92, 107, 110, 112, 114, 119, 120, 131, 163
Gilroy, Paul 3, 9–10, 16, 20, 28, 29, 33, 43, 52, 70, 71, 91, 107, 124, 173, 179
Grabar-Kitarović, Kolinda 152, 158
Greece 41, 59, 61, 80, 92, 93, 119, 143, 149, 156–7, 186

Guberina, Petar 109–10, 118
Guinea 2, 113, 119

Hall, Stuart 33, 53
hip-hop 3, 27–8, 34, 36, 43, 47
hooks, bell 45, 52
human exhibitions 26, 40, 55, 99–101
Hungary 10–11, 46, 48, 55–6, 60, 61, 67, 91, 100, 104, 114, 117, 134, 146, 148, 157–8, 162, 163, 164, 172, 187; *see also* Empire, Habsburg

Imre, Anikó viii, 10, 32–3, 179–81, 184
India 6, 15, 61, 101, 107–8, 112, 119, 127, 128, 131, 145, 163
indigeneity 21, 29, 30, 33, 55, 57, 63, 73, 78–9, 87, 102–3, 129, 173
interpreters 60, 131–3, 159–60
intersectionality 9, 13–16, 29, 71, 86, 179, 181, 185
intervention, international 79, 123, 127–33, 147–55 passim, 185–6; *see also* peacekeeping
Iraq 119, 131, 141–3, 147, 149–52, 154–5, 156, 161, 164, 165
Islam
  ethnicity and 21, 59, 62–3, 66–9, 72, 84–5, 126–7, 142
  Europe and 20, 85, 101, 116, 145–6, 156, 161–2
  migration and 88–9, 122, 138–42, 158, 160–1, 163–4
  racialisation of 20, 21, 23, 24, 69–70, 73, 84–5, 97, 125, 136–8, 140–1, 147, 149, 156, 161, 176
  security and 72, 84, 97, 136–8, 141–2, 146–7, 149–50, 156, 161, 175
  see also antemurale myth; Empire, Ottoman
Islamic State in Iraq and Syria (ISIS) 85, 141–2, 163–4, 165

Islamism 73, 85, 117, 138–40, 152–4, 163–4, 165
Israel 88–9, 137, 139
Istria 60, 70–2, 96, 102
Italy 34, 54, 55, 64, 68, 70–2, 77, 84, 92, 95–8, 101, 115, 124, 143–4, 156, 172
Iveković, Rada 118, 120

Karadžić, Radovan 125, 144, 162
Kardashian, Kim 44
Kilibarda, Konstantin viii, 19, 111–12, 120, 154
Korčula 77–9, 93, 97, 119
Kosovo 61, 63, 72, 85, 123, 142, 144
    Albanians of 44, 55, 84, 135
    ethnic relations in 39, 54–5, 64, 91, 129, 163
    international intervention 79, 131, 144, 149, 152–3, 162

language 19, 21, 40, 50, 77, 99, 102, 110, 159–60
    English, use of 2, 36, 187
    identity and 4, 15, 51, 62, 69–70, 71–2, 83, 118, 175
    see also interpreters
Li, Darryl 88–9, 154
Libya 119, 139, 144, 156, 161, 164
Longinović, Tomislav 21, 66, 125, 177, 178
Lumumba, Patrice 111, 118, 121

Macedonia 64, 66, 72, 81, 114, 125, 149, 151, 153, 155, 157–9, 164, 165
    Roma in 48, 83, 144
masculinities 24, 37–8, 55, 80, 103, 108, 140, 151–2, 161, 163
Middle East, *see* Asia, West
Mignolo, Walter 15, 21, 119, 171, 172
migration 57–8, 72–3, 79, 89, 94, 125, 160
    conflict and 57, 60–1, 123, 138–9, 157–8
    forced 1, 57–8, 62–3, 123, 155–62

foreign fighters 138–42, 153–4, 163–4
from Global South 1, 71, 74–8, 79, 122, 134–5, 143–7, 155–62
guest workers 52, 88, 92, 113–15, 123
labour 79–81, 89, 93, 113–15, 135–6, 154–5, 165
postcolonial 10, 18, 28, 52, 134–5
racism and 18, 24–5, 52, 81, 83, 86, 134–5, 142–7, 156, 158, 161
study of 27, 57–8, 73, 79, 84
visas and 58, 80, 88, 113–14, 134–6, 143, 144–5, 156–7, 176, 181
migration-security nexus 21, 133–6, 142–7, 154
Mills, Charles viii, 16, 21, 52, 129, 171, 174, 180–1, 186
Milošević, Slobodan 38, 39, 55, 80, 116, 117, 123, 149
modernity 28, 70, 85, 114, 122, 125
    colonialism and 26, 51–2, 55, 58, 100, 172
    Cold War and 29, 104, 107, 114, 120
    Europe/Balkans and 2–3, 34, 72–3, 107, 129, 170, 185
    gender and 13, 49, 58, 180
    identifications with 2–3, 33, 45, 53, 116, 130, 184
    race and 7, 16–17, 21–2, 33, 49, 53, 73, 89–90, 101, 104, 129, 168, 170, 175, 180
    spatialised hierarchies of viii, 17, 22, 32, 127, 129, 135–6, 168, 170, 179, 180, 186
    urban/rural divide and 72–3, 85
    see also balkanism
Montenegro 21, 40, 55, 60, 66–7, 74–7, 93, 164, 168
music
    folk traditions and 32, 37–8, 45, 66
    popular 2, 27–8, 31–56 passim, 106, 115–16, 128
    transnational 33–4, 35, 51
    see also hip-hop

nationalism
  empire and 27, 43, 61–2, 91, 155, 183
  gender and 12–13, 38, 43, 103, 128
  history of 40, 58–9, 61, 119, 141
  postsocialism and 12–13, 20–1, 73, 118, 122, 123–4, 133–4, 150, 173–5
  race and 11, 12, 22, 28–9, 32, 43, 63, 65, 68–70, 89, 92, 122, 126–7, 173
  study of 4–5, 9, 118, 167, 169, 182, 185
  Yugoslav Wars and 4, 9, 48, 54, 71, 118, 126–7, 128, 132, 137, 140, 169
Nehru, Jawaharlal 107, 108, 112
Netherlands 10, 11, 23, 25, 38, 41–2, 82–3, 96, 98
Nkrumah, Kwame 110, 111, 114
Non-Aligned Movement 2, 95, 129, 184
  forgetting of 9, 15, 49–50, 116–19, 123, 164
  race and 47, 106–16
  Yugoslav leadership in 107–8
North Atlantic Treaty Organization (NATO) 56, 130, 147–53

Ora, Rita 44, 55
orientalism 40, 188
  balkanism and 6–7, 19–20, 88, 173, 187
  gender and 43, 92
  nesting 6, 71, 116–17, 122, 168, 176, 179, 186
  Said and 6, 15, 19
  south-east Europe and 43, 98, 128, 170, 177

Palestine 65, 88–9, 141–2
peacekeeping 7, 24, 123, 127–33, 150
  racialised peacekeepers 56, 127–33, 163
  sex work and 79–80, 135–6
Plavšić, Biljana 125, 162

postcolonialism
  empire and 22, 32, 95, 105
  postsocialism and 2, 7–9, 29, 50, 95, 118, 123, 145, 167, 172, 176–87
  race and 7, 9–10, 15, 16, 22–9, 52, 94, 152, 162
  south-east Europe and 6–7, 9, 11, 12, 15–16, 19–20, 32–3, 88, 116, 118, 122, 145, 170, 176–87
  state socialism and 95, 105, 109, 113, 118, 120
  study of viii, ix, 12–13, 19, 57, 117–18, 166–7
  theory 6, 53, 71–2, 116, 167–8, 170
  race separated from 15, 186
'post-racial' society 2, 16, 18, 47, 105, 106, 109, 111, 117, 168, 175
postsocialism viii, 13, 80
  gender and 12–13, 123–4, 180, 181
  migration and 80–2, 124, 155–62
  post-conflict and 8, 133, 154, 155
  postcoloniality and 2, 7–9, 29, 50, 95, 118, 123, 145, 167, 172, 176–87
  race and 16, 28, 40, 45, 73, 81–2, 116–19, 122–65 passim, 166, 175
  reversals and 42, 122–3, 127, 129, 147

queer politics 3, 14, 23, 29, 124, 147, 180–1

racialisation
  skin colour and 84–5, 89, 106
  south-east Europeans' experiences of 18, 33, 82–9, 92, 102, 155–6, 163, 168, 171, 175–6, 179, 182
  study of 91, 166, 170–1, 173–4
raciality, global 2, 11–12, 14, 25, 57, 65, 166–87
racism 4, 11, 19, 31, 47, 116, 119, 126, 177–8
  anthropology and 17, 21, 48, 66–7, 74–7, 100–1
  biological 67, 69–70, 95, 99, 106, 169

'cultural' 20, 71, 73, 83, 95, 106, 120, 122, 124, 135, 150, 156, 162, 162
  media and 10, 41, 45, 48, 52, 100, 161
  multiple forms of 17–18, 67, 71, 84, 95, 124, 127, 171, 174
  police and 81, 85–6, 160
  scientific 66, 67, 94–5, 106, 124–5
  sport and 4, 96, 98
  state socialism and 12, 27, 45, 46, 53, 105, 111, 113, 120
  structural 24, 45, 135, 142, 185–6
  study of 16, 17, 28, 184
  see also anti-racism; colonialism
refugees 122–3, 125–6, 133–4
  'refugee crisis' 18, 145–6, 155–62
  Yugoslav wars and 83–5, 87–8, 123, 125–7, 134–5, 138, 140–1, 163, 181–2
religion 1, 124, 138–42
  conflict and 1, 8, 135, 137–8, 141–2, 149–50, 162
  identity and 20, 59, 61, 79, 94, 106
  race and 4, 21, 65, 69, 79, 84–5, 161
  south-east Europe and 8, 19, 59, 61, 85, 138, 142, 162, 166
  see also antemurale myth; anti-Semitism; Christianity; Islam
Republika Srpska 124–5, 131, 162, 169
Rijeka 54, 78, 92, 96–8
Roma
  blackness and 48, 106, 115–16
  citizenship and 36, 81, 92, 125, 160, 163
  feminism and 14, 45
  music and 35, 43, 45, 47–8
  see also antiziganism
Rucker-Chang, Sunnie ix, 81, 92, 120
Russia 15, 80, 81, 119, 148
  race and 25–6, 90–1, 104, 117
Rwanda 39, 70, 123, 128

Sarajevo 46, 50, 56, 59, 92, 124, 127, 129–30, 137, 139, 162, 172, 177, 183

Sardelić, Julija viii, 20, 73, 124
Sea, Adriatic 60, 67, 70, 71, 77, 79, 96, 98
  'black Adriatic' 10, 16, 74
security 5, 21, 73, 79, 117, 123, 133, 135, 136, 138–9, 142–62 passim
Serbia
  Europe and 3, 55–6, 121, 130, 143–4, 146, 149, 151, 157–60, 164, 168
  popular music 37–8, 41, 48–51, 55, 151
  race and 4, 14, 39–41, 48, 50–1, 54, 64, 81–2, 112, 121, 168, 178
  Yugoslav Wars and 39, 55, 80, 91, 117, 123, 126, 139
Serbs
  racialisation of 21–2, 66–9, 168
  unification of 61–3, 65–6, 72, 91
sex work 79–80, 120, 135–6
sexuality 41, 43, 44–5, 49, 115
slavery
  Atlantic slave trade 21, 42, 57, 77, 110, 150, 172, 173, 180, 183, 185
  Eastern Mediterranean 18, 74–8, 110, 119
Slovenia
  national identity of 6, 20–2, 40, 72–3, 116, 122, 148–9, 177
  refugees and 79, 144, 145–6
solidarity, interracial 35, 48, 50–1, 85–6, 123, 158–60, 187
  unmaking of 129, 178
Somalia 119, 123, 128, 129–31, 162
Spain 40–1, 78–9, 97
sport 4, 42, 51, 56, 96–8
state socialism 1
  geopolitical identities and 45, 75–6, 118–19
  Global South and 4, 29, 95, 104
  internationalism of 25, 95, 104–5, 120, 126, 158
  racial politics of 46, 75–6, 89, 103–19, 174–5
  see also Non-Aligned Movement; postsocialism

Stoler, Ann 24, 32, 155, 167
Sweden 23-4, 55, 61, 82, 84, 135, 156, 173
Syria 119, 141-2, 146, 156, 158-9, 163-4

television 4, 38, 76, 102, 106, 151
territory 4, 9, 15, 16, 25, 56, 57, 59, 61-4, 70, 73, 81, 90, 94, 101, 107, 124-5, 126, 149, 151, 169, 171, 175, 186; *see also* modernity, spatialised hierarchies of
terrorism 21, 117, 137-62 passim, 165
Tito, Josip Broz 2, 54, 59, 95, 107-9, 111-14, 116, 120, 123, 124, 146-7, 164
Tlostanova, Madina 15, 172
Todorova, Maria 6-7, 19, 21, 88, 94, 119, 174, 176
Todorova, Miglena viii, 5, 12, 17, 19-20, 89, 95, 105-6, 111, 184
translations of race 20, 29, 34-5, 38, 45, 48, 84, 89, 94, 96, 115, 166, 169, 173-4
travel 9, 18, 25-6, 29, 78-9, 96, 98-101, 105, 112-14, 123, 128, 138-44, 156-7, 163, 164
  travelling theory 15, 71-2, 89, 186
tribalism 27, 36-8, 55, 64, 128-9
Tržan, Tomislav 3, 55
Turkey 59, 63, 74, 80, 83, 88, 97-8, 107, 114, 119, 120-1, 156
Tuzla 47, 56, 131-2, 163

Ulcinj 74-8, 110, 113
Union of Soviet Socialist Republics (USSR) 12, 25, 27, 95, 104, 120; *see also* Russia; state socialism
United Kingdom (UK)
  black history of 50, 80, 99, 140
  Brexit 160-1, 176, 183
  colonial history of 3, 14, 22-4, 26, 34-5, 41-2, 61, 76, 87, 99-101, 131, 150, 163, 167, 182, 184
  east Europeans in 83-4, 135, 163
  racism in 3, 83, 124, 135, 139-40, 160-1, 163, 184
    anti-racism x, 2, 13
  Yugoslav region studied in 76, 182, 184
United Nations 105, 109, 153
  peacekeeping 127-8, 130-1, 149, 163
United States of America (USA)
  cultural diplomacy of 33-4, 49
  labour history of 55, 86, 89, 155
  military intervention and 56, 131-3, 152-3, 155-6
  racial politics of 28, 34, 41, 46, 53, 82-4, 95, 103, 104, 111, 132-3

Veličković, Vedrana 9, 118, 184
Venice 59-60, 70, 79, 91, 93, 96-8, 168, 172, 174

War on Terror 85, 143, 146, 147-55, 162, 185
Wekker, Gloria 10, 23, 28, 31-2, 41, 106
whiteness
  academia and viii, 104, 167, 180-1, 182, 186, 188
  conditional 86, 87, 108, 120, 136, 168, 171, 175-6
  identifications with 64, 83, 111, 150, 173, 175

Yugoslav wars 8, 13, 15, 20, 32, 37, 47, 122-9, 163-4, 187; *see also* Bosnia-Herzegovina; Croatia; Kosovo; Serbia
Yugoslavia
  1980s crisis in 4, 9, 20-1, 46-7, 103, 116-19, 125, 166

break-up of 32, 183; *see also* Yugoslav wars
differences from Soviet bloc 29, 46, 108, 111
global hierarchies and 113–14, 146–7, 155, 166, 168–9, 182, 185
imperialism and 1, 10, 161, 166, 172, 186
racial theories about 21, 65–6, 69–70, 171–2
social inequalities in 8–9, 72–3
unification of 66, 111, 119
see also state socialism

Yuval-Davis, Nira 13, 84

Žižek, Slavoj 19, 176–9